Fraynham 68-16382 (6-11-69)

THE ROYAL
PROVINCIAL INTENDANTS

A Governing Elite in Eighteenth-Century France

"The administration of intendants, save for a few abuses, is the best feature of my Kingdom; the major defects in the State do not lie in the intendancies."

Louis XVI

15 February 1788

THE ROYAL PROVINCIAL INTENDANTS

A Governing Elite in Eighteenth-Century France

VIVIAN R. GRUDER

CORNELL UNIVERSITY PRESS

ITHACA, NEW YORK

For My Mother and Father

Preface

The royal provincial intendants were the administrative cadre in the French state of the eighteenth century. Much has already been written about them, but, with a single exception, all the studies that have been done up to now examine administrative or institutional history. This is true whether they treat the creation of the system of intendants, the evolution of administrative functions within the intendancies, or the lives of individual intendants. The exception is *Les intendants de province sous Louis XVI,* a work by the Russian historian Paul Ardascheff, published in France in 1907. Ardascheff was the first historian to relate the intendants to the milieu in which they lived and worked and to analyze their family origins and social status. He succeeded in the first half of this endeavor, which constitutes the bulk of the book. He offers a treasure of information about the intendants' place in provincial and national society in late eighteenth-century France, their activities and thought, and contemporary attitudes toward them. But his analysis of the intendants' origins and status rests upon certain misapprehensions. Ardascheff uncritically accepted genealogies that claimed ancient and exalted noble origins for the families of Louis XVI's intendants, unaware that such pretensions were common in that aristocratically snobbish age. Moreover, he repeated assertions by the Duc de Saint-Simon that the ministers and intendants of Louis XIV, notably Colbert and Louvois, were baseborn commoners, and he did not examine the intendants of the intervening period from Louis XIV to Louis XVI. He thus drew a sharp contrast between the intendants of the late seventeenth century and early eighteenth, and the intendants of the late eighteenth century. The conclusion was clear: the members of the high administration in the last years of the monarchy were all nobles, and a greater number of them were of old noble lineage.

In the present century, studies in administrative history and in social history have multiplied, and each of these disciplines has contributed knowledge to the other. Historians, increasingly aware of the primacy of the state in modern society, have concentrated on examining the origins of the state system and on evaluating the operation of its institutional framework, the centralized bureaucracy. They have also borrowed theories and methods from sociology in an attempt to identify the social groups that exercised political power in the evolving modern state and to relate these ruling groups to the larger society in which they lived. This intellectual interchange has been fruitful in broadening the historian's perspective and in substantiating general theories and imaginative insights with concrete evidence. Yet it may also prove baneful if historians accept sociological hypotheses as axioms and merely seek historical evidence to prove the theory instead of using the theory to explore the past more deeply and imaginatively.

This book is an attempt to bridge the fields of administrative history and social history. The corps of royal provincial intendants is the focus, and the aim of this study is twofold: to evaluate the quality of French royal government before its demise, and to understand the character and transformation of French society in the *ancien régime* and the role that royal government played in the process of change. Part I examines the intendants' practical training and intellectual formation before they assumed their responsibilities in the provinces in order to estimate the administrative preparation and governing qualities of the Crown's principal agents. Part II examines the social origins and evolution of the intendants' families and the status of the individual intendants, tracing the social and professional groups to which these families belonged from their beginnings to the moment when the intendants began their careers; these family histories represent a microcosm of society in the *ancien régime* evolving under the pressures of economic forces and of political needs. In contrast to Ardascheff's book, which was limited to the reign of Louis XVI, the present study covers a broader span of time, including periods from the beginning, middle, and latter parts of the eighteenth century. Hence we may more accurately assess the changes in administrative caliber and in social recruitment of the intendants throughout the century, and we may relate these changes more closely to the character and policies of the regimes and to the underlying transformations within French society during the eighteenth century.

Ultimately, administrative history and social history bear upon political history. The most important political event in eighteenth-century France was the French Revolution, and the outbreak of the Revolution remains its most perplexing problem. My analysis of the provincial intendants in the eighteenth century—of their role in government and their place in society—has led me to speculate on the causes of the Revolution and to question certain accepted interpretations. In my conclusion I have drawn upon evidence from this study of the intendants and from other studies of French government and society in the eighteenth century to suggest a reappraisal of the ways in which royal government and aristocratic society contributed to the coming of the French Revolution.

The idea for this book grew out of studies in early modern European history, especially French history, begun at the University of Chicago and continued at Harvard University, which opened to me the fascinations of the *ancien régime* and led me to examine the eighteenth-century intendants. My appreciation goes to Professor Franklin L. Ford, who guided me through the complexities of the *ancien régime* and supervised the writing of my doctoral thesis. A Fulbright award in 1961–1962 enabled me to go to France to do research in the Bibliothèque Nationale; the delights of working in the Salle des Manuscrits, with its varied collections of documents, I shall long remember. In Paris I was privileged to attend a research seminar directed by Professor Roland Mousnier. I thank him and the members of this seminar whose reports enriched my knowledge of the social and administrative history of the *ancien régime;* Professor Mousnier also kindly advised me about genealogical sources and methods which enormously facilitated my own research and, it is hoped, guarded me from going too far astray in the labyrinth of genealogical studies. Conversations with Professor David Bien clarified and developed my ideas about eighteenth-century France.

My thanks to Doris Platzker and Irwin Kramer, who read portions of the manuscript, and to my nephew Howard Rosenhoch for last-minute assistance. Special thanks to my brother Arthur Gruder, who not only helped with some of the statistics but who, many years earlier, awakened my interest in history and set me to studying it. Professor Norman Cantor kindly recommended this manuscript to Cornell University Press, and Professor Kenneth Scott generously aided in preparing the index. I owe a special debt of gratitude to Professor Sidney A. Burrell for his advice and help over the years. He read the entire manuscript of this book and made suggestions from which I benefited.

V. R. G.

New York
September 1967

Contents

Preface   vii

Introduction: Royal Absolutism and Its Agents   1

PART I
THE ROYAL INTENDANTS AS AN ADMINISTRATIVE ELITE:
THEIR TRAINING AND RECRUITING

1 Students and Lawyers: The Legal Education and Apprenticeship of Intendants   17

2 Magistrates in the Courts: The Judicial Experience of Intendants and the Crown's Policy of Recruitment   34

3 From Sovereign Court to Royal Council: Admission as *Maîtres des Requêtes*   52

4 *Maîtres des Requêtes* Serve the King: Justice, Administration, and Politics   71

PART II
THE ROYAL INTENDANTS AS A SOCIAL ELITE:
THEIR FAMILY ORIGINS AND SOCIAL EVOLUTION

5 The Family Roots of the Intendants: Geographic and Social   97

6 Nobility, Robe, and Pen: The Rise of the Intendants' Families   117

7 Rank and Prestige within the Administrative Nobility: The Family Histories of Several Intendants   142

8 Social Mobility and "Aristocratic Reaction" within the High Administration in the Eighteenth Century   167

Contents

Conclusion: Some Thoughts on the *Ancien Régime* and the
French Revolution 208

APPENDIXES

I Comparative Incomes of Magistrates of the Paris Parle-
     ment and Members of the Royal Council 237
II Breakdown of the Income of a Councilor of State dur-
     ing a Period of Twenty-one Months, 1754–1755 241
III Proportions and Nature of the French Nobility in the
     Eighteenth Century 243
IV The Intendants Studied and Their Intendancies 246

     Bibliography 253
     Index 281

List of Tables

1 Exceptions to legal requirements for *licences,* apprenticeship, and judicial office   26

2 A comparison of natives and magistrates of Paris to provincial magistrates in the corps of intendants   43

3 Proportion of magistrates from different Paris courts among the intendants in each of the three periods   48

4 Changes in social-professional status between the documented first ancestors and the proven and presumed first ancestors   114

5 Noble origins of the intendants' families   132

6 The family origins and social evolution of the total group of intendants sampled   138

7 The comparative proportions of "new Parisians" among the three groups of intendants   182

8 Comparative status of the first ancestors of the eighteenth-century intendants sampled   186

9 Comparative status of the grandfathers of the eighteenth-century intendants sampled   186

10 Comparative status of the fathers of the eighteenth-century intendants sampled   188

11 A comparison of the social origins and evolution of the intendants' families in each of the three periods   191

12 Succession into the high administration of sons of the intendants sampled   194

13 A comparison of the noble lineage of the intendants in each of the three periods   196

14   A comparison of the intendants' lineage in the nobility, robe, and pen in each of the three periods   203

15   A comparison of the intendants' family status   204

THE ROYAL
PROVINCIAL INTENDANTS

A Governing Elite in Eighteenth-Century France

Royal Absolutism and Its Agents

I

Proceeding solemnly and majestically through the Galerie des Glaces in the Palace of Versailles, the King of France, whether Louis XIV, Louis XV, or Louis XVI, might see his decorated and imposing reflection along the entire length of the gallery: an image to inspire confidence and a sense of power for the individual monarch, a vision to evoke awe, perhaps fear or pride, among his millions of subjects throughout the kingdom. The king rules; he is the fleshly embodiment of sovereignty.

The king might then turn off into one of the adjoining rooms, where he lives and works. Some of his attendants continue the long walk through the corridor, down the stairs to the first floor, across the inner courtyard known as the Royal Courtyard, past the equestrian statue of Louis XIV to the outer courtyard, then turn to the right or to the left and enter one of the two wings on either side of the courtyard. The interior of these rooms is not as impressive or pleasing as those they have just left: there is no wall of mirrors to multiply the human figure and enhance its bearing. Majesty and authority are unadorned in these rooms, yet present in their actual and active forms, for these two wings house the royal ministries. Here sovereignty is put to work and becomes administration.

The meetings between the king and his ministers, the comings and goings between the king's bureau in the palace and the rooms in the outer courtyard, represent the inner workings and decisive activity of the French monarchy. In these relations sovereignty and administration unite. The Royal Council convenes; the king is seated, and gathered around him are his ministers and sometimes other government officials as well. There are actually several royal councils; the members may be the same, with a few new faces, but each council deliberates on different issues. The official calendar at Versailles would list at least four sessions of different royal councils during a single week. During these hours and among these few men decisions are made which determine the law of the land.[1] The king is absolute, his will is law; but to clarify his will, the sovereign seeks the advice of his ministers. Together or singly they guide and counsel him, so that the law in fact may be the will of one or several ministers.

The law is declared and must now be executed; for this the king depends absolutely on his ministers. At the end of a meeting of a royal council they retrace their steps and return to the two wings of the outer courtyard. There the ministers have their offices, which are at the same time the administrative departments of state. Except for an occasional royal prince, prince of the blood, marshal, or cardinal, all the royal ministers are also secretaries of state, and all the secretaries of state serve on one or another of the royal councils. Next to the king, these men collectively and singly embody the highest governmental authority in France: the ties of command and dependence that extend throughout the realm join together in their offices. Surrounded and assisted by secretaries and deputies, each minister and secretary of state drafts dispatches, transmits decrees, resolves problems not of paramount importance to be forwarded to the king and Council for decision, and oversees the enforcement of all royal orders

[1] Details of the organization and activities of the royal councils are found in Chapter 5 below.

2

relating to his department. By their work, the king's will becomes act.

From the palace and courtyard in Versailles, law proceeds to the provinces of France. Here the need is for men to receive the ministers' directives and execute the ruler's commands. These agents are the royal intendants, whom the Crown dispatches to the provinces. They embody royal sovereignty to Frenchmen far from the presence of the monarch; daily they transform royal authority into concrete acts; they are royal power and policy in their personal contacts with the people. As the direct representatives of the Crown in the provinces, the intendants link the king with his subjects.

There is, then, a direct chain of command: sovereignty begins with a silken-robed and powdered king, flows through ministers and secretaries of state gathered together in council and working apart in their bureaus, and ends its course with an intendant seated at a desk, with quill in hand, signing an order or a letter. In the reality of practical affairs, sovereign authority assumes the mundane guise of administrative work, and royal absolutism becomes centralized administration.

II

The direct origins of the eighteenth-century provincial intendants lie in the second quarter of the seventeenth century.[2] These were the decades when Cardinal Richelieu and

---

[2] Two general accounts of the origins and development of the intendancies may be found in Paul Viollet, *Le roi et ses ministres pendant les trois derniers siècles de la monarchie* (Paris, 1912), and Léon Aucoc, *Le conseil d'état avant et depuis 1789: Ses transformations, ses travaux, et son personnel* (Paris, 1876). The study by Gabriel Hanotaux, *Origines de l'institution des intendants des provinces* (Paris, 1884), deals with the years 1550–1631, that is, the period before Richelieu's innovations, in order to prove the thesis, no longer disputed, that the Cardinal did not "create" the system of intendancies but made use of officials and practices inherited from several of the preceding reigns. E. Esmonin, in "Observations critiques sur le livre de M. Hanotaux," *Bulletin de la*

Cardinal Mazarin were first ministers to Louis XIII and to the minor-king Louis XIV. More importantly, these were the years when France was engaged first in undeclared war and then in open war against the Hapsburgs of Spain and the Empire. Whether to subsidize allies or later to finance her own armies, the French Crown needed money, as much as it could obtain, and as quickly as it could be collected.

The traditional collectors of taxes, the *trésoriers, élus,* and *receveurs,* regularly delayed assessing taxes and delivering the revenue to the appropriate bureaus. Once they did act, they diligently proceeded to decrease the levy they imposed on themselves, their relatives, their friends, neighboring lords, and other influential individuals—in short, the local rich and powerful—and compensated for these losses by raising the levy an equivalent amount on those who could not pressure or buy such favors—namely, the weak and poor in towns, villages, and countryside. This disproportionate and heavy burden of taxes which impoverished peasants and townsmen were forced to pay (while soldiers who fought, wandered, or were quartered in their neighborhoods despoiled their homes and fields) excited them to riots and

---

Société d'Histoire Moderne, 7ᵉ série, No. 40 (Dec. 1932–Jan. 1933), refutes some of Hanotaux's assumptions based, as he believes, upon fallacious terminology, and presents some of his own thoughts on the subject. These last two works tend to rely excessively on the use of official titles as a means of tracing the origins and development of the intendancies. In an age when administrative practice was in the process of formation and constantly in flux, the business of government was far more varied and complex than precise titles reveal. Roland Mousnier, in contrast, focuses on the actual functions exercised by the several intendants during the ministries of Cardinals Richelieu and Mazarin in order to explain why the Crown employed these men increasingly until they became the central agents of royal government. See his *La vénalité des offices sous Henri IV et Louis XIII* (Rouen, 1945), 604–21, and especially his article "Etat et commissaire: Recherches sur la création des intendants des provinces (1634–1648)," *Forschungen zu Staat und Verfassung, Festgabe für Fritz Hartung* (Berlin, 1958).

revolts. Thus, the problem initially introduced by the Crown's need for revenue to fight the Hapsburgs became more complicated. Not only did the monarchy need to ensure efficient and speedy collection of taxes, but it also had to eliminate tax privileges or exemptions, equalize the levies and assess taxes in some proportion to the subjects' ability to pay, and forestall or repress disorders and uprisings which would further retard tax collection and divert troops who were fighting the Spaniards and Germans.

Faced with a national crisis precipitated by France's unequivocal entrance into the Thirty Years' War in 1635, Richelieu reverted to the men and methods that he and his predecessors hitherto had used on occasion: intendants, with various titles, had been dispatched previously to towns and provinces to enforce particular edicts, investigate and supervise normal administrative affairs including tax collection, suppress local riots, and judge particular malefactors. Beginning in 1632, more intendants went with greater frequency and regularity into the provinces, principally to supervise tax collections and, in extreme situations, to restore order. The continuing war emergency and persistent tax irregularities and inefficiencies further compelled Richelieu in 1637 to authorize the intendants to apportion and collect taxes themselves rather than simply to supervise collections. Cardinal Mazarin introduced a further, decisive innovation by a royal order in August 1642, followed by a royal edict in April 1643. Only after a ten-year period of essays and partial measures did the Crown finally decide to delegate major responsibility to the intendants sent to the provinces.

The edict on the *taille* of April 1643 gave the intendants the right to attend meetings of the tax agents in the *bureau des finances* of each fiscal administrative unit—the *généralité*—as presiding officers; the *trésoriers, élus,* and *receveurs* were no longer equal colleagues but became subordinate agents. The intendant chose from among them several officials to accompany and assist him in assessing and collecting taxes in all the cities, towns, and parishes of the provincial region; he also had authority to judge tax disputes and to investigate and punish corrupt tax officers. By these means the Crown aimed to hasten and make more equitable the collection of taxes. More importantly, this edict fundamentally changed the status and power of the intendants. Before 1643 they had been present on an extended basis in all the *généralités* and had accumulated judicial, police, and financial functions. The specific provisions of the edict definitively transformed them into executive financial officers—hereafter their most important role—and established the legal precedent by which they became the regular, superior administrative agents in the provinces.[3]

[3] A century after Mazarin issued this edict, royal officials continued to recognize its significance. Jean Louis Moreau de Beaumont, intendant and councilor of state under Louis XV, wrote in 1768–1769 an encyclopedic *Mémoire concernant les impositions et droits en Europe,* and in it devoted a few pages to explaining the edict of 1643. According to Moreau de Beaumont, the edict was designed to attack the following abuses and to ensure the following results: "to enforce equity in the assessment and apportionment of imposts, to tax those ennobled for thirty years and officers whose exemptions had been revoked . . . , also the rich and powerful in proportion to their ability, business, and trade, this being the only means of enabling the weak to subsist and of maintaining the state; . . . the greatest proportion of the rich and powerful . . . were the ones who resisted and were exempted under different pretexts and by different means; . . . several officers, collectors, clerks, and others appointed for the assessment, levying, and collection of these monies tolerated and even contributed to the overtaxing of some and the undertaxing of others, which resulted in indebtedness, excessive charges, and rioting in communities and among individuals who paid taxes; the purpose of the declaration of 1643 is to ensure more exact obedience to the preceding laws concerning the assessment, levying and collection of these taxes."

These several goals would be achieved through the agency of the royal commissioners, the intendants, who were appointed in the provinces and *généralités*. Moreau de Beaumont then explains the intendants' new tax-collecting powers: the intendant was to "preside at and have the principal voice" in the meetings of the Bureau of Finance

The forces that operated during the decade of the 1630's and the early years of the 1640's, compelling Richelieu and Mazarin to use intendants, to augment their functions and enhance their power, prevailed in the following years and produced similar results. Yet, in its course, the Crown's policy suffered serious setbacks. Parlementary magistrates and nobles, *trésoriers, élus,* and *receveurs* clamored against these new officials. The fiscal agents opposed the intendants because the latter were assuming functions they themselves had hitherto exercised untrammeled; magistrates and nobles became hostile because the intendants, by directly enforcing royal policy, diminished their influence and abridged their autonomous activities in the provinces. The system of intendants was one of the first targets of the Fronde rebellion, and in the winter of 1648–1649 the Paris Parlement forced the Crown to suppress all but six of these posts. Neither verbal outbursts nor revolts, however, could prevail against sheer political necessity, and, ironically, these actions strengthened

which receives the royal orders for the levy of the *taille;* the members of the Bureau would expedite the necessary ordinances for tax-collection in the intendant's presence and deliver them to him; to avoid delay in tax-collection, as soon as the authorization for taxes arrived the Presidents and Treasurers of France of each Bureau delegated one among them for each tax district who would be available at the stipulated time to assist the intendant; together with a Treasurer of France and several Presidents, the intendant would go to each of the tax districts within his jurisdiction, and aided also by the public prosecutor and clerk of the court of the district, the collector of the *taille,* and several tax agents of the district chosen by the intendant himself, would "proceed to assess and apportion the levies on the taxable towns, villages and parishes with requisite equity. . . . The intendants and all fiscal officers are to tax as a matter of routine privileged persons whose exemptions have been revoked by the declaration of November 1640, powerful residents [of the region], as well as tax farmers who maintain their exemptions and moderate rates by the authority and the fear which they inspire." Cf. Jean Louis Moreau de Beaumont, *Mémoire concernant les impositions et droits en Europe,* ed. Poullin de Vieville (5 vols., rev. ed.; Paris, 1787–1789) , II, 22–24. The translation is mine.

7

the forces promoting royal centralization and absolutism. Civil war now combined with foreign war to press upon the resources and responsibilities of the royal government. The need for revenue, the urgency of suppressing disorders and conspiracies, and of combating the enemy, gave Mazarin his opportunity and obliged him to insinuate the intendants back into the royal administrative system and gradually to restore their full powers.

Peace finally came to France in 1659, but it did not eliminate the need for intendants. Peacetime problems and measures now superseded the emergency priorities of war. Revenue had to be obtained, and the Crown continued to rely on the intendants, who had proven themselves to be quick, firm, and incorruptible in collecting taxes; moreover, they alone, not the local fiscal agents, attempted to reduce the burdensome taxes on the poor by collecting larger quotas from the local notables. Judicial abuses too had to be remedied, and this task also fell to the intendants. Ordinary judges often delayed decisions for long periods, charged exorbitant fees, and frequently decided in favor of local lords and influential families; increasingly, individuals brought cases before the intendants, who judged swiftly and without fee or favoritism.

In the last decades of the seventeenth century, and particularly during the ministry of Jean-Baptiste Colbert, the system of intendants became fully institutionalized and was introduced throughout the kingdom. Intendant followed intendant without lapse, each residing permanently in his *généralité* during the period of his tenure, except for periodic visits to the capital on government or personal business; each newly gained territory—Alsace, Franche-Comté, Flanders—received an intendant, and in 1689 the last autonomous province, Brittany, came under the administration of a royal intendant. As the intendants spread over the kingdom, so too their powers were enlarged to include direction of economic affairs. From 1672 to 1714 France was either directly engaged in war or preparing for war, and the need for strong and efficient government grew apace. The persistent economic depression during this period led the government to intervene more actively in the economy in order to revive and increase production. Mercantilism—or Colbertism—transformed the intendants into the prime agents of national economic policy; they became actively engaged in promoting and regulating trade and manufactures, and in supervising the repair and construction of roads and riverways.[4]

Whatever problems arose, whether in particular provinces or throughout France, became the intendant's responsibility and added to his many functions. And why not? This administrative procedure proved itself the best yet devised by French kings and ministers: it assured the most efficient and honest government then available. Even the Regency government of 1715, which, under the influence of Saint-Simon, had replaced the ministries with largely aristocratic councils (*polysynodie*), still retained the intendants as the Crown's direct agents in the provinces. Moreover, these men were capable, trustworthy officials and loyal to the king. They were trained and chosen from the governing elite on the royal councils, and the Crown, which appointed them to their posts, could dismiss them as well.

The intendants thus fulfilled important needs in French government and society while promoting and strengthening administrative centralization; the services they performed and the system that evolved were indivisible in their historical unfolding. No passion for unlimited power, no single

[4] A comprehensive general survey of the administrative functions of the intendants during the reign of Louis XIV may be found in Charles Godard, *Les pouvoirs des intendants sous Louis XIV* (Paris, 1901). See also Roland Mousnier, "La participation des gouvernés à l'activité des gouvernants dans la France du XVIIe et XVIIIe siècles," *Schweizer Beiträge zur Allgemeinen Geschichte*, XX (1962–1963), 216. Nora Temple, in "The Control and Exploitation of French Towns during the Ancien Régime," *History* (London), Feb. 1966, 16–21, examines the powers intendants assumed over municipal affairs during the last decades of the seventeenth century.

chimera of ideal unity and centralism beckoned particular kings and ministers to establish this form of government. Absolutism developed in response to national crises and as a means of solving stubborn, complex, practical problems; it corresponded to the interests of both the monarchy and the mass of French subjects.

III

To find men who could administer: that was the Crown's central concern in selecting its intendants. The king's men must perform the king's business ably and loyally, or else endanger the effective assertion of royal authority. The danger and the need were lessons of the mid-seventeenth-century crisis; loyalty and ability remained constant prerequisites during the later seventeenth century and the eighteenth for an administrative system in which active power was delegated to the direct agents of the central government.

Childhood experiences, memories of fleeing before rebellious nobles, had seared the mind of Louis XIV; he was keenly aware that royal authority depended on the character of its servants, that capable, trustworthy agents must be selected. Yet he did not introduce radical innovations or depart from established procedures for appointing intendants. As he had inherited the practice of using intendants, so Louis continued the method for selecting these agents that Richelieu and Mazarin had bequeathed and that his successors, Louis XV and Louis XVI, were to perpetuate.

No civil service regulations defined the requirements for becoming an intendant, no educational institute trained them, and no examination served to qualify them. Yet, beneath the indeterminateness and inconstancy of the *ancien régime*'s practices was a pattern of recruitment that revealed a rational procedure for preparing and selecting intendants. Moreover, it highlights the adaptability and traditionalism characteristic of the Bourbon regime which, paradoxically, both strengthened and enfeebled it. In short, the absolute monarchy innovated only partially and, in the main, used existing materials to serve its own purpose: the construction and maintenance of the system of administrative centralization. The merits and defects embedded in these traditional techniques remained in the revamped institutions of royal government, constituting its advantages and shortcomings during the final century and a half of its existence.

IV

The testimony of Saint-Simon and Boulainvilliers and the reputation of Alexis de Tocqueville support the view that the intendants were men of low birth or, less scornfully, mere bourgeois. But how reliable are these authorities? Saint-Simon, a duke and peer of the realm, arrogantly disdained all men (including noblemen) who were not princes and peers—whatever else they might have been. Boulainvilliers, exalted by the antiquity and feudal origin of his family, refused to consider as noble those families not equally old and similarly sprung from knightly service. Tocqueville demands greater respect as the pilot historian of the *ancien régime;* nevertheless, his upbringing and experience molded his image of that government and society. On the one hand, his antipathy to Louis Napoleon's government caused him to exaggerate royal absolutism and centralization; equally true, his background as a country nobleman from an old Norman family limited his understanding of the pre-Revolution nobility.

From the extreme of one interpretation historians have traveled to the opposite point of view. In recent years the theory of "feudal reaction" has been invoked to characterize events and developments in the second half of the eighteenth century that "naturally" led to the outburst of the Revolution. According to this school of thought, the nobles' determination to defend and promote their interests became greater and had widespread effect. *Seigneurs* recovered medieval rent-rolls and searched in feudal law to exact higher rents and fees from peasants; nobles monopolized all high positions in the army and the Church, in the sovereign courts, in some municipal governments, and even in the high administration of the royal government, excluding those without pure pedigree and ancient lineage. Society became increasingly closed and fixed, and government was a self-perpetuating aristocratic preserve. In the nation, hostility, resentment, and frustration engendered revolutionary ideas and fervor among the *bourgeoisie,* peasants, and town workers. How direct and persuasive an argument! To be sure, this interpretation embodies many truths, but there are some half-truths and oversimplifications as well, applied too universally.

Two contrasting images of the intendant emerge from these interpretations: at the beginning of the century a humble commoner, obsequious before his royal master who grants all honors and may withdraw them at will; at the end of the century a proud nobleman with lengthy titles and lineage, a lordly proconsul before subjects and sovereign. Neither is the true image, the first reflecting personal prejudices about society and government, the second expressing preconceived theories of historical change.

In the course of the eighteenth century many men filled the posts of intendants. Some came from old, distinguished, and traditional groups in society. Their presence in the corps indicates the firm hold those groups had on positions of power and, conversely, the limits that the *ancien régime* imposed upon the professional and social advance of individuals lower in the hierarchy. Other intendants came from new and different groups born of changes in French society. Their presence, in contrast, reveals the opportunities available in the *ancien régime* for professional and social advancement, and highlights the royal government's role as a vehicle for social mobility within the hierarchical society.

Their important functions as administrators and their prestige as officers of the Crown gave the intendants elevated status in society; they were outranked only by the king, the royal family, princes of the blood, royal ministers, and the highest court nobility. Such dignity was a powerful inducement to men seeking administrative careers in a society where notions of hierarchy regulated life and molded thought. To some among the intendants this exalted place in society was merely an extension of the status inherited from their families. To others, the status acquired through office signified a radical change from their family's place in society and transformed their personal fortune and the future of their children. Yet despite these differences among the intendants due to their social origins, all of them by their official functions and status constituted a single service elite.

Thus, there is no single model of the eighteenth-century intendant; nor may intendants be viewed from one sole perspective. They differed in origin, some higher and some lower in society, but by their royal commission they shared an honored rank.

How one became an intendant or, from the point of view of the Crown, who were selected to be provincial intendants may be determined by studying the careers of some of the men who actually were intendants. So too the social origins and status of the royal intendants may be understood by examining the family histories of these men. Those whom I have chosen for this study functioned as intendants during the years 1710–1712, 1749–1751, and 1774–1776, in the reigns of Louis XIV, Louis XV, and Louis XVI respectively. Their total number is 94: 30 intendants for the first period, 32 for the second, and 32 for the third period.[5] The method em-

---

[5] There are 37 intendants whom I studied for the years 1774–1776; 5 of them previously had been intendants during the years 1749–1751 and therefore are not included a second time in calculating the total number. In the period 1710–1712 there were 32 *généralités,* 2 of them, Montpellier and Toulouse, administered by the single intendant of Languedoc. There were again 32 *généralités* in 1749–1751; however,

13

ployed should yield as much as would comprehensive coverage for the entire century, and it provides a basis for comparing the training and social character of the intendants during different periods from the late seventeenth century through the eighteenth.

Lorraine was now included, though not yet legally annexed to France, and Flanders was now divided into 2 *généralités* instead of 3 as in 1710–1712. In 1774–1776 the number of *généralités* increased to 34: Dombes had been annexed to France in 1762 and Corsica in 1768, each receiving an intendant. In this latter period there had also been changes involving the *généralités* of Pau-Auch and Bordeaux and the creation of a separate *généralité* of Bayonne; but by 1774–1776 Bayonne was first reunited to Pau-Auch and then to Bordeaux. The above information was obtained from the relevant volumes of the *Almanach Royal*. The discrepancies between the number of *généralités* and the number of intendants is due to the transfer of intendants from one district to another, so that in one instance there may be one intendant who served in two *généralités* during the single period, or in another instance there may be two intendants who administered the same district during the three years. I have not included in this list, nor have I investigated, those men who functioned as intendants for only a short time during each of the three periods.

PART I

THE ROYAL INTENDANTS AS
AN ADMINISTRATIVE ELITE:
THEIR TRAINING AND RECRUITING

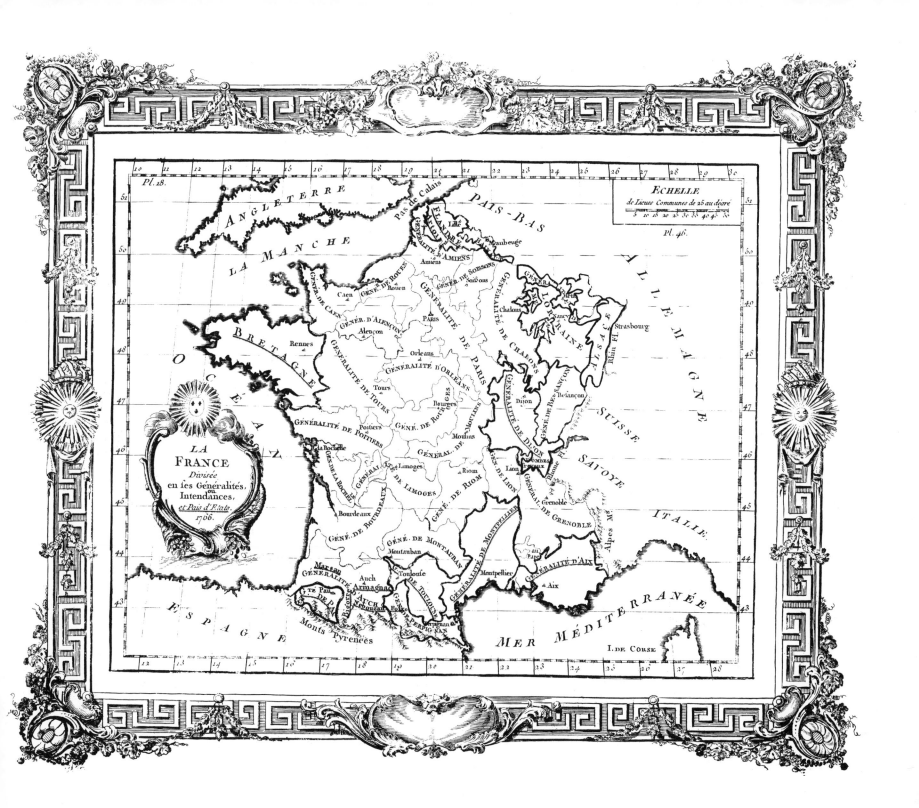

Pl. 18.

ECHELLE
de Lieues Communes de 25 au degré
5 10 15 20 25 30 35 40 45 50

Pl. 46.

ANGLETERRE

LA MANCHE

PAS-BAS

Pas de Calais

ALLEMAGNE

OCÉAN

BRETAGNE

GÉNÉ. DE CAEN
Caen
GÉNÉL. DE ROUEN
Rouen
GÉNÉ. D'ALENÇON
Alençon
Rennes
GÉNÉRALITÉ DE TOURS
Tours

GÉNÉ. DE SOISSONS
Soissons
GÉNÉRALITÉ D'AMIENS
Amiens
FLANDRE
GÉNÉRALITÉ DE FLANDRE
Lille
Maubeuge

GÉNÉRALITÉ DE PARIS
Paris

GÉNÉRALITÉ DE CHALONS
Chalons

LORRAINE
Metz
Nancy

ALSACE
Strasbourg
Rhin Fl.

SUISSE

Orleans
GÉNÉRALITÉ D'ORLEANS

Bourges
GÉNÉ. DE BOURGES

GÉNÉRALITÉ DE POITIERS
Poitiers

la Rochelle
GÉN. DE LA ROCHE.

GÉNÉRAL. DE LIMOGES
Limoges

GÉNÉRAL. DE MOULINS
Moulins

GÉNÉRALITÉ DE BESANÇON
Dijon
Besançon

GÉNÉRALITÉ DE DIJON

GÉNÉ. DE RIOM
Riom

GÉN. DE LION
Lion
DOMBES
TREVOUX
Rhone Fl.

SAVOYE

GÉNÉRAL. DE GRENOBLE
Grenoble

ITALIE

Bourdeaux
GÉNÉ. DE BOURDEAUX

Marsan
GÉNÉRALITÉ DE
Auch
Armagnac
GÉNÉRALITÉ D'AUCH
Pau
DE PAU
Arbouan
BIGORRE

GÉNÉ. DE MONTAUBAN
Montauban

Toulouse
GÉNÉ. DE TOULOUSE

Perpignan

GÉNÉRALITÉ DE MONTPELLIER
Montpellier

Alpes M.

GÉNÉRALITÉ D'AIX
au Pape
Aix

ESPAGNE

Monts Pyrenées

MER MÉDITERRANÉE

I. DE CORSE

LA FRANCE Divisée en ses Généralités, ou Intendances, et Pais d'Etats. 1766.

France, as divided into generalities or intendancies and *pays d'états,* 1766. From Louis Brion de la Tour, *Tableau Analytique de la France dans lequel on donne une connaissance générale et détaillée du royaume considéré sous ses différentes formes de gouvernement tant civil qu'ecclésiastique et militaire,* published in Paris, 1766. (Courtesy of the New York Public Library.)

Indicated as *pays d'états* in this map are: Aix (Provence), Alsace, Besançon (Franche-Comté), Brittany, Dijon (Burgundy), Flandre, Hainaut, Lorraine, Metz (Three Bishoprics), Montpellier and Toulouse (Languedoc), Pau (Navarre and Béarn), Perpignan (Foix and Roussillon). Indicated as *pays d'élections* in this map are: Amiens (Picardy), Auch (Gascony), Alençon (Normandy), Bordeaux (Guyenne), Bourges (Berry), Caen (Normandy), Châlons (Champagne), Grenoble (Dauphiné), La Rochelle (Aunis and Saintonge), Limoges (Limousin and Angoumois), Lyon (Lyonnais), Moulins (Marche, Bourbonnais, Nivernais), Montauban (Guyenne), Orléans (Orléanais), Paris (Ile-de-France), Poitiers (Poitou), Riom (Auvergne), Rouen (Normandy), Soissons (Ile-de-France and Picardy), Tours (Touraine, Anjou, and Maine), Trévoux (Dombes). The island of Corsica was annexed by France only in 1768 when it became an intendancy as a *pays d'états;* Avignon and the Comtat Venaissin were ruled by the Papacy until 1791.

The provinces of Alsace and Provence, for example, were considered *pays d'états* even though they did not have provincial estates in existence, as did Brittany and Languedoc; the estates of Provence had been suppressed in the seventeenth century and Alsace had been incorporated into the French kingdom after the establishment of the system of *élections* in the provinces. The province of Dauphiné had its provincial estates suspended in the seventeenth century; hence it is sometimes designated as a *pays d'états* although on this map it is considered a *pays d'élections.*

CHAPTER 1

Students and Lawyers: The Legal Education and Apprenticeship of Intendants

I

Information about the education of intendants is sparse. Of the ninety-four men here considered, there are references to the studies of only thirteen, and these data are vague and minimal, sometimes consisting merely of the word "student" or "studied." The nature of their studies is known for only ten men: nine studied law, and one studied medicine.[1] No data illumine the careers of four of these men before they became *maîtres des requêtes* or intendants.[2] Information

[1] The latter is Denis Dodart, intendant of Bourges (1728–1767), whose father was Louis XV's physician. Cf. J. Néraud, *Les intendants de la généralité de Berry* (Thèse pour le doctorat, la Faculté de droit de l'Université de Paris [Paris, 1922]), 180. Dodart's later career as a magistrate would indicate that he had some legal training, although there is no concrete evidence.

[2] These four were Marie Jean Baptiste Nicolas d'Aine, intendant of Limoges, 1774–1783; Antoine Jean Amelot de Chaillou, intendant of Dijon, 1764–1776; Etienne Louis Journet, intendant of Auch and Bayonne, 1767–1776; and Antoine Jean Terray, intendant of Montauban, 1773–1781. Two of the four men were from obscure, unknown families for whom contemporary genealogists would have no interest. The general decrease of biographical information in the late eighteenth century seems to indicate that there was diminishing concern for establishing genealogies or bringing them up to date except when particular circumstances demanded this, such as proofs of nobility required in the 1780's for entrance to military academies or participation in the

17

about the careers of ninety of them before they became intendants sheds light on the education they presumably received which enabled them to obtain their subsequent posts. Thus, we can attempt to reconstruct the character of the education for the entire group of ninety-four intendants and, by extension, for the intendants of the eighteenth century. (See Appendix IV for a list of intendants studied.)

All but one of the ninety men had been lawyers and magistrates prior to their appointments as intendants.[3] They must, therefore, have had legal training in order to be admitted to the bar and to the courts; educational prerequisites also attached to the judgeships in the sovereign courts. However, data about courses and examinations, necessary as they are for a concrete estimation of the character of their education, provide only a skeletal outline, a partial appreciation of the intendants' training. On the one hand, there was great disparity between the requirements as stated in law and in catalogues and the quality of university teaching and student performance. Equally true, the total process of learning and training, in short, the acquisition of knowledge and experience, cannot be neatly and simply gauged by its correspondence to periods of formal study and fulfillment of prerequisites.

At age sixteen, as stipulated by the royal ordinances of November 1690 and January 1700, a young Frenchman might enter a university faculty and begin his legal studies, having previously completed the traditional classical

---

honneurs de la Cour. Also, many family and personal documents were destroyed during the Revolution, leaving a permanent lacuna for this latter part of the eighteenth century.

[3] The career of François de Beauharnois before he was intendant of La Rochelle (1710–1715) was unique, being limited to service in the naval ministry and colonial affairs. Hence, I have not included his personal data with the information about the other 89 intendants since they are not relevant for determining the general professional formation of the corps of intendants.

studies—Latin and Greek language and literature, and rhetoric—and even modern subjects, such as French history and
literature, science, and geography, at one of the Jesuit or
Oratorian *collèges*.[4] Abuses distorted precise regulations
even at this initial stage: some students, ignoring the law or
obtaining exemptions, began their studies even earlier, although this was the least common malpractice.[5] Once enrolled, the young student faced three years of prescribed studies before obtaining his degree.

The curriculum of the law faculty in Paris, then as now
the best-attended law school in France, had been reformed
and enlarged in the early part of Louis XIV's reign. Until
1679 only canon law was taught there; a royal edict of that
year permitted the teaching of the whole body of Roman law
as well as French law—the customs, charters, and particu-

[4] François Bluche, *Les magistrats du Parlement de Paris au XVIII*
siècle (1715–1771) (Paris, 1960), 59, 245–46, and 262–63, nn. 64, 67, 68.
According to Baron François Delbeke, *L'action politique et sociale des*
avocats au XVIII siècle (Louvain, 1927), ch. 1, the Jesuits and Oratorians had already introduced some modern subjects into the classical
curriculum by the middle of the eighteenth century. The Jesuits taught
geography and the writings of the great French authors of the seventeenth century; the Oratorians, in addition to geography, taught the
French language, modern history (especially of France), physics, and
mathematics. Despite the criticisms that contemporaries, notably the
philosophes, voiced of their education in the *collèges*, Delbeke believes
the training and learning offered was quite good, especially in the
schools run by the Oratorians which he characterizes as the "best" in
eighteenth-century France (p. 26). Some of the intendants had outstanding records as students in the *collèges*. Calonne, the future intendant and controller-general, won prizes in Latin, Greek, and French
(cf. Robert Lacour-Gayet, *Calonne: Financier, réformateur, contre-*
révolutionnaire, 1734–1802 [Paris, 1963], 13).

[5] Bluche, 59–60. He cites Jean Baptiste Elie Camus de Pontcarré de
Viarme, intendant of Brittany (1734–1753), as one who obtained a
dispensation for age to begin his legal studies (p. 72, n. 141). The date
of this dispensation is given as 11 Jan. 1718; since Pontcarré was born
20 Mar. 1702 he lacked only two months of fulfilling the minimum age
requirement—an extremely minor abuse of the law.

larly the royal ordinances—as a means of improving the training of the large number of Paris students and thereby raising the quality of judicial administration.[6] Thus, in his first year the student had one course in Roman law, studying the *Institutes* of Justinian. During his second year he continued Roman law, studying the *Digest* or *Code,* and, in addition, attended a course in canon law; when this year ended he obtained his *baccalauréat* after successfully arguing a thesis. In his third and final year he studied French law and chose Roman or canon law as his second course. At the end of each year he took an examination designed to test his knowledge of each body of law; at the end of his third year he had to argue a second thesis in order to obtain his *licence.* By the time the student completed the required work at the law faculty, he was expected to have studied and learned "the four books of the Institutes; an exact précis of all of canon law; a part of the Digest; a certain number of treatises of the Decretals; and a résumé of the entire French law contained in the customs and ordinances." [7] If the student

[6] Charles M. Jourdain, *Histoire de l'Université de Paris au XVIIe et XVIIIe siècles* (2 vols.; Paris, 1862–66), I, 476, and Abbé G. Péries, *La faculté de droit dans l'ancienne université de Paris (1160–1793)* (Paris, 1890), 255, 257.

[7] Péries, 338. See also, Jourdain, II, 82, and Bluche, 60. One can argue, as does Péries, 312–13, that this heavy dosage of Roman law conditioned future judges to favor removing the privileges inherent in feudal custom and to substitute an "enlightened" and uniform base for the heterodox French law. One can furthermore assume that their early studies in Roman law served as political indoctrination and molded future intendants into firm advocates and promoters of royal absolutism. This interpretation is beguiling in its directness, but is not without serious weaknesses. Parlementary magistrates, for example, were also former students of Roman law, but were leading opponents of royal authority and of the agents of this authority. This view also rests on the presumption that, historically, Roman law served to lay the juridical base for royal absolutism. Two studies have shown that this tradition is partially fallacious—that men trained in Roman law were not unqualified absolutists and sometimes even used the terms and arguments of

followed the prescribed regulations strictly, he would be nineteen years old by the time he received his *licence*.

One of the most perplexing questions—and perhaps an insoluble one—is whether or not the student in the eighteenth century, the future lawyer, judge, and intendant, adhered to these forms during his passage through the law school and thereby obtained the full legal education that the requirements indicate. Equally important and as difficult to answer is the question whether the quality of the instruction offered at the law faculties, and above all at Paris, corresponded to the image that the enumerated course materials present. In short, exceptions and disparities abound, and the reality becomes more complex, at times even escaping our grasp.

Louis XIV had attempted several times to raise the caliber of the legal profession and of legal training by improving the quality of instruction, regulating the student body, and making the requirements for becoming lawyers and judges more strict. The most extensive of these edicts was the one issued in April 1679, introducing the teaching of Roman and French law, which also prescribed several other measures. It obliged students preparing for their examination in French law at the end of their third year to attend two daily lessons for three hours between July 1 and September 7; it prohibited law faculties from granting *licences* to those who had not completed the regular and full course of legal studies; it required a *licence* to become an *avocat*, with a minimum of two years' experience as an *avocat* before being received as a magistrate; and it prescribed that the Parlements examine candidates for the magistracy by having each present a harangue in Latin, dispute with two judges on a specific law prepared in advance, and explicate three legal texts chosen

Roman jurisprudence to defend feudal rights. Cf. Myron P. Gilmore, *Argument from Roman Law in Political Thought, 1200–1600* (Cambridge, Mass., 1941), and Franklin J. Pegues, *The Lawyers of the Last Capetians* (Princeton, N.J., 1962).

at random. A royal declaration of 26 February 1680 again stipulated that any member of a judicial court of whatever level had to prove that he had obtained a *licence* for legal studies and show evidence of his inscription on the roll of *avocats;* and the declaration of 6 August 1682 repeated the demand for a *licence* in order to be sworn in as an *avocat.* In November 1690 and again in January 1700 royal ordinances established a minimum age of sixteen for entrance into a law faculty; the declaration of 19 January 1700 required that students remain in residence at the university in which they studied, this being repeated in the declaration of 2 August 1712. The 1700 declaration further defined precisely the subject matter for entrance examinations administered to judges.[8] The contents of these edicts, ordinances, and declarations indicate the problems and abuses they were designed to attack and ameliorate; that several laws repeated some of these injunctions reveals that difficulties persisted despite legal pronouncements.

French university education, particularly in the law faculties, was poor in quality during the eighteenth century, historians claim, both the schools and the students being at fault.[9] Paris and provincial centers, Rheims, Orange, and Orléans—the latter renowned in the previous century for its law faculty—had extremely low academic standards. There was no regularized system of grading. More seriously, the study of French law—limited to one year and restricted to ordinances, some customary laws, and general legal principles—was too rapid and superficial. The law-school curricu-

---

[8] See Pierre Guyot, *Traité des droits, fonctions, franchises, exceptions, prérogatives et privilèges annexés en France à chaque office et à chaque état* (Paris, 1786–88), III, 78–81, 114; Bluche, 59, 61; Péries, 282–83; and Ernest Glasson, "Les examens d'entrée dans l'ancienne magistrature," *La Grande Revue,* I (1887), 51–52.

[9] See Bluche, 59 ff.; Péries, 284 ff.; Glasson, 45–46; and Delbeke, 56–65.

lum ignored criminal and administrative law and a variety of customs in the vast maze of French customary law; a graduate would still have much to study before being able to conduct a legal case. Moreover, students did little work and attended classes irregularly. They paid poorer fellow students or stand-ins to transcribe notes, and at the end of the year they quickly ran through review summaries to prepare for examinations. Worse still, law students sometimes paid to pass their examinations or even purchased their theses. These same students who ignored the law spent their time horseback riding, dancing, fencing, fighting, and pursuing and wooing young women.

Are the law schools and law students of the eighteenth century justifiably condemned? Their features may be overdrawn. The eighteenth-century law student appears not unique and inferior, but typical—a universal type, the gay, carefree, irresponsible young student. Professors and social observers or gossips in the eighteenth century, and writers and historians of a later age scorn such students, deride their behavior, and depreciate their intelligence and abilities. Yet no one has proof that all students were irresponsible and remained ignorant; the worst abuses, glaring in nature, probably characterized those who were in law school merely to pass time rather than to prepare seriously for a career. Days of jesting and jousting as a student, moreover, did not mark an individual for life as an ignorant and inept man of law. Lawyers in eighteenth-century France were esteemed. Their education and intelligence, as well as their profession, raised their status in society, and a number of them are renowned in history; they too were products of contemporary law schools. As the students varied in quality and diligence, so did their professors; on the faculties of eighteenth-century law schools were a number of jurists eminent in their day. One commentator concedes that the severe criticism of teaching and discipline in the law schools "is too general and unjust." [10] Furthermore, professional schooling did not complete legal training; after three years in the law faculty a student obtained his *licence* and at an early age began his career as a professional lawyer.

The exaggerated features of law schools and their students in eighteenth-century France may be modified without denying the problem that contemporaries and historians affirm: some students, if not all, were inadequately trained. Experienced senior magistrates blamed the universities for the poor preparation of young lawyers and judges. The professors, in turn, held the courts responsible or were intimidated and remained silent. Since many of their delinquent students were sons of prominent and powerful magistrates, they dared not reprimand them severely and ceased to demand exact performance. In this play of mutual recriminations, the universities had more valid arguments: the courts would recruit better lawyers and judges, they claimed, if the magistrates gave strict entrance examinations and refused to grant age dispensations to candidates, thereby obliging young graduates to know the law and gain practical experience as *avocats* before becoming judges. Royal laws repeatedly had prescribed the stages of preparation necessary before admission to the courts in order to assure that magistrates were qualified. Both the Crown and the universities thus attributed the flaw in legal training to the practices of the courts. The present investigation substantiates the responsibility of the magistrates.

II

A law student who followed the prescribed pattern of schooling would receive his *licence* at age nineteen. He would then become an *avocat* and enter the bar by presenting his credentials and paying a fee to the Parlement. Yet he remained at the outset an apprentice, still a student rather

[10] Delbeke, 58.

than a practicing attorney. He could not yet argue a case, but he was required to attend sessions of the court to learn the procedure and to deepen his knowledge of the law; he might also attend special conferences where a senior *avocat* would examine concrete legal questions. During this period of apprenticeship, varying from two to five years in the different Parlements, he would become better acquainted with those subjects to which he had been introduced at law school. Even at this early stage, however, exceptions appear; in some instances, sons of *avocats* were immediately inscribed in the roll of lawyers of the Parlement and were admitted to full practice without having to complete any apprenticeship.[11]

If the young lawyer attached to the Paris Parlement adhered to legal stipulations, he would become a fully certified *avocat* at age twenty-one, and after 1751 at age twenty-three. To be eligible for an office as magistrate, he had to attend sessions of the court for two years, according to the edict of April 1679. Moreover, another edict of November 1683 prescribed a minimum age of twenty-five for *conseillers* in all the Parlements; this was the legal age of majority and, in theory, no one below that age could exercise any public function.[12] All these regulations were designed to ensure a minimum apprenticeship so that lawyers and judges would be grounded in the law and in court procedure. Were they fulfilled? So far as the intendants were concerned, the answer appears to be: not at all, with very few exceptions.

For 84 of these 94 intendants we know the age at which they obtained their *licences*, when they became *avocats* and how long they served their apprenticeship, or when they assumed their first position as magistrates, generally as *con-*

[11] *Ibid.,* 66–76. Between 1693 and 1751 the Paris Parlement required an apprenticeship of two years; in May 1751 this term was increased to four years.

[12] Guyot, III, 78, 79, 81. It is unclear whether the required two years of attendance at court sessions fell within the period of apprenticeship or followed full certification as an *avocat*.

seillers in a Parlement. A total of 74 among them were exceptions to the rules, obtaining their *licences,* becoming certified *avocats,* or entering judicial office before attaining the minimum age or completing the full period of training. Neither their numbers nor their mean ages changed significantly from one end of the century to the other, as the figures in Table 1 indicate. Among the intendants for the years

Table 1. Exceptions to legal requirements for *licences,* apprenticeship, and judicial office

Years	*Licence* (below age 19)	Apprentice- ship *	*Conseiller* (below age 25)	Mean age as *conseiller*
1710–1712	3	12 [7]	21	20–21
1749–1751	1	21 [10]	29	21–22
1774–1776	4	21 [18]	21 + 3 †	21
Total	8	54 [35]	71 + 3 †	

* According to Guyot, *Traité des droits,* III, 81: "Si c'est un office de judicature, il faut, aux termes des articles 16 et 17 de l'édit du mois d'avril 1679, que le Candidat rapporte des lettres de licence en droit civil et canonique, un matricule d'Avocat, et une attestation d'assiduité aux audience [des Cours et Sièges] pendant deux ans." This can be interpreted in two ways. Before 1751 a lawyer had to serve two years as an apprentice, then two years as a certified *avocat,* and became a magistrate at age twenty-three. After 1751 the regulations for the Paris Parlement were changed; thenceforth a lawyer had to serve four years as an apprentice, then two years as a certified *avocat,* and became a magistrate at age twenty-five. Alternatively, the required number of years of apprenticeship, both before becoming an *avocat* and before becoming a magistrate, might run concurrently. In this manner, before 1751 the lawyer might serve a total of only two years as apprentice and become a judge at age twenty-one; after 1751, the lawyer in the Paris Parlement might serve a total of only four years as apprentice and become a judge at age twenty-three. The figures based on the latter calculation are bracketed.

† This figure of three represents the three intendants who became judges at age twenty-five or older but who were still below the legal age for their particular office; see note 13.

1710–1712, 21 ignored regulations, becoming magistrates at a mean age of twenty to twenty-one; of the intendants during the period 1749–1751, 29 were exceptions and assumed office at a mean age of twenty-one to twenty-two; and for the intendants of 1774–1776, 24 were again exceptions[13] and their mean age as magistrates was twenty-one years. The eighteenth century as a whole did not witness a deterioration of standards, for at all times regulations were uniformly ignored.[14]

Two sets of figures in Table 1 require initial examination. First, more intendants serving Louis XVI, in comparison with those serving Louis XIV and Louis XV, did not complete the required period of apprenticeship as lawyers before becoming magistrates: 18, as opposed to 7 and 10, respectively (assuming that all these intendants had served concurrent years of apprenticeship before becoming *avocats* and judges). Was discipline becoming more lax in the second half of the century, and were a greater number of the later intendants less well trained? The intendants in the latter part of the century faced the more stringent four-year requirement of 1751 for apprentice *avocats* in the Paris Parlement, whereas those before them needed only to complete a two-year apprenticeship. Louis XVI's intendants thus had greater temptation to overlook legal stipulations and speed

[13] Included in this last group of 24 for the years 1774–1776 are 2 who became *maîtres des requêtes* before twenty-five and were therefore even younger when they became magistrates, and three who were twenty-five or more when they became judges but were still below the minimum age for their particular office. The latter three were François Marie Bruno d'Agay de Mutigney, intendant of Amiens (1771–1789), and Claude François Bertrand de Boucheporn, intendant of Corsica (1775–1785), both *avocats-généraux* at ages twenty-five and twenty-seven respectively, well before the stipulated age of thirty; and Charles Antoine Claude de Chazerat, intendant in Auvergne (1771–1790), who succeeded his father as first president of the Cour des Aides of Clermont-Ferrand at twenty-five instead of the legal minimum age of forty.

[14] According to Bluche, 57–58, the entrance age for magistrates in the Paris court very clearly fell after 1704. From 1659 to 1703 the mean age was twenty-five and a half; from 1704 to 1770 the mean age varied from just below twenty-two to almost twenty-four.

up their careers. If the regulation of 1751 had not been introduced and a two-year apprenticeship had still prevailed, then only 8 intendants under Louis XVI would not have completed their apprenticeship as *avocats*—a number similar to those intendants under Louis XIV and under Louis XV who had not completed their apprenticeship as lawyers before becoming magistrates. Apprenticeship in the courts in the second half of the century would then appear no more irregular than in the first half of the century, and the intendants of Louis XVI would not seem more poorly prepared than the intendants of Louis XIV or of Louis XV.

Secondly, more of Louis XV's intendants became *conseillers* before the minimum age of twenty-five than did Louis XIV's or Louis XVI's intendants: 29 in contrast to 21 each, respectively. Among the 29 of Louis XV's intendants who had ignored the rules, all but 4 had obtained judicial office between 1716 and 1737. Louis XV, certainly not the assiduous monarch that Louis XIV was, assumed his loose control over government and ruled without a first minister only after 1743. The preceding years of the Regency and the ministries of Dubois and Fleury represented the period when the Crown was most ineffective or indifferent in overseeing court practices and enforcing judicial requirements.

All three groups of intendants evaded the law in a clear and constant pattern, as Table 1 indicates. The least number in each group received their *licences* and became *avocats* before age nineteen: a total of 8.[15] Many more failed to complete their apprenticeship, sometimes remaining as *avocats* merely a few months before gaining office in a sovereign court: a total of either 54 or 35. By far the largest number in

[15] The youngest recorded age is seventeen: Nicolas Prosper Bauyn d'Angervilliers, intendant of Grenoble (1705–1715), became a *conseiller* in the Paris Parlement, and Gaspard Louis de Caze de la Bove, intendant in Brittany (1775–1785), became an *avocat* in the Châtelet, both at seventeen. The other six either received their *licences* or became *avocats* or even *conseillers* at eighteen.

all three periods became magistrates before they attained their majority, at the legal minimum age of twenty-five: a total of 71.[16] The conclusion is striking and confirms the criticisms of contemporaries. Fewer evasions of the rules occurred while the intendants studied at the law faculties. Most of the abuses took place when they began their professional careers in the courts, first as *avocats,* then as magistrates, when they had to be approved and accepted by the assembled body of judges. Thus, the magistrates themselves were directly implicated at the moment when abuses multiplied: they condoned, sanctioned, indeed promoted such disregard of legal regulations.

How did this game of exceptions and exemptions operate? In two ways: by means of the court-administered examinations and by grants of dispensations. A candidate for the magistracy appeared before the court for a threefold examination. He presented a speech in Latin as proof of his broad culture; as proof of his legal knowledge, he answered questions on a law, prepared in advance; and as a practical test of his knowledge, he explained a legal text chosen at random.[17] However, after the harangue, the presiding first president could ask the judges to admit the young lawyer without further formalities; and he often did, according to historians. Moreover, the court might even eliminate the entire examination and automatically accept the candidate as a *conseiller*—as the Paris Parlement did in January 1701 when it admitted Bernard Chauvelin de Beauséjour, the future intendant of Tours.[18] That examinations remained generally

[16] The age range was seventeen years to twenty-four, the largest single group (14) consisting of those who were twenty-one upon becoming magistrates.

[17] Mousnier, *La vénalité des offices,* 93 (following page references to Mousnier are to this work).

[18] Cf. Carrés d'Hozier 181, "Chauvelin," f. 55, for the "provision de l'office de Conseiller du Roy en sa Cour de Parlement de Paris," and f. 56 for the dispensation from taking the examination for the office of *conseiller* that Bernard Chauvelin de Beauséjour obtained. The declaration

superfluous and perfunctory is indicated by the fact that, from the late seventeenth century on, the court set in advance a single day for examining candidates, administering the oath, and receiving them as new magistrates.[19]

By the ruse of dispensations, the judges also overlooked the regulation regarding age and the prohibition against admitting close relatives into the same court.[20] Candidates for any of the magistracies might receive a single dispensation or a letter exempting them from both requirements. Bignon de Blanzy, future intendant of Paris (1709–1724), offers one such example. He obtained a "lettre de dispense d'âge donnée par le Roy . . . 17 avril 1689 à Roland Armand Bignon avocat au Parlement de Paris, âgé seulement de 22 ans et demy . . . pour être reçu en l'office d'avocat-général de Sa Majesté en sa Cour des Aydes."[21] Paul Esprit Marie de La Bourdonnaye de Blossac, intendant of Poitiers (1751–1784), obtained a similar dispensation to become a *conseiller* in the Paris Parlement when he was only twenty years and ten

---

of January 1700, which defined the subject matter of this examination, also provided the means of exempting candidates from it: dispensations might be given to those "who have already given proof of ability" and moreover such dispensations are "of right for those who previously have been received in another [judicial] office . . ." (Guyot, III, 114). In this instance, Chauvelin de Beauséjour became a *conseiller* at twenty-eight, following nine years as an *avocat* in the Paris Parlement. So many years in the court obviously provided sufficient proof of his capacity, though this might not always be true of others who were exempted.

[19] Three authors describe the examinations for new magistrates as meaningless: Bluche, 61–62; Glasson, 51–52; and Franklin L. Ford, *Robe and Sword: The Regrouping of the French Aristocracy after Louis XIV* (Cambridge, Mass., 1953), 117.

[20] There were also "dispense d'études" allowing young men to become *avocats* in the courts before completing the full course of studies. The single example I found is that of Jacques Etienne Turgot de Soumons, who in 1688 at age eighteen became "avocat du Roi aux Requêtes de l'Hôtel." Cf. PO 2897, "Turgot," f. 108.

[21] PO 344, "Bignon," f. 844.

months.[22] Technically, these young judges merely had the right to hold the office and to attend sessions of the court, the right to participate and vote in the deliberations being withheld until they attained the minimum age of twenty-five. Even this reservation was overcome: François Marie Peirenc de Moras, intendant of Riom from 1750–1752, was admitted as a *conseiller* in the Paris Parlement with a "dispense d'âge" in July, 1737 when he was nineteen, and only four years later he was granted "voix délibérative," the right to speak and to vote.[23] When Jacques III Pineau de Lucé, future intendant of Hainaut-Meubeuge (1745–1752), became at age twenty-one a *conseiller* in the Paris Parlement, where his father was equally a *conseiller,* he obtained "lettres de dispense d'âge et de parenté."[24] Presumably, Jean François III Joly de Fleury de la Valette, intendant in Burgundy (1749–1760 or 1767), received a similar dispensation at age nineteen when he became *substitut* to the *procureur-général* in the Parlement, his father.[25]

[22] Carrés d'Hozier 122, "Bourdonnaie," f. 234.

[23] PO 2255, "Peyrenc," f. 20. Jean François Claude Perrin de Cypierre, intendant of Orléans (1760–1785), similarly received "voix délibérative" at age twenty-two when he was a *conseiller* in the Grand Conseil; cf. Louis Guérin, *L'intendant de Cypierre et la vie économique de l'Orléanois, 1760–1785* (Orléans, 1938), 18. According to Guyot, III, 79–80: ". . . with regard to the right to express opinions in judicial decisions, . . . the declaration of 20 May 1713 grants the right to speak and to vote to the minor holding a judicial office when he is a *rapporteur.*"

[24] DB 524, "Pineau," f. 21. The Roman numeral following the name of this intendant and of others in this book represents the form genealogists use to distinguish members of one family bearing the same name.

[25] Cf. Guyot, III, 81–83, for the prohibitions—and dispensations—regarding close family relations in the same court: "The edict of August 1669 prohibits relatives of the first, second or third degree, who are father and son, brothers, uncle and nephew, and relatives through marriage of the first and second degree, who are the father-in-law, the son-in-law, and the brothers-in-law, from possessing or

Letters of dispensation in effect were letters of the Chancellery, issued and authorized by the chancellor, a royal official, in the name of the king. The traditional formula was "dispense . . . donnée [or "accordée"] par le Roy"; and the staple reasons, expressed in these letters, were that the king desired to recognize the superior qualities and talents of the candidate or to reward the able and loyal services of his father and ancestors.[26] However, the rhetoric conceals the historical truth. These practices, in effect violations or forced manipulations of the law, resulted from the desires and interests of the magistrates themselves, which were embedded in the elemental mores, values, and goals of the *ancien régime*

---

exercising conjointly any office whether in the sovereign courts or in lower courts, on pain of invalidating the provisions which will be expedited as well as the receptions which will be made in contravention of these prohibitions, and of the loss of the offices.

"The same edict prohibits holders of offices received and serving at the moment in judicial bodies from contracting an alliance in the first degree, of father-in-law and son-in-law, on pain of confiscation of office of the last entrant.

"The letters of dispensation which are spoken of in that edict [i.e., 30 September 1728] and in that of January 1682, are given very easily today."

According to Bluche, 55, one of the first edicts prohibiting close relatives from being judges in the same court dates from January 1597. The Crown recognized, however, that it could not prevent such practices and instead tried to counteract its effects by another device embodied in the declaration of 25 August 1708: "The opinions of officers who are related in the following degrees; father and son, brothers, uncle and nephew" or "related through marriage in the following degrees; father-in-law, son-in-law and brother-in-law only, will count merely for one when they are the same."

[26] Carrés d'Hozier 122, "Bourdonnaie," f. 234, letter to the future intendant of Poitiers (1751–1784), Paul Esprit Marie de La Bourdonnaye de Blossac, July 1737; Nouveau d'Hozier 136, "Flesselles," f. 2, letter of 14 December 1751 to Jacques de Flesselles, future intendant of Lyon (1765–1784); and Chérin 24, f. 45, letter of 12 May 1741 to Henri Léonard Jean Baptiste Bertin de Bellille, future intendant of Perpignan (1750–1753) and controller-general (1759–1763).

society. Judges could purchase and sell their offices, own and bequeath them. They, or anyone with enough money, might buy an office for a son or transfer the rights to their own office to an heir or relative. A judicial office signified status, prestige, and wealth; men sought these positions and strove to retain their rights to these offices. Hence, the pressure was on the Crown to accede to their desires. When a candidate already possessed an office through transfer, purchase, or inheritance, the king could not easily bar him from becoming a magistrate, nor would the other judges refuse to admit him. The Crown as well turned this practice to its own advantage: the royal treasury always received part of the purchase price for the offices, and the king aimed to tie these officeholders to him in loyalty and dependence by such marks of recognition and reward.[27]

[27] For a thorough, penetrating, and definitive examination of this aspect of *ancien régime* society and government, see Mousnier, 101.

Royal edicts of Aug. 1669 and Feb. 1672 prescribed penalties for disobeying the age requirements: voiding of the acts of provision and reception to judicial offices, confiscation of the property rights and value of the office to the king's profit, and prohibition against holding a judicial office in the future. Yet these laws were never carried out. Moreover, immediately following the listing of various punishments in the edicts comes the phrase "without an explicit dispensation declared by special letter" (cf. Guyot, III, 79). Thus, with a single flourish the Crown threatened punishments and contravened its injunctions: in effect, it abdicated its authority to enforce these regulations.

CHAPTER 2

Magistrates in the Courts: The Judicial Experience of Intendants and the Crown's Policy of Recruitment

I

The young student and lawyer next became a magistrate. Of the ninety-four intendants studied, eighty-nine previously had been judges, sharing the experience of court work. Yet, their education did not cease nor was it ever limited to the few years of study in the law faculty. Regular schooling never monopolized professional preparation in the *ancien régime* as it does in the modern age; family tradition, the home milieu, and practical apprenticeship all served to educate young men and to train them for their careers. Fathers and grandfathers who were judges stood forth as models to emulate; fathers, uncles, and family friends imparted their professional knowledge and advice to these young men; and certainly individual tutors taught the young *collégiens* and law students in the privacy of family libraries or in small conference groups.[1] When a student became a young lawyer, and more significantly, when he became a *jeune magistrat*, he was considered competent and sufficiently mature for his

---

[1] Cf. Bluche, 247.

job, but not yet fully prepared and still in the process of training.[2]

The young judges, whether aged eighteen or twenty-five and whether or not they could vote, were supposed to attend sessions of the court to hear the senior magistrates deliberate legal cases and decide administrative questions; if they were members of a Parlement, they would also hear their colleagues debate the merits of edicts the Crown submitted for registration.[3] Thus, during their first few years, the court was, for the younger members, an extension of the law faculty, and its discussions replaced their professors' lectures, perhaps to better effect. The junior magistrate would broaden his knowledge of the contents of laws, become familiar with complex legal procedures, and learn to apply written laws and customs to a variety of complicated legal problems. If he also had the right to express his opinions and present reports regarding cases before the court, he then had the opportunity, and was obliged, to examine issues more thoroughly and to defend his conclusions logically and lu-

[2] Men of the *ancien régime* conceived of age as well as education in ways profoundly different from the views held by men of the twentieth century. Just as they did not consider education to be synonymous with schooling, so they believed that maturity was not strictly determined by legal age and accepted youths as adults at ages that today still render them adolescents. These ideas undoubtedly served to rationalize their extralegal practices, such as the admission of "child-judges"; but apprenticeship and learning apart from formal schooling undoubtedly served to counteract these defects. For a historical survey of the various conceptions of age, education, and the roles of different age groups in Western society, see Philippe Ariès, *Centuries of Childhood: A Social History of Family Life,* trans. by Robert Baldick (New York, 1962) .

[3] It should be remembered that the courts of the *ancien régime* had general judicial authority as well as administrative competence. See Bluche, 51–53, for the functions of the Paris Parlement, and Ford, 37–41, for a precise account of the various activities of all the sovereign courts—Parlements, Chambres des Comptes, Cours des Aides, Cours des Monnaies, and the Grand Conseil.

cidly.[4] Since each court had numerous magistrates as members—the most active generally being the most capable and experienced—and decisions resulted from general vote, the relatively inexperienced young magistrates would be advised, instructed, and counterbalanced by their seniors; their

[4] The following excerpt from the edict of 20 May 1713, which conferred upon *rapporteurs* below twenty-five the right to speak and to vote and justified these dispensations, concisely expresses the view that the presence of young judges in the courts provided them with legal training and practical experience. "The concern which we have always had to confer the administration of justice only on judges capable of rendering it well to our subjects has caused us to seek with care the most proper means for instructing those who enter the magistracy in all their duties; it is with this end in mind that we have . . . granted dispensations more easily, and at a younger age than previously, on condition nevertheless of having the right to speak and vote only at the age prescribed by our ordinances, so that before they undertake their functions they can learn all that is necessary in order to judge worthily; and while attending court proceedings and seeing how judges render decisions, they can model themselves according to the worthy examples before them and imbibe the spirit of the true principles of jurisprudence; we have had the satisfaction of seeing this succeed. . . . We may contribute still more to the instruction of young magistrates if we permit them to deliver reports on the proceedings and present their own views, because the necessity which this imposes to examine and discuss an entire case in order to report and vote on it will make them used to work at an early age and prevent them even from falling into frivolous ways; we believe we should grant them this permission, all the more as we are convinced that the litigants will not suffer any prejudice, because the desire of the young judges to distinguish themselves and to make a reputation for themselves, together with the love of their duty, will be sufficiently strong motives to oblige them to examine with scrupulous exactitude the lawsuits which they are encharged with, and furthermore if something escapes their attention the [senior] judges appointed to assist them at the time of their report will not fail to notice it and to call their attention to it." (Cf. Guyot, III, 80, n. 1. My translation.) Certainly this edict is laden with rhetoric, for the Crown attempted to put the best interpretation on a measure that social pressure forced it to take in order to legitimize prevailing practices; nevertheless, it does concretely describe the potential benefits that might result and perhaps actually did.

judgments would therefore not cause irreparable harm.[5] Moreover, an ambitious magistrate who wanted to advance his career had to be assiduous and was most likely to benefit from court work. Thus, this stage in the *cursus honorum* of future intendants proved valuable for their professional development: it provided their apprenticeship in the practical workings of the law, which in turn initiated them into concrete problems of individuals and of government.

II

The judicial careers of these intendants were neither uniform nor totally disparate; while the sequence of their professional advance varied, certain distinct patterns reveal themselves. Throughout the century these patterns remain generally constant, but from one period to the next the few changes in the character of their judicial offices may indicate subtle changes in the Crown's policy of recruitment and in the balance of political and social forces in the nation which determined or influenced this policy.

Eighty-six of the 89 intendants were former magistrates who had served in the sovereign courts. At all times, judges—*conseillers*—from the Paris Parlement predominated: there were 15 Paris parlementarians out of 26 former magistrates among the intendants for the period 1710–1712; 24 out of 32 former magistrates among the intendants for the period 1749–1751; and 13 out of 28 former magistrates among the intendants for the years 1774–1776, plus 2 who had been *substituts* in the Paris Parlement before advancing to higher office in another sovereign court.[6] Thus, of the total of 89 intendants who were former judges, 58 percent came into the corps from the Paris Parlement.

[5] Bluche, 282, states that the actual work of the Paris Parlement was done by a handful of the best judges in that body. See also Ford, 47, n. 24.

[6] The *substituts* assisted the three *avocats-généraux* and the *procureur-général* who represented the king's interest in the parlementary deliberations.

Among the other thirty sovereign courts in eighteenth-century France, only fourteen sent their former members into the ranks of the intendants during these three periods. The provincial Parlement of Metz had the highest representation, and, indeed, it served as a testing and training ground for young magistrates who wished to prove their ability and advance in the government hierarchy. Two former *conseillers,* one later serving in a more important court, were intendants during the first period; this was exactly repeated for the intendants of the second period; and among the intendants serving in 1774–1776, one had been a *conseiller* and *avocat-général* in Metz. The other provincial Parlements whose former members were represented among the intendants included in this study were: 1710–1712—Rennes (Brittany), Aix (Provence), and Rouen (Normandy), one *conseiller* each; 1749–1751—Toulouse (Languedoc), Dijon (Burgundy), Grenoble (Dauphiné), and Aix, again one *conseiller* each, the latter magistrate succeeding first to a more prominent court following his service in Provence and before becoming an intendant; 1774–1776—Douai (Flanders) represented by a former *procureur-général* who previously had been *avocat-général* in the Conseil Provincial of neighboring Arras (Artois), Besançon (Franche-Comté) with a former double officeholder, its *avocat-général* and *procureur-général* among the intendants, Dijon with one *conseiller,* and Dombes with a former member who had held the offices of *avocat-général, conseiller,* and first president.[7]

Only three of the sovereign courts that were not Parlements had former members who became intendants during these three periods. Among these was the Paris Cour des Aides: a former *avocat-général* and a former *conseiller* were

---

[7] The magistrate from Dombes who became an intendant was a unique case. Dombes was an autonomous principality until France annexed it in 1762 and integrated it into the French administrative system by establishing an intendancy there; at the same time the Parlement of Dombes was suppressed and its first president, Jean Benoît Cachet de Garnerans, became the new intendant of Trévoux.

among the intendants during the years 1710–1712, and a member who previously had been both its *avocat-général* and a *conseiller d'honneur* was among the intendants for the years 1749–1751.[8] Only one other Cour des Aides is included in this group: Clermont-Ferrand had its first president among the intendants during the years 1774–1776. The last of the sovereign courts whose members became provincial intendants during the periods studied was the Grand Conseil in Paris. Among the intendants for the years 1710–1712, five were former *conseillers* of the Grand Conseil, one of whom was previously a magistrate in the Parlement of Metz; for the period 1749–1751, three of the intendants had served on the Grand Conseil, and one of them was a former provincial parlementarian from Aix; during the years 1774–1776, the number of former magistrates of the Grand Conseil among the intendants increased to nine, one of these having served as *avocat-général* on this body after having been a *conseiller*.

Success undoubtedly lay in Paris for the future intendants. Parisian magistrates—from the Parlement, the Grand Conseil, and the Cour des Aides—who advanced directly from those courts first into the ranks of the *maîtres des requêtes* and then into the corps of intendants numbered: 22 out of the 26 intendants for the years 1710–1712 who had been sovereign-court judges, plus 3 from other Paris courts;[9] 28

---

[8] An honorary councilor in any of the sovereign courts was one who had resigned his office of councilor but continued to bear the title and retain its privileges, and to attend, participate, and vote in the sessions of the court; he could not, however, receive the income and emoluments of the office, since he had sold it to another party whose property it became. Royal letters patent conferred this privilege on the former magistrate. Cf. Guyot, IV, 21, for the legal basis of this practice; and AN, X¹ᴬ8781, f. 151–52, for the precise contents of such a letter granted 12 October 1766 to Antoine Jean Baptiste Jullien, intendant of Alençon (1766–1790).

[9] Of these three, one came from the Châtelet, a presidial court directly below the Parlement in rank, and two came from the Requêtes de l'Hôtel, the tribunal exercising jurisdiction over members and officers of the royal household.

out of the 32 intendants for 1749–1751; and 22 of the 28 intendants for the years 1774–1776. In short, of the total of 89 intendants for these three periods whose judicial careers can be determined, only 14 had not been judges in any of the Paris courts.

Native Parisians, of course, by birth and residence and with relatives or long-standing friends and acquaintances in the capital, were better placed to obtain judgeships in Paris and later higher positions. Yet, even these figures do not fully indicate the predominance of Paris, the quasi monopoly of Parisians, in the royal administration. Several intendants who were in provincial courts before obtaining Paris magistracies, and even more who were provincial *conseillers* before becoming *maîtres des requêtes,* actually were Parisians. They had become members of provincial courts instead of those in Paris for one of two reasons: either judicial offices in the provinces were easier or cheaper to obtain than those in Paris; or, in some instances, their fathers were royal officials in the provinces, and their families resided there for the time, so they could conveniently serve in the provincial court while remaining with the family.[10]

[10] Jean Charles Doujat, intendant of Flanders, i.e., Hainaut-Meubeuge (1708–1720), and Jean Moreau de Séchelles, intendant of Lille from 1743 to about 1754, had both been *conseillers* in the Parlement of Metz before advancing to a Paris court, the former to the Grand Conseil and the latter to the Parlement. Louis Claude Le Blanc, intendant of maritime Flanders, i.e., Dunkerque and Ypres (1708–1716), and Jean Louis de Bernage de Vaux, intendant of Moulins (1744–1756), were Parisians who served as provincial magistrates only, the former at Metz and the latter in Toulouse. Cardin II Le Bret, intendant of Aix (1704–1734), and Louis Arnaud de La Briffe des Ferrières, intendant of Caen (1740–1752), were *conseillers* in Aix and Dijon, respectively, because their fathers were then intendants in the same provinces. Charles Jean Baptiste des Gallois de la Tour, intendant of Aix (1744–1771 and 1775–1790), had been a *conseiller* in Aix while his father was there as intendant; but he then became a *conseiller* on the Grand Conseil in the same year he entered the ranks of *maîtres des requêtes,* and so he is listed as a Paris magistrate. Taking into account

A young provincial—born and raised in *province*—who wanted to make his career in government knew that he had to go to Paris. Only in the capital could his intelligence and ability, his wit or charm, possibly catch the eye of a minister, courtier, or royal official who would be willing to favor him and had the power to promote his fortune. And so Paris drew to itself these ambitious provincials and quickly made them Parisians; but for those among them who dreamed of important, powerful government posts, the most coveted rewards came slowly, after years, decades, or generations in the capital. Immediate success eluded the provincial who himself had moved from his distant native region in the hope of securing prominent office; he only began what his son or grandson could better and more easily accomplish. Many among these intendants, specifically those eighty-two who were natives of Paris or held judgeships there, came from families that had originated in the provinces. Few of the intendants themselves, however, had moved from the provinces directly to a Parisian court and immediately advanced into the ranks of *maîtres des requêtes* and then into the corps of intendants. Apart from the ten who graduated directly from provincial courts into the royal administration, only four or possibly five "new Parisians" succeeded in transplanting themselves from their province and becoming Paris magistrates and then royal intendants. All, as we shall see, were intendants in 1774–1776.[11]

Le Blanc, Bernage, Le Bret, and La Briffe reduces from 14 to 10 the number of non-Parisian intendants recruited outside of Paris. The corrected figures for the first two periods are: 24 out of 26, plus the 3 from the Châtelet and the Requêtes de l'Hôtel, for the years 1710–1712; and 30 out of 32 for 1749–1751. The figures for the years 1774–1776 remain the same: 22 out of 28 intendants.

[11] These were: Charles François Hyacinthe Esmangart (Bordeaux, 1770–1775); Christophe Pajot de Marcheval (Grenoble, 1761–1784); Jean Claude François Perrin de Cypierre (Orléans, 1760–1785); Jean Samuel de Pont de Monderoux (Moulins, 1765–1778); and possibly Antoine Jean Baptiste Jullien (Alençon, 1766–1790). Three others

Paris retained its hold as a recruiting ground for intendants for definite and significant reasons. Certainly the Crown, through its ministers, could "test" the abilities of magistrates if it could see them at work in the courts of the capital; or it could easily hear about able young magistrates performing in the nearby courts. From among the intelligent judges close at hand, the ministers could conveniently select the more gifted for the posts of *maîtres des requêtes* and higher positions in the royal administration. Subtler social and political forces also operated, influencing and reinforcing the effects of the Crown's rational calculations. Sovereign-court judges, and Parisian magistrates in particular, had much power and greater prestige. Their ambitions certainly did not remain limited to the *palais de justice;* they coveted high posts in the royal service for themselves or for one of their sons. Perhaps they knew a minister or had a relative or friend in Parisian society who knew one; more opportunities fell to them to solicit favors and to request appointments than to their provincial colleagues. Certainly individuals and families who had lived for some time in the world of Paris society had more connections and important contacts for their benefit than did newly arrived young provincials. Where could the Crown presume to find better-trained judges, potentially better administrators, than in the Paris courts, which conducted the most important judicial business in the kingdom? Moreover, from the little-known or equally capable candidates, ministers would prefer to choose magistrates who were relatives, friends, or acquaintances—

---

might be added to this list, but with reservations since they had relatives (a father, uncles, or a cousin) in the Parlement or on the Royal Council: Henri Léonard Jean Baptiste Bertin de Bellille (Perpignan, 1750–1753, and controller-general, 1759–1763) ; Paul Esprit Marie de La Bourdonnaye de Blossac (Poitiers, 1751–1784) ; and Louis Gabriel Taboureau des Réaux (Valenciennes, 1764–1775) . See Part II, Chapter 5 below for a comparative analysis of the geographic origins of the intendants' families.

those who would feel personally indebted to them for their advancement. In this way, they could staff the administration with their favorites and their clients, thereby assuring themselves of support in government deliberations, and through personal fidelity to themselves, committing these royal officials to loyal service to the king.

The predominance of Parisian magistrates (both those

Table 2. A comparison of natives and magistrates of Paris to provincial magistrates in the corps of intendants

Years	Paris	Provinces	Total	Percentage of Parisians
1710–1712	27	2	29 *	93%
1749–1751	30	2	32	94%
1774–1776	22	6	28 *	78.5%

* The judicial careers of four of the intendants in the third period are unknown, and biographical data about one intendant in the first period indicate that he was never a magistrate; their place of birth or their families' residence, however, can be adduced from the available evidence. The father of François de Beauharnois, intendant of La Rochelle (1710–1715), lived in Orléans; Marie Jean Baptiste Nicolas d'Aine, intendant of Limoges (1774–1783), was born in Paris; Antoine Jean Amelot de Chaillou, intendant of Dijon (1764–1776), and Antoine Jean Terray, intendant of Montauban (1773–1781), were both of families prominent in Paris. With these men included, the number of Parisians among the intendants becomes: 27 out of 30 (90%) for the first period, and 25 out of 31 (80%) for the third period.

who were born in the capital and those who had served in the Paris courts) over the provincials clearly fluctuated during the eighteenth century, as Table 2 indicates. These data may be examined from two points of view: the deliberate policy of the Crown regarding administrative preferment; and the ministers' response to pressure which the Paris magistrates in general, and the parlementarians in particular, brought to bear upon the Crown's actual procedures.

The higher proportion of Parisians among the intendants

in the first two periods indicates that the Paris magistrates were most effective in influencing the ministers' choices in the first half of the century; the parlementarians especially exercised greatest weight during the earlier part of Louis XV's reign, the period when the intendants of 1749–1751 entered the corps of *maîtres des requêtes*.[12] In numbers and percentage there were fewer Parisians in the later period, either because they were less eager for these posts or because the Crown was more reluctant to bestow the offices on them. The first explanation seems improbable: why should they willingly slacken their pursuit of this important office? Most likely, the appearance of more non-Parisians as intendants indicates that in the second half of the century the Crown altered its recruiting practices.

There was no preponderant change in personnel. A few more provincials entered the corps, four more than in the preceding two periods: a total of six among the thirty-two intendants. Their proportionate increase was somewhat greater, provincials constituting 21 percent in the third period compared to 6 or 7 percent in the first two periods, a not insubstantial total gain of 15 percent. Nor was there any enunciated policy change; indeed, the king's ministers might not have been fully conscious of the total import and final results of their individual actions. Nevertheless, beginning approximately in the 1760's, slightly more non-Parisian magistrates entered the royal administration as *maîtres des requêtes,* eventually to become intendants.[13] Why in particular

[12] The intendants of the second period, except one who became a *maître des requêtes* in 1710, all entered the latter corps between 1719 and 1745. It was a known fact at the turn of the eighteenth century that the Chambre des Enquêtes of the Paris Parlement was "the necessary training-ground in order to become a *maître des requêtes* in Paris"; cf. J. Marchand, *Un intendant sous Louis XIV: Étude sur l'administration de Lebret en Provence, 1687–1704* (Paris, 1889), 23.

[13] Of the six provincials among the intendants in 1774–1776, the earliest entered the royal administration in 1759 and the latest in 1771; the last, Charles Antoine Claude de Chazerat, became intendant in his

instances would ministers select such individuals? Perhaps they hoped to counteract the influence of the Paris high robe in general, and more specifically, the latter's influence on recruitment into the administrative service, by favoring the provincial robe; after all, the Crown was soon to attack directly the political pretensions of Paris magistrates. Perhaps the ministers also believed that former provincial magistrates would be more pliable and loyal servants of the Crown, more influential in their own or neighboring provinces, and less apt to support the political claims of the Paris judges.

Precise information about individual cases tends to confirm this interpretation. Two among the six intendants in 1774–1776 who were former provincial magistrates were appointed to the provinces where they had served as judges and in which they resided. Undoubtedly, the Crown chose them because of the influence they wielded in their provinces, enabling them to exact from the inhabitants, especially from the magistrates, obedience or at least acquiescence to royal policy. In one of these two instances the Crown appointed as intendant, at the time of the Maupeou reforms, the first president of the Cour des Aides of Clermont-Ferrand, who was willing to establish the new Conseil Supérieur and to recruit his colleagues for this tribunal; in contrast, his predecessor, a former Parisian magistrate, supported the Paris parlementarians and had refused to co-operate in suppressing their court.[14]

---

native province of Auvergne in 1771 (previously having been first president of the Cour des Aides), and only two years later, in 1773, did he become a *maître des requêtes*.

[14] The dismissed intendant was Antoine Jean Baptiste Robert Auget de Montyon, intendant in Auvergne (1767–1771), who refused to combine the functions of intendant with those of first president of the new Conseil Supérieur, which the Crown desired. Subsequently, he was appointed intendant of Aix and of La Rochelle, but his career in the royal administration was henceforth compromised because of his opposition to this judicial reform. The Auvergnat was Charles Antoine Claude

A striking contrast between the kinds of provincial judges who became intendants in the first two periods and in the last period further underscores the significance of this change in recruitment. All four during the years 1710–1712 and 1749–1751 had been *conseillers* in their Parlement. Of the six during the years 1774–1776, four had been either *procureurs-généraux* or *avocats-généraux;* one of the latter plus a fifth had been *premiers présidents;* and only one had been a *conseiller.* In the organization and functions of a Parlement, the *avocats-généraux* and *procureurs-généraux* were the *gens du roi:* they represented the king's interests and argued for the Crown. Moreover, these two magistracies and the post of first president were not venal charges, held as personal property. They were conferred as royal commissions, so that by law the Crown retained its authority over these posts, and in practice these judges remained dependent on the king's good will.[15] Consequently, they would have to demonstrate loyal service to retain their posts, and in performing their work they would more likely adopt the Crown's outlook. Such was the role assigned to the *avocats-généraux,* the *procureurs-généraux,* and the first presidents, and with few exceptions this was the traditional role they played between Crown and court. Among the sovereign-court magistrates, the "king's men" and his first presidents would obviously make the best

---

de Chazerat; he remained intendant from 1771 to 1790, when the Revolution suppressed these offices. For various accounts of this episode see René Allisan de Chazet, *Vie de M. de Montyon* (Paris, 1829), 15–16; Fernand Louis Edmond Labour, *M. de Montyon* (Paris, 1880), 32–35; and Louis Guimbaud, *Un grand bourgeois au XVIII⁰ siècle: Auget de Montyon, 1733–1820* (Paris, 1909), 129. The second of the intendants referred to above was Cachet de Garnerans, intendant of Trévoux (1762–1782). When the principality of Dombes was annexed to France and its Parlement suppressed, he as the first president was the obvious choice as intendant of this new province.

[15] Cf. Ford, 118; Bluche, 49; and Paul Bisson de Barthélémy, *L'activité d'un procureur général au Parlement de Paris à la fin de l'Ancien Régime: Les Joly de Fleury* (Paris, 1964), 29, n. 50.

intendants. Not until the last years of the monarchy did some of these officials betray their trust and, allied with the corps of venal judges, attack or condone attacks on the royal government.[16] But this reversal occurred years after the *gens du roi* in this study had entered the corps of intendants; at that earlier date the Crown could still reasonably assume that *avocats-généraux* and *procureurs-généraux,* by their training, might make more trustworthy agents than simple *conseillers.*

The presence of more provincial magistrates among the intendants in the later period, especially of the nonvenal *gens du roi* and first presidents, is not alone sufficient evidence that the Crown modified its recruiting practices. Yet these two changes parallel a third: the proportions among the several groups of Paris magistrates represented in the corps during the years 1774–1776 also shifted. The same significance attaches to the three series of changes.

The percentage of former Paris parlementarians within the corps of intendants varied substantially: 50 percent for the years 1710–1712; 75 percent for 1749–1751; and 41 per-

[16] The Breton La Chalotais is the first glaring exception among the *gens du roi;* in the 1760's he attacked the royal governor and, by extension, royal authority in defense of provincial and corporate privileges and powers. When the Maupeou reforms to suppress the Parlements were introduced in 1771, some of the *avocats-généraux* and *procureurs-généraux* refused to support the Crown and defended the existence of the courts. After this date it was not until the middle and late 1780's, notably in 1788, that some of the "king's men" joined in or led the sovereign-courts' insistent demands for political power, and most of them lost directing control over the magistrates. The *procureur-général* of the Paris Parlement, Guillaume François Louis Joly de Fleury, torn between responsiblity to his sovereign and loyalty to his colleagues, was powerless to sway the judges and, because he could do nothing else, passively supported their claims. (See Bisson de Barthé-lémy, 9–10, 40, 49–51, 55, 58.) In contrast, the first *avocat-général* of the Paris Parlement, Séguier, actively took the lead in the parlementary campaign against the Crown. (See Jean Egret, *La pré-Révolution fran-çaise, 1787–1788* [Paris, 1962], 208–10.)

cent for 1774–1776. The intendants for the first period included one who entered the corps directly from the Paris Châtelet and two who entered following service on the Requêtes de l'Hôtel; in the two later periods, all the intendants were drawn from the sovereign courts. Moreover, a decreasing number of former members of the Paris Cour des Aides became intendants: two for the first period, one for the second period, and none for the third. At the same time, the intendants who were former *conseillers* of the Grand Conseil decreased in numbers during the second period and then increased in the third. Table 3 illustrates the changes in the pattern of recruitment among the Paris judges:

Table 3. Proportion of magistrates from different Paris courts among the intendants in each of the three periods

Years	Parlement	Cour des Aides	Grand Conseil	Châtelet	Requêtes de l'Hôtel
1710–1712	15	2	5	1	2
1749–1751	24	1	3	0	0
1774–1776	13	0	9	0	0

The sovereign courts in the capital clearly acquired a monopoly among the Paris judges who entered the royal administration and became intendants. This can be explained in two ways. On the one hand, magistrates in the sovereign courts undoubtedly pressured the ministers more forcefully and effectively to grant these posts to them; the parlementarians in particular were most successful during the first half of Louis XV's reign, which accounts for their exceptionally large numbers among the intendants for the years 1749–1751. On the other hand, the ministers seemed to become more discriminating in their choice. They ceased to recruit judges from the lower courts of Paris, such as the Châtelet, or from special tribunals, such as the Requêtes de l'Hôtel, and selected only those from the sovereign courts where magistrates gained experience in judging more complicated and significant legal problems which their work as future intendants demanded. This also explains why judges from the Cour des Aides ceased to appear in the ranks of the intendants: their work in this court limited them to adjudicating only appeals of tax cases.[17] Yet the last and most significant change in the recruitment of Paris magistrates concerned the Grand Conseil: in the second half of the century, the Crown increasingly recruited judges from the Grand Conseil as opposed to magistrates from the Parlement.

What accounts for the appeal of the Grand Conseil to the royal government? There are two conceivable answers. First, judges on this court decided select judicial problems, which gave them more valuable professional experience. The Grand Conseil adjudicated three categories of cases: those involving jurisdictional conflicts between courts; those withdrawn or on appeal from all other tribunals, including the Parlements; and those, whether civil or criminal disputes, which the Royal Council sent to it. Moreover, its judgments were supreme, bearing greater authority than decisions of all other sovereign courts and having effect throughout France. Thus, the character of the Grand Conseil's functions made it technically a supreme court. More importantly, it received disputes for which the Crown sought equitable or favorable judgment and thereby became the king's favorite among the sovereign courts. As a result, its members would tend to adopt the royal outlook, and so from the Crown's point of view they were pre-eminent judges and promising administrators (though they remained the least prestigious among the magistrates in eighteenth-century France).

Second, the Crown had more direct control over the Grand Conseil than over the other sovereign courts. From 1738 on, the several presidents of this court were no longer venal officeholders but royal officials—*conseillers d'état* and *maî-*

---

[17] Cf. Ford, 39–40.

tres des requêtes—whom the king appointed to serve for a designated period of years. Undoubtedly, the king's agents guided the work, channeled the energies, and influenced the views of their subordinates in the court. The magistrates on the Grand Conseil, therefore, would absorb from their seniors a sympathetic appreciation of royal interests and a strong sense of faithful service to the king: in short, they were molded to suit the Crown's needs. Whether by foresight or chance, they received a model apprenticeship for royal administrators.[18]

III

The overwhelming number of intendants during the eighteenth century had been sovereign-court magistrates before entering the royal service. Yet not all came from the same courts or held the same judgeships; and depending on the location of their courts or the nature of their offices, some could more easily gain high office at all times, while others had greater promise as royal servants. Thus the corps of intendants included a variety of former magistrates, and the proportions among them altered in the course of the century.

During the first three decades of Louis XV's reign, sovereign-court magistrates in the capital obtained a greater number of important coveted positions in the central administration as a result of forceful influence which they exerted on ministers who selected recruits. This reflects the greater political power the courts accumulated during this period. In the

---

[18] On the Grand Conseil see *ibid.*, 40 and 53, n. 36; Chérin 24, "Bertin," f. 65; Aucoc, 36–37; and René Kerviler, "Etudes sur les Bignon," *Le bibliophile français*, (Nov. 1872), 337. In Volume VIII[2] of the *Histoire de France* (ed. Ernest Lavisse), H. Carré describes the Grand Conseil as "instituted . . . to execute the will of the King . . ." (241). This proved true when in 1771 the members of this court agreed to replace the recently suppressd Paris Parlement by serving on the new superior court established in Paris. Socially, Carré states, "they . . . hardly counted in the world of the salons" in the capital (397). This was perhaps another reason why the Crown increasingly turned to these judges in selecting intendants.

final three decades of the *ancien régime,* however, the Crown decidedly modified its policy: Paris parlementarians continued to become intendants, yet royal ministers gradually selected more men from provincial courts and from the Grand Conseil. All three groups of judges shared traits that enabled them in general to enter the corps: competence allied to influence and ambition. By mid-century however, the government had strong reasons for favoring the provincials and the *Grand Conseillers.*

Periodically in the last half of the century, the Crown and the Paris Parlement became embroiled in conflicts of policy and competing claims to power. By deliberate calculation or perhaps by intuitive reaction, the king and his ministers awakened to the danger of excessive recruitment into the administrative service of Paris parlementarians. The experiences of these magistrates might have developed within them deep commitments to or strong sympathies for the parlementary point of view. Whether willfully or not, this might weaken their loyalty to the Crown and check their support of its interests; in practice, these men might then be lax in enforcing royal laws or might oppose executing royal programs that aroused the easy hostility of the Paris Parlement. Consequently, the government had to seek and appoint men more politically reliable, whose trustworthiness and attachment to the king might be presumed. Clearly, the monarchy needed administrators tutored in royalism, removed from the imbroglio of Paris politics, and unnurtured by the pretensions of stalwart Paris parlementarians. At the same time, the central government was assuming greater responsibility in national life and undertaking more active measures of reform and improvement. Therefore, it required agents acquainted with broad and complex governmental affairs. The few changes in the pattern of recruiting intendants that occurred from 1760 on reflect these central political and administrative concerns, and indicate the initial response of the royal government. The Crown would not jeopardize its invaluable means of command.

CHAPTER 3

From Sovereign Court to Royal Council: Admission as *Maîtres des Requêtes*

I

The young magistrate in a sovereign court had an alternative before him: to remain a judge and rise in the judicial hierarchy or to become a *maître des requêtes* and begin an administrative career. The profession of judge in the powerful and prominent sovereign courts was certainly appealing: magistrates were honored in society; they were the undisputed, lionized spokesmen of the political opposition; and they constantly magnified their claims to political power and national leadership, even succeeding at times in wresting more administrative authority and forcing the king to submit to their will. Why then did some of these judges desert the Parlements and enter the royal administration? What were the greater advantages of a career in the king's service, in the national government?

The corps of *maîtres des requêtes* was only the first level of the monarchy's bureaucratic hierarchy. The young judge entered and served in its ranks because he knew that from there one passed into the higher posts in the royal government: the king selected from the *maîtres des requêtes* his most trusted and most powerful servants. The young officer hoped that he too would be among those chosen to be an intendant in the provinces, an intendant of finance or of commerce in the central bureaus, a councilor of state on the

Royal Council, and ultimately a secretary of state or a minister of state. This prospect could not help but impress the young magistrate when he had to decide upon his career.

His quest for success began in earnest when he became a *maître des requêtes;* rarely could prominence be achieved in the government without such prior service. Of the ninety-four intendants studied, eighty-nine previously were *maîtres des requêtes,* two became *maîtres des requêtes* following their appointments as intendants, two never held the post, and one remains unknown.[1] Indeed their hold upon these posts in the seventeenth and eighteenth centuries imbued them with an *esprit de corps* which at times led them to oppose openly the appointment to intendancies of men who were not *maîtres des requêtes.* In 1717 the members of the corps presented a petition to the Regent in an effort to prevent the nomination of a president of the Cour des Aides as intendant in Auvergne. Royal statute, they claimed, assigned to them the functions of intendants: article 3 of the edict of October 1674 stated that *"maîtres des requêtes* will be sent to all the provinces and armies."* But legal right was not the only basis of their argument; they had historical rights and superior qualifications. The *maîtres des requêtes* were the oldest royal judicial officers and direct agents of the king in the realm. They were, they averred, not only the best trained men for these functions but also those most attached to royal interests, serving only to merit their sovereign's ap-

[1] Chazerat became *maître des requêtes* after serving two years as intendant in Auvergne; Jean Etienne Bernard de Clugny de Nuis, intendant of Perpignan and Roussillon (1773–1775) and of Bordeaux and Bayonne (1775–1776), had been an intendant in the French Caribbean islands and a naval intendant in Brittany before becoming a *maître des requêtes,* although his service as a provincial intendant followed his entrance into that corps. The two who never became *maîtres des requêtes* were Beauharnois, whose training and service were completely in the naval ministry, and Cachet de Garnerans, whose appointment as intendant was unique; for these two see Chapter 1, n. 3, and Chapter 2, n. 7.

probation. To be passed over would mean for them a serious loss of wealth and of professional repute; the value of their office would diminish and so destroy the major part of their fortune, and doubt would be cast on their capacity and zeal, which would be an unwarranted reproach. Undoubtedly, they also feared being closed off from posts higher in the government. The Regent ignored their petition, however, and appointed his own candidate, replying that "he would take good subjects wherever he found them." By force of circumstance these "good subjects" or best candidates continued to be found among the *maîtres des requêtes*.[2]

Promotion into the upper ranks of the administration and the Royal Council awaited many of these *maîtres des requêtes,* including more than half of the ninety-four studied. Sixty-six attained positions higher than that of provincial intendants in the regular bureaucratic hierarchy of the central government.[3] Thirty ended their careers as councilors of

---

[2] See "Mémoire pour M^{rs} les Ms. des req. Pretendants quils sont seuls in Droict et en possession destre envoyés dans les provinces en qualité dintendants . . . Janvier 1717" (BN, ms. fr. 7-013, f° 558r°–566v°). The eighteenth-century jurisconsult Guyot also states that the *maîtres des requêtes* derived their right to the intendancies from art. 3 of the edict of 27 Oct. 1674; cf. his *Traité des droits,* II, 245. Georges Livet (*L'intendance d'Alsace sous Louis XIV, 1648–1715* [Paris, 1956], 657) refers instead to a rule of 1654 which required that intendancies be withdrawn from all those who were not *maîtres des requêtes.* For the training and qualifications of the *maîtres des requêtes* to be intendants, see below, Chapter 4.

[3] These 66 do not include 2 who did not advance beyond the level of provincial intendants but had been intendants of commerce after having served as *maîtres des requêtes* and before becoming provincial intendants. These were Gaspard Henri de Caze de la Bove, intendant in Champagne (1749–1750), and Jean Nicolas Mégret de Sérilly, intendant in Franche-Comté (1744–1750) and in Alsace (1750–1752), both of whom died while in their last provincial posts. This total also excludes Gabriel Sénac de Meilhan, intendant of Aix (1773–1775) and of Valenciennes (1775–1790), who served as war intendant in 1775 for the war minister, Comte de Saint-Germain; however doggedly he tried, Sénac

state; one was a councilor of state and also served as special plenipotentiary ambassador representing France in peace negotiations ending the War of the Spanish Succession; and one became lieutenant-general of the police in Paris. Five more who were councilors of state also obtained appointments as *prévôt des marchands* of Paris—head of the municipal government in the capital; of these five, two also served as presidents of the Grand Conseil before becoming intendants, and one of the latter was also president of the Conseil Supérieur of Lyon while intendant. Eighteen in all became presidents of various sovereign courts—most often the Grand Conseil, but also the Parlements of Paris, Aix, and Brittany, as well as of the superior councils established by the Maupeou reforms. Apart from their presidencies on the Maupeou courts, all but three of the eighteen had been presidents of the Grand Conseil before becoming intendants, and three were first presidents of Parlements during their tenure as intendants in the same provinces. Ultimate success came to eleven of these *maîtres des requêtes* who gained the highest posts in the royal government: one became secretary of state for the royal household and Protestant affairs; three were controllers-general; three were controllers-general and ministers of state; two were secretaries and ministers of state for war; and two accumulated all three of the most important offices—controller-general, minister, and secretary of

---

never succeeded in being appointed a councilor of state. (Cf. Gabriel Sénac de Meilhan, *Considérations sur l'esprit et les moeurs* [London, 1787], vii.) All the posts of intendants were approximately on a par: the functions of intendants of the army and of the navy were most often attached to the regular provincial intendant in the region, particularly in border areas during wartime; and appointment as intendant of commerce or of finance might precede or follow service as provincial intendant and therefore ranked neither higher nor lower, although the greater complexity in the work of intendants of commerce and of finance in the second half of the century caused the Crown to bestow them on former provincial intendants and councilors of state.

state, one for war and the other for agriculture and manufactures.[4]

The regular administrative bureaucracy was not the only source of offices for this group of *maîtres des requêtes*. Four became officers in charge of the households or councils of members of the royal family, and six became officials of the royal military Order of Saint-Louis. Even lower offices, vestiges of the feudal past, adorned the intendant's name, lengthening his accumulated titles and adding to his honors; one intendant, later in his career, would become the *grand bailli d'épée et sénéchal du comté de Forêt*. Whatever governmental or honorific position the king could bestow, he gave to his able and trusted administrative agents.[5]

Royal offices signified prestige and power, which were alluring qualities. Young magistrates pondering the choice of a career, novice *maîtres des requêtes* striving for advancement, might envision the honor they would attain as functionaries serving the king. In the *ancien régime*, those who performed the acts of the sovereign power shared in the majesty attached to the sovereign; the closer the office was to the ultimate source of sovereignty, the higher it was in the governmental hierarchy, the greater was the dignity attached to it and its holder. The individual's functions gave him importance in society: the authority he exercised, the majesty he shared, removed him from the body of ordinary subjects and elevated

[4] Three of the above had also served as presidents on the Grand Conseil before becoming intendants, and one of the three was also lieutenant-general of the police in Paris after his tenure as intendant and before he became one of the principal members of the Royal Council. The controllers-general, being in charge of the important business of taxation, generally attended the highest Council of State and thus were ministers; however, I have no designation for three of them as ministers and so simply listed them as controllers-general.

[5] The question of wealth as an inducement to work in the royal administration is discussed in Appendix I, where there is a comparison of the incomes of Paris parlementarians and royal administrative officers.

56

him to a special status which his countrymen acknowledged, his king extolled, and he himself esteemed. Material advantages intermingled with spiritual ones, and the converse of prestige was privileges—not merely in mores, but in law. For all public officials in France, position conferred exemption from onerous taxes and duties.[6]

Yet as a member of the Royal Council the *maître des requêtes* would be singular and pre-eminent, belonging to what was "incontestably *the first company of the kingdom*," where he would be continuously in the presence and under the eye of the royal ministers and the king.[7] A token though not a distinguishing attribute of a post on the Council was that it conferred on its holder immediate hereditary nobility.[8] The Council member, moreover, lost none of the privileges he formerly enjoyed as a magistrate, including entry, seat, and deliberative voice in all the sovereign courts, and he gained additional ones in his new capacity.[9]

Symbolic acts, formal rites, and titles signified exalted rank to men whose ways of thought and of behavior still bore a feudal imprint. As *maître des requêtes*, the young officer would be regarded both as a *courtisan* (courtier) and a

[6] For the special status of public officials, see Guyot, III, 168–76, and also p. 109 below.

[7] Guyot, II, 200; the quality of "first company of the kingdom" was expressly given to the Council by a regulation of Louis XIV in May 1657.

[8] This privilege members of the Royal Council shared with the notaries and secretaries of the king, royal household, and Crown of France; the presidents of sovereign courts if they served on the Royal Council; and the governors, commanders, and lieutenants of the king in the provinces. After 1715, the judges in the Parlement, Chambre des Comptes, and Cour des Aides of Paris also obtained immediate hereditary nobility by virtue of their office. See Guyot, II, 234–35; Jean Richard Bloch, "L'anoblissement en France au temps de François 1er: Essai d'une définition de la condition juridique et sociale de la noblesse au début du XVIe siècle," *Bibliothèque de la Revue Historique* (Paris, 1934), 75 and 87; and Chapter 6 below.

[9] Cf. Guyot, II, 231 ff., 234, 246, 250–51.

magistrat, and was entitled to present himself in person before the king and the royal family during ceremonies; to attend the king's awakening—the *lever du roi;* to follow the king to and from mass; and to sit beside the monarch's throne during religious services.[10] Then as a councilor of state he would have the honor of accompanying the king whenever the latter appeared in public, and of dining with the king at his table.[11] Were he ever to become a secretary of state he would enjoy "[les] plus grand honneurs." By law and custom a secretary of state acquired the rank of "chevalier" and obtained a title of nobility; when spoken or written to, he was entitled "monseigneur"; the king personally addressed him as his *"amé et féal";* and he had the right, along with the military nobility, to carry a sword at his side when entering the king's apartment or the Council meetings. If ever the king asked him to attend meetings of the Council of State as a minister, he would then be called "Excellency" and would bear the title of minister for the rest of his life, even when he ceased to attend the Council.[12]

To sup with the king, carry a sword, have various titles adorn one's name—prerogatives that traditionally belonged to the oldest and highest nobility—all this was only the glistening shell that encased and glorified what was paramount: a position of power. Serious, ambitious, energetic

---

[10] *Ibid.,* II, 250.

[11] The rights that councilors of state had to accompany the king and dine with him are prescribed in royal regulations of 1413, 1585, and 1628 (cf. *ibid.,* II, 224). In its origins this was meant to be a political duty and precaution: the king aimed to preclude possibilities for social and political relations between his advisers and his opponents among the powerful nobility and so obliged the councilors of state to attend him and dine with him only. By the eighteenth century this political danger no longer existed and the original purpose of the law became transformed. We can imagine councilors of state, or aspirants to that post, viewing this provision as a gratifying privilege and not as an obligatory tie.

[12] *Ibid.,* II, 212, 216, 219–21; and J. R. Bloch, 75.

young men want to act and contribute to life; what they accomplish will provide personal satisfaction, advance their fortune, and leave a mark for posterity. And what more important, more impressive work could a young magistrate perform than to participate in the activities of that body which determined law and policy for the entire kingdom? [13]

The Royal Council was the actual government of France, the locus of national power. To be on the Council meant belonging to the small governing elite in the monarchy, being numbered among the 125 men who ruled France.[14] Whatever task he would be given, whatever post he would attain, so long as he remained a member of the Council his work would involve him in acts of sovereignty: deciding or executing the king's will. These royal laws and policies, furthermore, aimed at promoting the national interest and affected all the subjects in the realm. The Crown would then command his energies, and he in turn could commit his efforts to the king and the nation. Ambition, service, and

[13] The following quotation from the memoirs of an eighteenth-century nobleman and *pair de France,* Baron de Frénilly, reveals how he, and undoubtedly his contemporaries, regarded the posts in the royal government for the triple opportunities they offered young men—industrious work, public service, and professional advancement. "The career of intendant was the best profession for a man who had an aptitude for work and love of the public weal; endowed with such traits . . . this career lifted you above your peers . . . you had wings and you rose to the heights." Quoted in Guillaume de Bertier de Sauvigny, *Le comte Ferdinand de Bertier (1782–1864) et l'énigme de la Congrégation* (Paris, 1948), 3.

[14] The members of the royal councils, in addition to the king, included 80 *maîtres des requêtes;* 30 councilors of state (3 representing the Church and 3 representing the *noblesse d'épée*); between 4 and 6 secretaries of state; the controller-general; the chancellor; and the ministers of state who were drawn from the secretaries of state, generally also the controller-general, and one to three marshals of France and/or royal princes; the marshals or princes and the six non-robe councilors of state were the only non-*fonctionnaires* on the councils. Cf. any volume of the *Almanach Royal* for the eighteenth century.

loyalty converged: to men with such desires and thoughts, an administrative career was unrivaled.

II

The decision made, the young magistrate had to become a *maître des requêtes* and begin his service on the royal councils. There were few legal prerequisites for entrance: the edict of February 1672 required a magistrate to serve ten full years in a court in order to qualify as a *maître des requêtes;* this term of service subsequently was reduced to six years by the edict of November 1683.[15] The minimum age would then be thirty-one years; but since lawyers became judges before age twenty-five, they might serve six years and qualify as *maîtres des requêtes* before age thirty-one. Moreover, the ruse of dispensations again came into play. Of 88 intendants whose age and dates of service as magistrates and *maîtres des requêtes* are known, only 33 had served six or more years in a sovereign court, and only 16 were at least thirty-one years old when they entered the Royal Council.[16] The majority, in short, had obtained dispensations for age or for service: the youngest became *maîtres des requêtes* at ages twenty to twenty-two, and the shortest period of judicial service ranged from one month to one year. All three monarchs of the eighteenth century granted dispensations, although Louis XIV was somewhat less generous while Louis XV and XVI showed equal liberality. In precise terms, the median age for becoming a *maître des requêtes* was twenty-eight years for the intendants of the first period, and twenty-five years for the intendants of the later two periods; the median period of

[15] Guyot, II, 238, and III, 81; and Bluche, 66.

[16] The breakdown for each of the three periods is as follows: 1710–1712—of a total of 29, 8 attained the minimum age and 13 served the minimum time; 1749–1751—of 32, 3 attained the minimum age and 11 served the minimum time; 1774–1776—of 27, 5 attained the minimum age and 9 served the minimum time. Again there is a proportionately higher concentration of exceptions for the second period.

prior judicial service was five years for the first group and four years for the last two groups.[17] Personal and family interests, combined with royal temporizing, again explain this disregard of legal requirements. A young judge who was keenly ambitious and sought to advance quickly, or whose family eagerly pushed his career in order to promote its fortune or secure acquired office and status, might seek admission when he desired and if he could fulfill other nonstipulated prerequisites. Age and length of experience might easily be ignored, but wealth, influence, and family ties were indispensable.

The process for acquiring an office of *maître des requêtes* was almost exactly the same as that for obtaining a *charge* in the sovereign courts: usually a judge or his father purchased the office from a current *maître des requêtes*. The price was never cheap. The legal values, set by edicts of November 1674, February 1689, and June 5, 1708, were 180,000 livres, 190,000 livres, and 200,000 livres respectively; its estimated market value, indicated in a testament of 1709 and a marriage contract of 1714, was 150,000 livres.[18] In 1719 the inflation induced by Law's "system" precipitously raised the price, and Urbain Guillaume de Lamoignon de Courson sold his office for 220,000 livres to the father of the future intendant of Bordeaux, Louis Urbain Aubert de Tourny.[19]

[17] The full range of ages and terms of service were as follows: 1710–1712—ages 20 to 37, and a year and a half to 21 years; 1749–1751—ages 22 to 33, and one month to 11 years; 1774–1776—ages 21 to 51, and less than one year to 20 years. For copies of royal dispensations for age, service, or both, see: Carrés d'Hozier 70, "Bauyn," f. 125; PO 300, "Bernage," f. 65; Chérin 24, "Bertin," f. 49 and f. 56; PO 344, "Bignon," f. 857; DB 150 (3837), "Camus de Pontcarré," f. 44; Carrés d'Hozier 181, "Chauvelin," f. 56; and DB 237, "Dodart," f. 1.

[18] Aucoc, 71; Nouveau d'Hozier 141, "Foullé," f. 2, testament of Hiacinthe Guillaume Foullé de Martargis, November 1709; and Minutier Central (hereafter MC), LXI:337, marriage contract of Louis Bazile de Bernage, 11 February 1714.

[19] Cf. Michel Lhéritier, *L'intendant Tourny, 1695–1760* (2 vols.; Paris, 1920), I, 45.

With the return to more normal financial conditions following the tightening of the money market in the 1720's, and the subsequent expansion of trade and industry after 1730 offering alternative opportunities for investment and gain, the price for the office of *maître des requêtes*, as for all the sovereign-court offices, began to fall: in 1742 the purchase price was 95,000 livres, and between 1748 and 1750 the market value varied from 79,000 to 82,000 livres.[20] An edict of August 1752 fixed the price at 100,000 livres, which remained the market price for transactions in following years.[21] In all instances the new *maître des requêtes* had to spend an additional amount for the cost of his official reception by the Paris Parlement; in a letter to his father, the future intendant and controller-general Calonne lamented the 10,000 livres spent for his reception as a "pure loss."[22] In comparison to these prices, numerous magistracies in the sovereign courts and other venal offices were more expensive, some commanding as much as 500,000 or 700,000 livres.[23] Moreover, a purchaser rarely used his personal funds to pay

[20] The 1742 price was specifically 95,775 livres; cf. MC, LII:315, "Compte, liquidation et partage de la succession de Messire Jean Louis Thiroux de Lailly . . . , 26 janvier 1744." For the other two figures see Bluche, 164. See also Ford, 148–51.

[21] This edict of Aug. 1752 which set the price on the office of *maître des requêtes* at 100,000 livres is mentioned in the *lettre de provision* which Antoine Jean Baptiste Jullien (intendant of Alençon, 1766–1790) received on 14 Dec. 1765 when he became *maître des requêtes;* cf. AN, V⁴ 1504, f. 192⁴. In 1780 Antoine Chaumont de la Galaizière (intendant of Lorraine, 1766–1777) purchased the office for his son at 100,000 livres (cf. Pierre Boyé, "Le Chancelier Chaumont de la Galaizière et sa famille," *Le Pays Lorrain*, XXX [1938], 481); and Jullien himself sold the office to his nephew in 1784 for the same price (cf. Angot des Retours, "Le dernier intendant de la généralité d'Alençon," *Bulletin de la Société Historique et Archéologique de l'Orne*, XII [1893], 504).

[22] Quoted in Pierre Jolly, *Calonne, 1734–1802* (Paris, 1949), 35.

[23] Comparative prices of various venal offices—judicial, financial, and administrative—may be found in Bluche, 164–68.

the total price immediately; instead, he would pay periodic installments, borrow money to pay a portion of the price, or in less frequent and most favored cases obtain a credit from the Crown to cover part of the expense. Despite these qualifications, however, the fact that a *maître des requêtes* had to buy his office and pay a relatively high price meant that only wealthy men could attain these positions. Such was the consequence and law of venality.

Since the entire corps of *maîtres des requêtes* numbered only eighty,[24] vacancies were infrequent. Magistrates searching for sellers might find their efforts frustrated; holders of these offices might not want to sell to strangers and deprive their kin of this honored post. Families therefore sought alternatives to random sale and instinctively resorted to practices that habit or law had sanctioned.

Individuals who had contact with the king or with ministers might solicit aid to ensure that vacant offices of *maîtres des requêtes* would be offered to them. The father of the famous Tourny was business manager to Pontchartrain; in 1719 the Chancellor showed his favor by offering him the sale of an office of *maître des requêtes* for his son, then only twenty-four years old and a *conseiller* on the Grand Conseil for merely six months.[25] Friendship was the common, but not the sole, medium for influence. A war debt of over four million livres that the Crown owed Antoine Chaumont became his lever for obtaining offices for himself and his sons; within four months Antoine Chaumont de la Galaizière, the future intendant of Lorraine, became at age twenty-three first a *conseiller* in the Parlement of Metz and then a *maître*

---

[24] In the mid-seventeenth century there were 80 *maîtres des requêtes*. Their numbers were increased to 88 by an edict of Feb. 1689 and again were reduced to 80 by an edict of Aug. 1752. At the very end of the *ancien régime* an edict of November 1787 further reduced their numbers to sixty-seven. Cf. Michel Antoine, *Les Fonds du Conseil d'Etat du Roi aux Archives Nationales: Guide des recherches* (Paris, 1955), 12.

[25] Lhéritier, I, 44. Tourny previously had been a *conseiller* in the Châtelet for five years.

des requêtes.[26] Usually, however, a father who himself held an honorable position would request his senior colleagues in the ministry to bestow this favor upon his son; so Pierre Cardin Le Bret, intendant of Provence and first president of the Parlement of Aix, began his entreaties in 1694 when his son was twenty-one years old, and two years later Cardin Le Bret, future intendant in Provence, became a *maître des requêtes.*[27]

Venality, when first introduced for judicial and financial offices, did not remain limited to simple purchase and sale; other practices immediately attached themselves and became accepted.[28] The traditional cycle which began with the sale of offices was now repeated. Offices of *maîtres des requêtes* began to be inherited. Individuals who had secured an office of *maître des requêtes* kept it within the family by transmitting it to relatives. Usually, fathers would resign in favor of young sons; those who became *maîtres des requêtes* in this way were Louis Claude Le Blanc, intendant of Dunkerque and Ypres, 1708–1716; Charles Blaise Méliand, intendant of Soissons from 1743 to perhaps 1751; and Henri Léonard Jean Baptiste Bertin de Bellille, intendant of Perpignan, 1750–1753, and controller-general, 1759–1763.[29] César Charles de L'Escalopier, himself intendant in Champagne

---

[26] Boyé, "Le chancelier Chaumont de la Galaizière et sa famille," *Le Pays Lorrain*, XXVIII (1936), 118. Undoubtedly having this example of Chaumont de la Galaizière in mind, the famous eighteenth-century lawyer Barbier caustically remarked about both the Parlement of Metz and the corps of *maîtres des requêtes*: ". . . the *charge* of *maître des requêtes* . . . is the refuge of men of disrepute and of low birth. For one is received in it after having had professional experience considerably different from that of a magistrate, then passed a year as *conseiller* in the Parlement of Metz, which is the stepping-stone, and from there *maître des requêtes*." Barbier, quoted in *ibid.*, XXVIII, 448, n. 4.

[27] Cf. Marchand, 23.

[28] Cf. Mousnier, *La vénalité des offices*, xxviii–xxix and Book I.

[29] Cf. DB 99, "Le Blanc," f. 13; DB 440, "Méliand," f. 10ᵛ; and Chérin 24, "Bertin," f. 49 and f. 56.

(1711–1730), resigned his office of *maître des requêtes*, which he had held for twenty-five years, in favor of his son Gaspard César Charles de L'Escalopier, the future intendant of Montauban (1740–1756).[30] The Bernage family held and bequeathed the office during three generations: Louis de Bernage, intendant of Amiens (1708–1718), was *maître des requêtes* from 1689 to 1714, when he passed it to his son Louis Bazile, who later became a provincial intendant and *prévôt des marchands* of Paris; in 1740 the latter resigned his office in favor of his son, Jean Louis de Bernage de Vaux, the future intendant of Moulins (1744–1756) and of Metz.[31] Fathers-in-law did the same: Jacques Etienne Turgot de Soumons, intendant of Moulins (1709–1713), resigned his office of *maître des requêtes* in 1711 to his son-in-law, Jean François de Creil de Bournezeau, who later became intendant of Metz (1721–1751).[32] Sometimes the father transmitted his office to his son as part of the latter's marriage dowry; this was how Louis Bazile Bernage succeeded his father as *maître des requêtes.*[33]

Other subtle traditional methods similarly were adopted. Some *maîtres des requêtes* obtained their office *à titre de survivance:* they had the right to cede it to their heirs or to other designated successors. Louis de Bernage, Antoine Jean Baptiste Alexandre Jullien, intendant of Alençon (1766–1790), and Antoine Jean Baptiste Robert Auget de Montyon, intendant of Auvergne, Provence, and La Rochelle under Louis XV and Louis XVI, legally acquired this privilege; the first two used it, but the Revolution occurred before the latter could dispose of his office.[34] Con-

---

[30] DB 390, "Lescalopier," f. 37 and f. 38.
[31] PO 300, "Bernage," fs. 56–57 and f. 65.
[32] DB 222, "Creil," f. 4.   [33] MC, LXI:337, 11 Feb. 1714.
[34] For Jullien, see AN, V⁴ 1504, f. 192ᵛ, "lettre de provision," 14 Dec. 1765 and V⁴ 1506, f. 184ᵛᵒ, letter as *maître des requêtes honoraire,* 30 Sept. 1784; on Aug. 18, Jullien had sold his office to his nephew, Cromot de Sougy. For Auget de Montyon, see Guimbaud, 28.

versely, some initially entered the corps as *maîtres des requêtes* "en survivance": they assisted their fathers on the
Royal Council for a number of years while the latter remained the legal officeholders and before they acquired the
office in their own names. Le Blanc served "en survivance"
for three years until his father resigned the office in his favor
in 1700.[35] Bertin de Bellille left his functions as a councilor
on the Grand Conseil in December 1741, and at twenty-one
joined his father, a *maître des requêtes* since 1724, on the
Royal Council. The latter continued to serve in his office
until February 1745, when he legally resigned it specifically
and solely in his son's favor; on April 30 Bertin received
from the Crown the legal "provision de l'Etat et office de
Conseiller du Roy en ses Conseils, maître des requêtes ordinaire de son hôtel," which he now "[held, exercised, and
enjoyed] à titre de survivance."[36] And so the cycle was
completed.

A *maître des requêtes* could easily obtain the right of
survivance. All he needed to do was pay an annual
tax—the *droit annuel*. This permitted him to resign his office
when he desired, placing it at the king's disposal, but with
the explicit and legal acknowledgment that the Crown
would in turn confer it on the holder's choice, granting
relevant dispensations if necessary. If the new *maître des
requêtes* should die before the original officeholder died, the
office would not be lost to the family but would revert to the
previous holder.[37] Similarly, if the *maître des requêtes* who
had the right of *survivance* died before designating a succes-
sor, the office remained at his family's disposal; they could

[35] Cf. DB 99 (2403), "Le Blanc," f. 13.

[36] Cf. Chérin 24, "Bertin," fs. 49, 50, 51, 56 ff., and 75. Bertin retained
the title, income, and legal ownership of his office on the Grand Conseil
although he no longer performed the functions after Dec. 1741; not
until Dec. 1745 did he resign and sell that magistracy.

[37] Cf. PO 300, "Bernage," fs. 56–67, a royal proclamation dated 1714
granting the office of *maître des requêtes* to Louis Bazile de Bernage.

bestow it on a relative or sell it to a stranger by requesting the king to invest their candidate with the office.[38]

Despite the reoccurrence of the same names among the *maîtres des requêtes* from one generation to the next, and the introduction of such usages as resignations in favor of designated successors and *survivance* that enabled offices to be transmitted to heirs or relatives, direct inheritance of these offices was not the most common means for entry into the corps. Some fathers bequeathed their own posts to sons, but most, even former or current *maîtres des requêtes*, purchased new offices for them. Inheritance of the office of *maîtres des requêtes* was only one recourse, occasionally used, among several in a social and professional reality which was more complex; family succession or family relations were more potent by their indirect effects. A young judge whose father or father-in-law, uncle, or brother-in-law was a prominent magistrate or royal official could more easily and promptly find an available place in the corps of *maîtres des requêtes* than could one whose father and family had no prestigious posts and consequently no fruitful connections. At some point, whether for the father, grandfather, or son, uncle, nephew, or in-law, an office had to be purchased and money paid: the family had to be sufficiently wealthy. Influence, wealth, and family ties, consequently, were an irreducible triad, and they cannot be separated and weighed apart.

Thus, the mores that originally characterized nobles and magistrates stubbornly persisted and spread their effects: personal and family interests which preoccupied the *maîtres des requêtes* were unmistakably the root causes. Yet this play of family, wealth, and influence was not entirely irredeemable, and it served the king's purposes as well.[39] Indeed, the Crown

[38] Cf. Mousnier, xxix.

[39] Cf. J. Russell Major, "Henry IV and Guyenne: A Study Concerning the Origins of Royal Absolutism," *French Historical Studies*, IV (Fall 1966), 363–83, where the author attributes administrative and political goals—greater royal control—as the motives for the introduction of the *Paulette* tax in 1604.

desired and promoted the succession of families within the corps of *maîtres des requêtes* from one generation to the next because of definite benefits that this practice produced. The examples of forebears who had worked for the king encouraged descendants to emulate them and inspired a sense of service which was inbred and intuitive. Private interests and public needs coalesced in this way. But individual emotions might prove capricious and fluctuating. The monarchy, therefore, did not depend solely on personal attachments to family traditions. One element remained which by its nature was unchangeable and which the Crown could use for its own purposes and at its own command.

Seemingly, an office of *maître des requêtes* was like other venal offices, and one acquired it as one obtained an ordinary venal *charge*. Yet in essential respects there were significant differences. This post was an *office*, a *charge*, for it involved public functions, conferred public power and personal dignity, and was purchased; the holder even received as part of his salary a *gages*—the interest on the capital that he invested.[40] But a notary, tax collector, and magistrate obtained their posts *en titre;* a *maître des requêtes* received his *par commission*.[41] This legal distinction had fundamental political implications and enormous practical importance for the Crown.

Sales and purchases of ordinary venal offices operated in an unrestricted open market. The Crown exercised no supervision except to ensure payment of the *droit annuel* and its share of the price. The sovereign courts superintended sales of their offices for the dual purpose of favoring their own members or relatives and testing the proficiency of new judges. In all cases the Crown's approval, embodied in a *lettre de provision,* was perfunctory. Once the office was

[40] Mousnier, xxvii–xxix; Guyot, II, 245; see also PO 583 (13,517), "Camus," f. 101, and PO 2897, "Turgot," f. 1699, for copies of receipts for the payment of *gages* to *maîtres des requêtes.*

[41] Guyot, III, 77.

purchased, the owner possessed it in fact and in law as private property, retaining the title and functions until he chose to resign or sell, or until he died. Hence, these officials remained in their posts for life. The king could not remove them unless their actions incurred forfeiture—an event which rarely occurred. They were, in short, independent agents.

Offices of *maîtres des requêtes* were bought and sold by individuals, but neither purchase nor possession transformed them into private property and the Crown consequently controlled the market. These offices were set apart from the thousands that entered the Bureau des Parties Casuelles, the royal agency which administered sales of venal charges; they were sold separately and individually, so the Crown was able to supervise the transactions. Furthermore, a *maître des requêtes* legally obtained his office by the grant of a commission and therefore did not have full property rights. He could not freely dispose of it as he desired, but had to obtain official authorization; thus even the practice of *resignatio in favorem* required the king's explicit approval.[42] When a *maître des requêtes* decided to sell his office, to resign and recover the money he invested, the Crown might indicate which of several buyers it favored or even offer the sale to its own candidate—and it had the right and power to impose its choice.

Most importantly, since the Crown conferred these offices by commission, *maîtres des requêtes* technically served only during good behavior—as long as it pleased the king. In turn, the king and his ministers, if they chose, could dismiss a *maître des requêtes* for lack of ability or diligence, or for

---

[42] Mousnier, 312–18. In 1779 Gaspard Louis de Caze de la Bove, intendant in Brittany (1775–1785), wrote to the minister Maurepas requesting permission to "faire passer sa charge" [i.e., of *maître des requêtes*] to a future son-in-law who was a councilor in the Parlement of Rouen; cf. Henri Fréville, *L'intendance de Bretagne, 1689–1790* (3 vols.; Rennes, 1953), III, 32 (drawn from AN, H.589).

poor judgment or disloyalty. Indeed one did suffer this disgrace. Jean Moreau de Séchelles, *maître des requêtes* since 1719, was arrested in 1723 with Le Blanc when the latter was forced out as minister of war. He was not reinstated until three years later, and subsequently became intendant of Lille (1743–1754), minister of state, and controller-general.[43] The law then was definite, and the example was instructive. A *maître des requêtes* harbored illusions at his own peril. If he wanted to remain in office or to advance, as every one of them did, he could be neither slothful nor disobedient—without jeopardizing his career and his social position.

Offices that the Crown granted as commissions, therefore, were fundamentally different in character from regular venal charges. The legal provision *par commission* gave the king and his ministers an adaptable and effective instrument which they could apply for admitting men into the corps, and above all for retaining individuals as *maîtres des requêtes*. In terms of the needs of the eighteenth-century monarchy, this served to repair some of the defects caused by private interests and enlarged by royal dispensations and public venality. In terms of the development of administrative procedures, this signified an improvement over previous traditional practices and a transition to the regularized promotions and advancement by merit that characterize modern bureaucracies.

[43] Cf. Antoine Jean Baptiste Robert Auget de Montyon, *Particularités et observations sur les ministres des finances de France les plus célèbres, depuis 1600 jusqu'en 1791* (Paris, 1812), 130–31, n. 1.

CHAPTER 4

Maîtres des Requêtes Serve the King: Justice, Administration, and Politics

I

Recruitment and admission completed, the *maître des requêtes* began his definitive training after he entered the corps. Now started the final and most important stage in the process of becoming "the king's man." His work would require him to exercise the king's authority and make him learn to value it; his new activities would draw him away from his former colleagues of the robe, and his responsibilities as a royal servant would diminish the sympathies he had acquired for the powers of the magistracy. Henceforth, he would be attached to the Crown. He would learn the work of monarchical government, identify with royal interests and adopt the royal outlook, and mold himself into a suitable and favored administrator.

In origin, the *maîtres des requêtes* were magistrates in the king's household, where they exercised specific judicial functions.[1] As officers in charge of the Requêtes de l'Hôtel, they had original jurisdiction for cases involving members of the royal household and for specially privileged officials, dignitaries, prelates, and religious communities. They were, in

[1] For what follows, see Guyot, II, 242, 248; Aucoc, 71; Antoine, 12, 26–27; and Roland Mousnier, ed., *Lettres et mémoires adressés au Chancelier Séguier (1633–1649)* (2 vols.; Paris, 1965), I, 42–45.

addition, members of the Chancellery. In their dual capacity as *maîtres des requêtes ordinaires de l'Hôtel* and as assistants to the chancellor, they received petitions from private persons or groups requesting royal letters patent and submitted the dossiers to the chancellor; the latter, presiding in the Audience de France, decided whether to accept or reject these requests. Furthermore, they advised the chancellor in granting pardons or reducing judicial sentences. A secondary task in assisting the chancellor, which recalled their origins during the medieval monarchy, was to guard the royal seals. Even these limited, technical functions served to broaden their view beyond that of sovereign-court magistrates: they came to appreciate the Crown's direct judicial authority.

For three months a year they served on the Requêtes de l'Hôtel; throughout the year they attended the Council, where they performed their key work.[2] The Royal Council consisted of several different councils, each with a distinct function and varied personnel. There was a total of five councils in the eighteenth century: the Conseil d'Etat, the Conseil des Dépêches, the Conseil Royal des Finances, the Conseil Royal de Commerce—permanently created in 1730—and the Conseil d'Etat Privé Finances et Direction. The *maîtres des requêtes* were members of the latter only. Never did they participate in meetings of the Conseil d'Etat, which was reserved solely for the king and for ministers whom the sovereign personally invited to attend; and only in special instances did they appear before the three other councils.[3]

The Conseil d'Etat Privé Finances et Direction was the

[2] Cf. Guyot, II, 245, and Aucoc, *loc. cit.*

[3] For the following discussion of the activities of the various royal councils, bureaus, and commissions, and the work of the *maîtres des requêtes* on these, see the *Almanach Royal* for the eighteenth century; Gabriel Sénac de Meilhan, *Du gouvernement, des moeurs, et des conditions en France avant la Révolution* (Hamburg, 1795), 132–33; Aucoc, 54–58; and Antoine, 5–23, 26–29, 39.

oldest of the councils, the continuator of the original "Conseil du Roi," and the nucleus from which the other councils had evolved; members of all the other royal councils still were considered as its members. Its pre-eminence symbolically remained: the date of entry into this Council determined seniority among *maîtres des requêtes* and councilors of state. Its authority, however, had been diminished with the periodic formation of superior, policy-making councils and in effect, although the king theoretically presided at its meetings, he never actually attended, and the presidency passed to the chancellor. Nevertheless, its importance remained; one of its members who later became a provincial intendant expressed his regard and appreciation for its work by characterizing it as "the guardian of the executive power." [4]

By the eighteenth century, this Council had two distinct parts: the Conseil Privé, also known as the Conseil des Parties; and the Conseil d'Etat et des Finances. The former Council, which consisted of all the councilors of state and *maîtres des requêtes,* presided over by the chancellor, met twice a week during Louis XIV's reign and only once, on Monday mornings, during the following two reigns. The latter Council, composed of eighteen councilors of state and all the *maîtres des requêtes* and intendants of finance, presided over by the controller-general, held its meetings on Tuesday mornings.

The Conseil Privé, in essence, exercised the justice which the king embodied. Although not the ultimate court of appeals in France, it was the supreme appellate tribunal for judicial and administrative disputes arising from decisions contravening established laws and legal processes; issues involving political problems or requiring changes in the law fell within the jurisdiction of the Conseil des Dépêches. A *maître des requêtes,* in the course of serving on the Conseil

[4] Sénac de Meilhan, *Du gouvernement, des moeurs, et des conditions en France,* 134.

Privé, would be responsible for a variety of cases. He might, for example, receive requests to resolve conflicts of jurisdiction between courts or to transfer cases from one court to another on grounds of judicial bias. Most cases, however, required more involved judgments by this Council. In these instances, the *maître des requêtes* would consider petitions to set aside or review court decisions in civil or criminal cases, and appeals directed against administrative orders or decisions made by intendants or other royal agents. The Conseil d'Etat et des Finances, on the other hand, had jurisdiction over all important issues concerning the administration of the royal domains and of national finances, including judgments of tax disputes; when policy decisions were required or issues of paramount importance were involved, problems were referred to the king and the Conseil Royal des Finances.

Within the general activities of the Conseil d'Etat Privé Finances et Direction and among its personnel, the *maîtres des requêtes* had specific tasks. The Council received a case in the form of a dossier of legal briefs constituting the petition for judgment. In the Conseil Privé the chancellor distributed each dossier to a *maître des requêtes* designated as *rapporteur* and assigned to examine the case.[5] The *rapporteur* was in command of the entire investigation. If he desired, he consulted authorities outside the Council who might advise him—the judge who originally reported the case, an intendant or other administrator concerned, royal *procureurs-généraux* or *avocats-généraux,* or the local bishop and town officers. The examination completed, two to four councilors of state together with the *maître des requêtes*

---

[5] Although all the *maîtres des requêtes* attended the Council for the full twelve-month period, they technically served only three months; thus, only those *maîtres des requêtes* who were "en quartier . . . au Conseil du Roy" at the moment were assigned to cases on the Conseil Privé; cf. Antoine, 13, and any volume of the *Almanach Royal* for the eighteenth century.

would examine all evidence and information. The latter then presented his report and his legal opinion before the entire Council; the councilors associated with him expressed their views, and the remaining members of the Council in turn stated their opinions. The final decision represented the vote of the majority of the entire Council. The *rapporteur* was now responsible for drafting the judgment entirely by hand—a formality highly regarded and uniformly observed.[6] When the *maître des requêtes* was not appointed *rapporteur* for a case—and he was rarely *rapporteur* on the Conseil d'Etat et des Finance, where the controller-general or the intendants of finance performed this task—he of course attended the Council sessions to hear the reports, present his opinion, and vote for the judgment.

Assisting the Royal Council were a series of bureaus and commissions to which the *maîtres des requêtes,* together with councilors of state and sometimes the chancellor and controller-general, belonged. Their work in these bodies served to initiate the men thoroughly into the technical details of administration and gave them an understanding of the varied responsibilities of royal government. Although the bureaus and commissions were confusing in their numbers and sometimes had overlapping titles—a commission sometimes was labeled a bureau—their legal status and competence were distinct.

The bureaus were permanent bodies attached to the Conseil d'Etat Privé Finances et Direction and received the petitions addressed to the Council. In the eighteenth century there were three classes of bureaus, each responsible for different kinds of disputes and each with varying degrees of authority. There were, first, five bureaus charged with handling petitions for annulment or revision of decisions in civil and criminal cases, and in ecclesiastical cases; these bureaus did not issue judgments but merely examined the requests in

[6] Cf. Antoine, 39.

order to advise the chancellor whether to accept them for deliberation by the Council or to reject them. The second kind, the Bureau des Postes et Messageries, examined disputes concerning the mail service whose administration was farmed out; it rendered final judgments of appeals from the intendants' decisions, but until 1777 it made preparatory studies for cases that the Conseil Privé would judge in first instance. The third bureau dealt with disputes resulting from regulations of the printing and sale of books and other printed matter; in this instance, it had authority to issue final judgments.

The commissions, in contrast to the bureaus, dealt with disputes that the Council accepted for adjudication and delegated to them. These were of two classes: ordinary and extraordinary. The ordinary commissions were permanent, numbering four in the eighteenth century, but the authority of each varied. The most important was La Grande Direction des Finance; it had full juridical powers and consequently was considered as a third meeting of the Conseil d'Etat et des Finances, thus often called the "Conseil de Direction." Its functions were threefold: it adjudicated disputes between individuals and the state in cases where private interests were greater than the government's interests; it regulated financial disputes between two private parties; and it prepared responses to the *cahiers* that provincial estates presented to the Crown. The second ordinary commission was La Petite Direction des Finances, which had the same competence as La Grande Direction and served only to relieve the latter by settling less important disputes. The last two, called Le Bureau des Domaines et Aides and Le Bureau des Gabelles, Cinq Grosses Fermes, Tailles et Autres Affaires de Finance, in effect were only preparatory sessions for La Grande Direction and La Petite Direction, examining cases before transmitting them for judgment. At times, however, the Crown empowered these last two commissions to give final judgments in particular cases.

The extraordinary commissions were more complicated. Their special status resulted from the circumstances of their creation: they were established to settle certain cases whose importance or particular circumstances determined the Crown to judge with greater dispatch and less cost than the regular procedures in the Council entailed. In theory all of them were temporary, but the longevity of some made them in effect permanent. Extraordinary commissions were further divided into two other categories. Some of them functioned outside of the Council, in whatever part of France the dispute arose and required settlement; they operated for short periods of time, only until the issue was resolved, and consisted of one or two officials or a larger group. Others, however, remained a part of the Council, attached in most cases to either the Conseil Privé or the Conseil d'Etat et des Finances, or sometimes to the Conseil des Dépêches or the Conseil Royal des Finances, and they regulated affairs in which the Crown was interested.[7] Some of these extraordinary commissions attached to the councils, and composed of a number of royal officials, exercised their important functions continuously over many years.

The quasi-permanent extraordinary commissions were numerous throughout the eighteenth century, and almost all included *maîtres des requêtes* among their personnel. Their jurisdictional powers, however, varied: some were consultative or conducted preparatory examinations to aid the several councils in rendering judgments or determining law; others either had limited powers of judgment, subject to appeal before one of the councils, or judged with sovereign authority. Among the more important extraordinary commissions were: the Bureau de Commerce, a consultative body which examined all affairs concerning commerce and manufactures; the Commission des Péages, which examined claims

---

[7] The practice of appointing extraordinary commissions serving these last two governing councils is discussed below in this chapter.

of individuals to feudal rights of passage on highways and waterways and then advised the Conseil Royal des Finances, or itself issued sentences verifying, annulling, or modifying rights to these tolls; and the Commission des Vivres et Etapes, which examined, verified, and liquidated the claims of private military suppliers, and issued final judgments in cases of disputes between the government and the concessionaires. Several extraordinary commissions were established immediately following the failure of Law's "system" in order to settle the financial crisis and restore stability. These consisted of the Commissions pour les contestations relatives aux actions de la Compagnie des Indes, aux concessions de terres à la Louisiane, aux écritures en banque, and the Commission aux dettes et affaires de Jean Law. Whatever political, judicial, financial, or administrative problem occurred, the Crown could easily bring together *maîtres des requêtes,* councilors of state, and other necessary royal officers in extraordinary commissions to examine the issue, advise the Council, or resolve it directly.

As a member of a particular bureau or commission, a *maître des requêtes* served in one of two ways: he might be designated *rapporteur* charged with investigating a specific problem and presenting his report before the Council, in the case of commissions, or to the chancellor, if it concerned a bureau; or he might be merely an ordinary member assisting in the assigned work and participating in the final decision of his group. A new member of the corps would be assigned to a bureau or to one of the commissions directly attached to the Council as a place became vacant. Gradually, he might become a member of two or more of them; this was particularly true of those who served during the reigns of Louis XV and Louis XVI, since increasingly during the eighteenth century the Crown established commissions to handle the manifold tasks of government. Aubert de Tourny and Bertin de Bellille, for example, both served on three of the quasi-permanent extraordinary commissions during their first few years as *maîtres des requêtes*.[8]

His work on any of these bodies would involve the *maître des requêtes* in numerous problems concerning tax disputes or printing regulations, military supplies or royal domain lands, finances of Paris guilds, religious establishments, or commercial companies, or feudal tolls and proofs of nobility. In exceptional instances an individual *maître des requêtes* might accompany an army in battle to oversee the discipline, payment, and provisioning of the soldiers, or even to draw plans for battles and sieges; Nicolas Lamoignon de Basville carried out such a mission for Turenne in Alsace in 1674, and Jean Louis Moreau de Beaumont did the same for his uncle Jean Moreau de Séchelles when the latter was army intendant in Bohemia in 1742.[9] Clearly the assignments that a *maître des requêtes* received covered a wide range and made him generally competent. In some instances he might concentrate on particular issues and become a specialist in judicial or financial affairs, or, like Antoine François Ferrand de Villemilan, in economic affairs.[10]

II

A variety of concrete administrative and judicial work was the core of experience for all *maîtres des requêtes*. Policy-making was not their responsibility, and politics directly involved them only in exceptional circumstances. National laws and policy were the responsibilities of the four governing councils—the Conseil d'Etat, the Conseil des Dépêches, the Conseil Royal des Finances, and the Conseil Royal de Commerce—and of the king, ministers, secretaries

[8] Cf. Lhéritier, II, 45 ff., and Chérin 24, "Bertin," fs. 49 ff., 65.

[9] Louis Vian, *Les Lamoignon, une vieille famille de robe* (Paris, 1896), 172, and Moreau de Beaumont, *Mémoire concernant les impositions et droits en Europe*, I, ii.

[10] Fréville, I, 110.

of state, controller-general, and chancellor who were members of these councils. Nevertheless, *maîtres des requêtes* participated, though peripherally and occasionally, in the work of all these councils except the Conseil d'Etat, but only a few in the entire corps were selected for these secondary yet important roles.[11]

The Conseil des Dépêches was the supreme governing council for domestic policy and the highest, final court of appeals in the kingdom. It decided all internal affairs except finances, settled all outstanding political problems, and judged on appeal or in first instance the most important administrative and legal disputes involving the government which the Conseil Privé transmitted. The Conseil Royal des Finances determined all fiscal policy—setting the amounts of annual revenue and expenditure, reforming old taxes and introducing new ones, and arranging contracts with tax farmers. In addition, it set policy for the administration of domain lands and of roads and bridges, and until 1730 for all economic affairs; and it was the supreme court for financial matters, adjudicating the most important fiscal disputes sent to it by the Conseil d'Etat et des Finances. The last of the governing councils, the Conseil Royal de Commerce, was the least prominent and had the shortest life: it was created in 1730, and in 1787 united with the Conseil Royal des Finances; and it prepared decrees and regulations for commerce and manufactures, but even in this sphere competed

[11] The Conseil d'État consisted only of the king and those whom he invited to attend: a *dauphin* or prince of the blood, a marshal, always the secretary of state for foreign affairs since this Council decided diplomatic policy, other designated secretaries of state, and sometimes the chancellor and controller-general. Under Louis XIV the Conseil d'État directed all foreign and military affairs as well as the most important domestic affairs; under Louis XV and for the remainder of the *ancien régime* it confined itself solely to diplomacy and war. Cf. Antoine, 5; Sénac de Meilhan, *Du gouvernement, des moeurs, et des conditions en France,* 132; and any volume of the *Almanach Royal* for the eighteenth century.

with the policy-making authority of the Conseil Royal des Finances and the advisory capacity of the Bureau de Commerce.

Among all the issues presented to these councils, some were particularly important to the government or involved complex problems; for such matters the Council appointed a commission to study the dispute and present its recommendations, and on the bases of these reports it rendered final judgment, determined policy, or promulgated law.[12] The Conseil des Dépêches in particular frequently used this procedure beginning in the reign of Louis XV, undoubtedly as a result of its increased authority in domestic affairs and because of the more frequent and venomous clashes between the Parlements, on the one side, and ecclesiastical officials or the Crown, on the other side.

Members of these commissions were councilors of state and a *maître des requêtes* who always served as *rapporteur*. On the day the Council discussed the issue that the commission had examined, its members appeared before it and the *maître des requêtes* delivered the report; since the latter was not a member of a governing council, he could not vote for the decision as he did on the Conseil d'Etat Privé Finances et Direction. But this was unimportant: the work of a *maître des requêtes* for the Council and his appearance before it would be a memorable event in his life and perhaps also significant for his career. He would have the distinction of addressing and displaying his talents before the secretaries of state, chancellor, controller-general, and perhaps even the king himself. Henceforth they would know him personally; they might even honor and elate him with their compliments; and in exceptional instances the king might show his satisfaction by promoting him forthwith to an intendancy.

[12] The following is based on Michel Antoine, "Le Conseil des dépêches sous Louis XV," *Bibliothèque Ecole des Chartes* (Paris, 1953), 193–95.

Guillaume Joseph Dupleix de Bacquencourt, intendant in Burgundy from 1774 to 1780, had this rare good fortune. In 1765 he and a councilor of state were sent to Navarre as royal commissioners to resolve difficulties concerning the Parlement of Pau. They returned to Paris and on December 27 appeared before the Council to deliver a report of their efforts; following this they were presented to the king, and Dupleix de Bacquencourt immediately heard the sovereign announce his appointment to his first intendancy.[13]

The fruits of such work, however, were not merely personal. A *maître des requêtes* might impress officials and obtain a promotion, but from the Crown's point of view he gained invaluable experience in the most important matters of government. His tasks for the governing councils required him to examine and evaluate crucial, paramount problems—political or administrative, judicial, financial, or economic—and enabled him to witness how and upon what grounds the king and his secretaries of state determined royal policy. This training transcended the regular work of learning administrative details: it was the initiation of the *maître des requêtes* into actual policy-making.

A novel procedure introduced into government deliberations under Louis XV provided additional opportunities for *maîtres des requêtes* to learn about law-making.[14] During the reign of Louis XIV the royal councils transacted all government work. Beginning in the 1720's, however, individual ministers and secretaries of state periodically met in general committees, in the king's absence, to co-ordinate the work of all administrative departments. After Cardinal Fleury's death in 1743 these committees increased their work, membership, and significance. Now they became preparatory committees, convened before or after Council sessions to

---

[13] *Ibid.*, 200.

[14] This paragraph is based on M. Antoine, "Les comités de ministres sous le règne de Louis XV," *Revue Historique du Droit Français et Étranger*, 1951, 193–230.

draft or examine texts of laws and treaties; the results of their work, which they submitted to one of the governing councils, became the basis for its final decision—for the determination of national law or policy. Several councilors of state and *maîtres des requêtes* assisted the secretaries of state in these committees; on occasion, specialists who were not members of the Royal Council attended committee sessions to discuss particular problems and present their advice. These committees offered a less formal atmosphere, freed of the rigors and protocol of Council meetings, which might encourage a more open exchange of views further enriched by the knowledge of specialists. *Maîtres des requêtes* who participated in these committees undoubtedly deepened their knowledge of the general considerations that determined law and those that the monarchy judged most important for national and royal interests.

As the king's intimate and trusted judicial officers, the *maîtres des requêtes* were thrust into the center of the political conflict between the Crown and sovereign courts, a conflict that raged throughout the eighteenth century. In 1715 the Parlements regained their right to remonstrate; thereafter the Crown and the courts engaged in a series of verbal duels interrupted only by more intense clashes. Periodically the Paris Parlement vetoed royal legislation, and in response the king would appear before the court in formal sessions known as *lits de justice* to admonish his magistrates and compel them to register edicts. Or sometimes judges in a sovereign court would go on strike, refusing to perform their judicial and administrative functions, and the king would then send them into forced exile on their estates or to provincial towns until idleness or loss of income would cause them to resume their work. Whether on strike or in exile the result was the same: the courts were closed and law suits remained unsettled. As the source of justice and protector of its subjects, the Crown could not remain passive; moreover, it had to demonstrate that its judicial opponents could not paralyze essential government activities. Hence, the government deputized *maîtres des requêtes* to hear and judge cases; these special tribunals replaced not only the Paris Parlement but recalcitrant provincial Parlements as well. Aubert de Tourny's first assignment as *maître des requêtes* was as a member of a royal *chambre de vacations* established on September 27, 1720, to substitute for the Paris parlementarians then exiled in Pontoise; and in 1753 both Bertin de Bellille and Antoine Chaumont de la Galaizière served on the Chambre Royale de Justice, which again replaced the exiled Paris Parlement.[15] In 1765 the La Chalotais affair precipitated a judicial crisis in Brittany: the entire body of parlementarians resigned to demonstrate emphatically their sympathy for their colleague and to protest against the actions of the royal government and its agents. The Crown responded immediately and dispatched *maîtres des requêtes* to Rennes: Gaspard Louis de Caze de la Bove, a future intendant in Brittany (1775–1785), and François Pierre du Cluzel, soon to be intendant of Tours (1766–1783), served on this judicial commission.[16]

The Crown resorted to this stratagem not only in dire emergencies when Parlements ceased functioning. Special courts composed of *maîtres des requêtes* also judged in first instance or on appeal controversial and politically significant cases that had aroused the bias of sovereign courts and determined the Crown to remove from their jurisdiction. La Chalotais himself, the *procureur-général* of the Parlement of Rennes, would certainly escape judgment before his fellow magistrates, yet the Crown would risk political humiliation before all the sovereign courts and the nobility if it did not take action against him in response to his abusive criticism of the royal governor, the Duc d'Aiguillon. Hence the government created a special commission in 1766 to judge La

---

[15] Cf. Lhéritier, I, 45, and Boyé, "Le chancelier Chaumont de la Galaizière et sa famille," *Le Pays Lorrain*, XXIX (1937), 132.

[16] Fréville, II, 217.

Chalotais' actions; among the commissioners was Charles Alexandre de Calonne, then a *maître des requêtes,* who served as *procureur-général.*[17] The Calas affair occasioned the formation of a special tribunal in 1765 in response to Voltaire's demand for a retrial; Louis Thiroux de Crosne, future intendant of Rouen (1768–1785), was a member and Dupleix de Bacquencourt was *rapporteur.* The latter, according to Voltaire, used his pivotal role to convince the other members to annul the judgment of the Toulouse Parlement, rehabilitate the memory of the dead Calas, and indemnify his family. Both Dupleix and Thiroux earned Voltaire's plaudits for their sincere and successful efforts in this case.[18]

Public esteem was not always the recompense of the *maîtres des requêtes;* magisterial hostility and popular scorn, which judges calculatingly stirred up, resulted more frequently. Their efforts were portrayed not as earnest attempts to execute justice and assure equity, but as the groveling efforts of obsequious servants or the arbitrary actions of rigorous agents of a despotic master—the king and royal ministers. Calonne never succeeded in obliterating from the memories of parlementary magistrates his role as judge of La Chalotais, and their bitterness erupted against him during his tenure as controller-general. Yet the *maîtres des requêtes'* service as extraordinary judges and the hostile reaction of magistrates ironically produced a single result that served the Crown's purpose. Acting in the name of the sovereign in the face of critical outrage, *maîtres des requêtes* would more consciously embrace royalist views and unqualifiedly promote royal interests: royalism would be their mark. As the king's agents against their fellow magistrates, their former colleagues, their actions would mark a definitive break, polit-

---

[17] M. Michaud, *Biographie universelle ancienne et moderne* (rev. ed.; Paris, 1843), VI, 424. See also Charles Alexandre de Calonne, *Mémoire presenté au roi, par M. de Calonne, maître des requêtes: pièces sur l'affaire du duc d'Aiguillon et de La Chalotais* (Paris, 1766).

[18] Fréville, II, 348, and Bluche, 373, n. 7.

ically and psychologically, between the two groups. For those *maîtres des requêtes* who never engaged personally in these forays, their sympathy and support for their colleagues, their corporate solidarity, served equally to stamp their outlook. Parlementary opposition did not separate but soldered their attachment to the Crown.

III

Most *maîtres des requêtes* advanced directly from the Council to provincial intendancies; some, however, performed other functions in the interim as extensions of their duties as *maîtres des requêtes,* or following promotions to higher ranks. In one case or the other, their additional service further deepened their knowledge of administrative or judicial affairs and their understanding of the workings and aims of monarchical government. A total of twelve of the ninety *maîtres des requêtes* became presidents of the Grand Conseil; all of them were intendants of the periods 1749–1751 and 1774–1776, since only after 1738 did this post become appointive. In effect, this assignment took the form of a special commission conferred on a *maître des requêtes* for a stated period of time, a year or more, after which he resumed his regular functions on the Royal Council or, in a few instances, immediately became an intendant.[19] Only four served as intendants of commerce and one as intendant of finance—offices that were distinct and more prominent in the administrative hierarchy; three held these intendancies during the first period and two during the second. The small number of *maîtres des requêtes* who were intendants of commerce or finance before becoming provincial intendants and their disappearance from these posts in the last period probably only indicate that these offices acquired higher status with their increased responsibilities owing to greater government activity in financial and economic affairs after

[19] Cf. Chérin 24, "Bertin," f. 65, for a copy of a commission to a *maître des requêtes* as president of the Grand Conseil.

mid-century; the Crown increasingly assigned these offices to former provincial intendants or councilors of state who unquestionably had more experience.

The last two decades of Louis XV's reign witnessed an innovation in administrative practices: the introduction of *maîtres des requêtes* who served as *intendants adjoints* in the *généralités*. A total of five who were intendants in the years 1774–1776 held the position. An automatic assumption would be that family ties accounted for this: fathers wanted to guarantee professional advancement for their sons and therefore associated them in the work of their intendancies. Such is the empire of social habits and interests. But this is only partly true.

Of the five *intendants adjoints,* only two assisted their fathers, who were intendants, and directly succeeded them in the same *généralité:* Guignard de Saint-Priest in Languedoc and Bertier de Sauvigny in Paris.[20] The experience of Antoine Chaumont de la Galaizière as *intendant adjoint* illustrates the dual character of this new post. While still *maître des requêtes,* he went in 1751 to Lorraine where his father, the intendant Antoine Martin Chaumont de la Galaizière, initiated him in the affairs of the province. Stanislas, the former Polish king, father-in-law of Louis XV, and currently ruler of Lorraine, requested in 1756 that the son succeed the father to the intendancy, but the Comte de Belle-Isle, minister and secretary of state, replied that he should gain prior experience in a less important intendancy. So the younger

[20] Jean Emmanuel de Guignard de Saint-Priest, intendant in Languedoc (1751–1785), and Marie Joseph Emmanuel de Guignard de Saint-Priest, *intendant adjoint* in Languedoc (1764–1785) and intendant from 1785 to the end of the *ancien régime;* and Louis Jean Bertier de Sauvigny, intendant of Paris (1744–1776), and Louis Bénigne François Bertier de Sauvigny, *intendant adjoint* of Paris (1768–1776) and intendant from 1776 until July 22, 1789, when he was attacked and killed by a mob aroused by their fears of a royalist plot and the news of the taking of the Bastille. For a recounting of this incident see G. Bertier de Sauvigny, 4 ff.

Chaumont became intendant of Montauban in that year. Two years later he returned to Lorraine, where he was *intendant adjoint* until 1766 and then provincial intendant in his own right until 1777, afterward succeeding to other posts in the royal administration.[21] That Antoine Chaumont de la Galaizière succeeded his father was designed but neither automatic nor direct, since first he had to serve independently as an intendant elsewhere and thereby demonstrate his administrative skills. The last two *intendants adjoints,* in contrast to the others, had no family ties to account for their positions as assistants or for their accession in full status to the same intendancies.[22]

Sending *maîtres des requêtes* as *adjoints* to assist intendants in the provinces, whether or not they were sons, was a practice that reversed the views the Crown had expressed earlier in the century. When André Jubert de Bouville, intendant of Orléans, requested in 1703 that his son Louis Guillaume, recently made *maître des requêtes,* be attached to him in order to learn the administrative practices of an intendancy, Chancellor Pontchartrain responded that his work on the Royal Council would serve him better; and after five years of service there, Louis Guillaume became intendant of Alençon.[23] The government's acceptance or adoption of this procedure later in the century may reflect its solici-

[21] Boyé, "Le chancelier Chaumont de la Galaizière et sa famille," *Le Pays Lorrain,* XXIX (1937), 132 ff.

[22] These two are Nicolas III Dupré de Saint-Maur, *intendant adjoint* of Bourges (1764–1767) and intendant (1767–1776); and Louis Thiroux de Crosne, *intendant adjoint* of Rouen (1767–1768) and intendant (1768–1785). For a further analysis of the practice of appointing *intendants adjoints* in its relation to family succession see below, Chapter 8.

[23] Ironically, Louis Guillaume Jubert de Bouville was named intendant of Orléans in 1713, only six years after his father had left the post in that *généralité;* cf. Charles de Beaucorps, "Une province sous Louis XIV: L'administration des intendants d'Orléans, de Creil, Jubert de Bouville, de la Bourdonnaye, 1686–1713," *Mémoire de la Société Archéologique et Historique de l'Orléanais,* XXXIII (1911), 98, n. 3.

tousness to personal appeals, or may indicate one aspect of its response to the greater burdens and complexities of provincial administration which its own vigorous domestic policy produced. Perhaps the Crown sought to lighten the labors of particular intendants. More likely, it aimed to initiate younger officers in the affairs of their future provinces, and before they assumed full and independent responsibilities, to provide them with their most meaningful apprenticeship: actual work in the intendancies. That some families also used this procedure for their own advantage only further highlights a fundamental paradox of the *ancien régime:* private and government interests often coincided and were mutually beneficial, even if the former aimed at personal gain and the latter at public need.

IV

The importance the Crown attached to the experience that *maîtres des requêtes* obtained reveals itself in the number of years they served in this office before the government assigned them to provincial intendancies. The intendants for the years 1710–1712 served a median number of five years as *maîtres des requêtes;* those of 1749–1751 served a median of seven years; and those of 1774–1776 served a median of eight years. Age, moreover, served to indicate both experience and maturity: the median age for the intendants of the first period was thirty-four; for those of the second period thirty-three; and again thirty-four years for the intendants of the third period.[24] In all, their periods of service ranged from ten months to twenty-eight years, including the years spent as intendants of commerce or finance, or as *intendants adjoints;* and their ages ranged from twenty-five to fifty-one years.

Few became intendants when they were inordinately young or after minimal experience as *maîtres des requêtes,*

[24] The minimum age for an intendant, as stipulated in the law, was thirty-six years, but as was usual, legal provisions were not always literally observed; cf. Jolly, 28.

and of these only one fits the exaggerated stereotype: Antoine Jean Terray, after serving only two years as *maître des requêtes*, was appointed intendant of Montauban in 1773 at age twenty-five by the Abbé Terray, his uncle and the controller-general. Eight others became intendants before age thirty, three in each of the first two periods, and one in the third, yet they previously had been *maîtres des requêtes* for several years; and two who were *maîtres des requêtes* for only one year or less had served a number of years as magistrates in sovereign courts before entering the Royal Council, and became intendants when they were thirty-seven and fifty-one years old.[25] Clearly the intendants of the eighteenth

[25] The eight, apart from Terray, who became intendants before age thirty were: 1710–1712—Nicolas Prosper Bauyn d'Angervilliers, intendant of Grenoble (1705–1715), who served as *maître des requêtes* for five years before his first appointment as intendant at age twenty-seven; Cardin Le Bret, intendant of Aix (1704–1734), also five years as *maître des requêtes* before his first intendancy at age twenty-six; and Jacques Etienne Turgot de Soumons, intendant of Moulins (1709–1713), six years as *maître des requêtes* before his first intendancy at age twenty-six; 1749–1751—Jean Louis de Bernage de Vaux, intendant of Moulins (1744–1756), Louis Jean Bertier de Sauvigny, intendant of Paris (1744–1776), and Denis Dodart, intendant of Bourges (1728–1767), all three having served four years as *maître des requêtes* before their first appointments as intendants at age twenty-eight; and 1774–1776—Antoine III Chaumont de la Galaizière, intendant of Lorraine (1766–1777), *maître des requêtes* for seven years before his first intendancy at age twenty-nine, and Antoine Louis François Le Fèvre de Caumartin, intendant of Lille (1756–1778), *maître des requêtes* for five years before his first intendancy at age twenty-nine. The two who were *maîtres des requêtes* for very short periods were Yves Marie de La Bourdonnaye, intendant of Orléans (1709–1713), who was *conseiller* in the Parlement of Rennes for ten years and *maître des requêtes* for one year before his first appointment as intendant at age thirty-seven; and Antoine Jean Baptiste Jullien, intendant of Alençon (1766–1790), first *conseiller à la table de marbre* and *procureur-général des eaux et forêts à la table de marbre* in the royal administration for eight years, then *conseiller* in the Paris Parlement for fourteen years, and *maître des requêtes* for only ten months before becoming intendant at age fifty-one.

century were neither untried administrators nor callow youths when they first went to the provinces to rule the king's subjects. For its own purposes the monarchy succeeded in counteracting, even correcting, the defects that marred the sovereign courts and potentially threatened the royal administration, whose personnel came from the body of magistrates.

No substantial differences, whether regarding their length of service as *maîtres des requêtes* or their ages when they began their tasks in the provinces, distinguish the three groups of intendants. Evidently, there was no deterioration during the century in the standards for selecting provincial intendants and consequently in their quality as administrators, which only experience and age could determine and assure. It was almost as if the work of administration and the game of politics operated in two separate spheres. Louis XIV had died; ministers whom he had chosen and trained no longer directed affairs. Louis XV was young, later indolent and indecisive; his ministers frequently changed, often quarreled or ignored each other; and his mistresses and favorites assumed importance, freely bestowing places and privileges. Despite all this, the Crown did not relax its rigorous oversight or disregard its need for able administrators. Political rivalries and favoritism produced weak government, whetted personal ambitions, and indulged social habits; yet the central administration, personified by its provincial agents, the intendants, remained untarnished.

V

Maîtres des requêtes undeniably received the best practical training for administrators and underwent the surest intellectual formation for royal agents. In school they studied the contents of the law and in court they began to apply it. On the Council they judged disputes with concern for the interests of the Crown and the benefit of the king's subjects, and they evaluated legal decisions and established laws; they learned to administer, make law, and decide policy; [26] they became habituated to the operations of royal government,[27] identified with its actions, and stamped with monarchical sympathies and aspirations. Among no other group in eighteenth-century France could the Crown find men with similar

[26] A description of Moreau de Beaumont's zest for work and intellectual disposition illustrates the mental habits and discipline he acquired in the course of his professional experience as a magistrate and *maître des requêtes;* the following was written by the editor of Beaumont's study of European taxes (cf. Moreau de Beaumont, I, vii) : "He had no greater pleasure than to be occupied with work. He talked about it ceaselessly: in the [royal] councils among men who understood and in society with men who loved these matters. One can judge how well he was suited to it by the ineffaceable imprint which it produced on his mind. When he heard a case he could later recall it as exactly as if he had studied it himself. *His memory was astounding, resembling a file of records always open, where one could find in order, at every hour of the day, the laws and all the issues of the administration."* (The italics are mine.)

[27] The following judgment of a contemporary reveals the high regard for the administrative experience available to *maîtres des requêtes* and intendants, and for the value of the entire administrative *cursus honorum.* The author had advanced from magistrate to *maître des requêtes,* intendant, and finally *conseiller d'état,* so his statement reflects his personal experience: "In order to exercise successfully any art or profession you must have practice in all its aspects in an orderly progression, so as to improve and extend your abilities. The gradation established in France for administrative functions, although not as well marked out as it could have been, would have conferred excellent instruction if it had been followed exactly. The basic ideas of administration were gained in the judicial courts invested with the sanction and execution of laws, to which principles administrative practice must always conform. From this first level you passed to the [Royal] Council, where you did not judge individuals but judicial decisions; and the reports drawn up regarding the complaints against administrative abuses enabled you to learn the regulations and inculcated a spirit that differed from the spirit of the judiciary. This experience prepared you for the functions of royal commissioner in a province; transfer from the administration of one province to the administration of another enabled you to compare them and to become aware of their essential and different characteristics. Success in these posts enabled you to become an intendant of

talents and sentiments. They were a select and loyal corps—an unrivaled governing elite.[28] Their work on the Council not only gave them concrete experience, but their political outlook set them apart from

finance, having within your jurisdiction a particular sector of financial affairs, and in order to excel in this you had to concentrate your studies on these matters. Intendants of finance met in conferences in which were summed up all the knowledge that could be made into general principles. Thus in many respects they were, on the one hand, excellent inspectors of the provincial intendants, and on the other hand useful assistants to the controller-general who, in case of change, could be replaced by one of them." (Auget de Montyon, *Particularités et observations,* 384 f.). The translation is mine.

[28] An evocation of the historical tradition of royalism which *maîtres des requêtes* imbibed from their service, as well as gaining superior technical training, follows in this excerpt from the petition the corps presented to the Regent in 1717 claiming pre-emption for the posts of intendants. Cf. "Mémoire pour M^rs les Ms. des req. Pretendants quils sont seuls en Droict et en possession destre envoyés dans les provinces en qualité dintendants . . . Janvier 1717," BN, ms. fr. 7–013, fs. 560r°-v°, 561v°: "The French monarchy during the first centuries of the Third race had rather narrow limits, several princes although vassals having usurped almost all the regalian rights. Thus there were few provinces which were under the immediate administration of officers of the king and during this period eight *maîtres des requêtes* sufficed. But they were always near the person of the king, some to bring the petitions of his subjects and to attend his councils, others to carry his orders to the few provinces in which he ruled, and still others to serve in the Chancellery and in the parlement when he remained in one place. Subsequently, royal power having caused the princes to render full obedience and the last kings having made great and glorious conquests, the number of provinces subject to the government having increased and the needs of the state having caused several taxes to be imposed of which some have remained permanent, the needs of government service thereby multiplied and required an increase in the number of *maîtres des requêtes* finally to eighty-eight, the number currently in the Company.

"Your Royal Highness will permit them to add that if the Kings have regarded them as alone capable of this function which combined the magistracy and the ministry, the people have thought the same. . . .

"Nourished in the [Royal] Councils, the ordinances of our kings have

the magistracy and the nobility. Contemporaries considered them as different, and the language of historians reflects this reality: they were neither *noblesse d'épée* nor *noblesse de robe;* they were, instead, *noblesse d'Etat, noblesse de la plume.* The Crown gained and French subjects benefited as a result of their distinct political character. For in all other essential aspects—their family life and social relations, their legal status and economic interests—the provincial intendants were equally magistrates and noblemen: the pen belonged as well to the robe and to the sword.

---

been their principal study and the foundation of their decisions; they have derived their ideas from the science of laws, the maxims of the state, and the views of the government. Your Royal Highness will have difficulty in finding among his subjects raised in another company all this knowledge combined together and the qualities which are necessary to fill the posts which have been assigned to them at all times."

For other general evaluations of the administrative and political training of the *maîtres des requêtes* see Bluche, 66–67, and Fréville, III, 335–36.

PART II

THE ROYAL INTENDANTS AS A
SOCIAL ELITE: THEIR FAMILY
ORIGINS AND SOCIAL EVOLUTION

The Family Roots of the Intendants: Geographic and Social

I

A Frenchman, when introduced to a Parisian, often asks: "But were you born in Paris?" The same question may be asked of eighteenth-century residents of Paris, among them the intendants who as *maîtres des requêtes* served on the Royal Council in the capital. Throughout its history Paris has had its native-born and its provincials; as the capital it offers more and greater opportunities, and beckons the ambitious who seek fortune and a future. The presence of provincials and their ultimate success or failure in a strange city reflect a society's power of assimilation. Thus the movement from province to capital is one measure of mobility in a society.

Genealogies inform us where the families of the intendants originated and approximately when their ancestors settled in Paris; these facts are known for ninety-three of the ninety-four intendants. Families classified as native Parisian include those whose earliest direct ancestor resided there. Along with these Parisian families and those originating in the provinces is a third group: families whose oldest *direct* ancestor lived in Paris but whose earlier *probable* ancestor was from the provinces.[1] For all the families in each of these

---

[1] Genealogists accept *direct* filiation only when original documents attest to the specific relation between father and son, or to the relation between members of different generations in the same family which may aid in determining that between father and son. For example, if one

three categories we may calculate their years of residence in Paris and determine whether they were long established or new in the capital.

At least 56 families, perhaps as many as 79, were originally from the provinces, while 14 were native to Paris. Among the 30 intendants for the years 1710–1712, 7 came from families of Parisian origin, 14 were originally provincial—one even from Switzerland—and 9 were probably provincial in origin. The numbers of families originating in the provinces increased in the succeeding two periods. During the years 1749–1751, out of 32 intendants only 4 of their families were originally from Paris, 16 were definitely provincial in origin, and 12 were of probable provincial origin. For the years 1774–1776, of the 31 families whose geographic origins can be determined, 3 alone were Parisian in origin, 26 were of definite provincial origin, and 2 were of probable provincial origin.[2] With the increase of intendants from fam-

---

document reveals the relation between an uncle and a nephew, and another between the same uncle and his brother, whereas only a genealogical chart states that the nephew is son to the brother, we may presume the definite relation between the father and son. If no original documents confirm the family relations presented in genealogical lists or charts, the latter may be accepted only as *probable* filiation.

[2] There is no evidence that one intendant of provincial origin in the first period, Beauharnois, ever settled in Paris. Two of the twenty-six intendants in the third period—Cachet de Garnerans in Dombes and Chazerat in Auvergne—remained in their provinces and never settled in Paris; they obtained their appointments on the basis of provincial service and influence. Some of the intendants in each period were of the same or related families, and each of these families is repeated in the tabulation above. In the first period, Lamoignon de Basville and Lamoignon de Courson were father and son, and Turgot de Saint-Clair and Turgot de Soumons were cousins; in the second period, La Bourdonnaye and La Bourdonnaye de Blossac were distant cousins, Chaumont de la Galaizière and Chaumont de la Millière were brothers, and Moreau de Séchélles and Moreau de Beaumont were uncle and nephew. Moreover, the same families are represented in each of the three periods by different members and so again their numbers are repeated. In the first and second periods: Barberie de Saint-Contest, Bernage, La Briffe,

ilies originally provincial, there was an increase in the range of provinces represented in the corps: intendants or their forebears came to Paris from more distant provinces such as Languedoc, Dauphiné, and Gascony.

Regardless of their place of origin, the important matter was how long these families resided in Paris once they settled there. A family living in the capital for several generations became totally assimilated: after the passage of many years they no longer differed in speech or behavior from older Parisians. Moreover, time bred connections and gave prestige which promoted success. But a family newly established in Paris still had to make their way alone in strange and difficult surroundings: professional success and social esteem would be harder for them to achieve. Did the native and older families of Paris retain their grip on positions of power, or did new provincials rise to high positions in government—such as royal intendants?

Those intendants who were the first members of their families to establish themselves in Paris numbered only 15 out of the total of 93. From the late seventeenth century through the first half of the eighteenth century their fortune did not vary: only 3 were in the first group from 1710–1712, and 2 in the second from 1749–1751. The third quarter of the century witnessed a great increase of first-generation Parisians in the corps: there were 10 among the 31 intendants during the years 1774–1776. The thirteen or fourteen intendants, of the total group, whose families had recently settled in Paris during the fifty years preceding the intendants' ca-

---

La Bourdonnaye, Chauvelin, and Méliand. In the second and third periods: Bertier de Sauvigny, Caze de la Bove, again Chaumont, and La Porte de Meslay. If the figures are corrected to include each family only once, this yields a total of 48 provincials, 19 probable provincials, and 12 Parisians; and the tabulation for each group is as follows: 1710–1712—13 provincials and 8 probable provincials; 1749–1751—12 provincials, 9 probable provincials, and 2 Parisians; and 1774–1776—23 provincials and 2 Parisians.

reers increased to almost one-third the number of new Parisians in the corps. Under Louis XIV there were one or two, under Louis XV there were 7, and under Louis XVI there were 5. The total of new Parisians among the intendants, with one to three generations in the capital, was as follows for each of the three periods: Louis XIV, 4 or 5 (13%–17%); Louis XV, 9 (28%); and Louis XVI, 15 (48%). Thus, the proportion of new Parisians, lowest among the intendants serving Louis XIV, progressively increased during the century: they constituted almost half of the corps during the early years of Louis XVI's reign.

The number of intendants from old Parisian families, established in the capital for more than a century, totaled 20 or 21 of the 93. Conversely, their proportion in the corps gradually decreased in the course of the century: Louis XIV, 10 (33%); Louis XV, 7 or 8 (22%–25%); and Louis XVI, 3 (10%). Individuals from families living in Paris between fifty and a hundred years had the most persistent hold on positions in the corps. Although equal in number to the new Parisians, totaling 28 or 29 of the 93 intendants, their proportion remained relatively steady throughout the century. There were 9 of them in the first period, 11 or 12 in the second, and 8 in the third.

The latter group of families were fairly well established in Paris. During their three or four generations of residence they had acquired sufficient social prestige and political connections to assert themselves effectively in the ranks of the royal government. However, they had not assimilated into the oldest families or become totally transformed by aristocratic mores and ambitions. Hence they did not direct their full attention to the more prestigious or leisured offices such as court sinecures or military commands. Those Parisian families with more than approximately four generations of residence either did not exert preponderant influence on ministers and the king or were sufficiently entrenched in society to lack interest in powerful administrative posts and active government careers.[3] Provincials and recently settled Parisians understandably had the strongest urge to assert themselves in political life, and their fortunes continued to rise in the high administration during the eighteenth century: the native *pays* became less attractive as national life grew more active and men focused their energies and ambitions upon Paris.

At all times Paris was the political and economic center of France. Provincials arriving in the capital sought to establish themselves where business and finance were more active and gave promise of greater wealth than in provincial towns; during periods of prosperity they might come in larger numbers, tempted by the prospect of swift, large profits. Some newcomers sought careers in the judicial courts or the royal government, where they might gain prestige, even nobility. And where but in the capital could they hope to advance their careers without limit? Sometimes the monarchy abetted their ambitions: its administrative or fiscal needs caused it to create more offices to carry out necessary tasks of government or to bring more revenue into the needy royal treasury. What originally had drawn these forty-eight families, possibly sixty-seven in all, to the capital? What had enabled them to establish themselves there, so that within one to three generations they became members of the ruling elite?

More than four-fifths of these sixty-seven families had settled in Paris during six distinct periods beginning in the sixteenth century. Nine had arrived from 1540 to the 1570's; 8 came between 1600 and 1630; 9 followed from 1640 into the late 1650's; 8 settled from the mid-1670's into the 1690's and 13 between 1700 and the mid-1720's; and from the 1740's to the 1760's 12 arrived in the capital.[4] What forces—economic, political, or social—were at work during those

[3] Cf. Mousnier, . . . *Chancelier Séguier*, I, 121.

[4] The above figures include each family numbered only once, regardless of how many of their members are included among the ninety-three intendants.

decades to attract especially large numbers of provincials to Paris?

The mid-sixteenth century witnessed an artistic and cultural renaissance in France and an economic one as well; this was a time of vigorous and enriching economic activity, ended only by the outbreak of the Wars of Religion. At the same time the cost of foreign wars made the Valois kings indigent and caused them to create endless new judicial and financial offices. Men came to Paris to find both profit and office. Prospects changed somewhat during the seventeenth century. Economic activity was relatively less intense; instead, the lure was primarily government office. The peace that Henry IV brought allowed the monarchy to turn its attention to administrative tasks which required more personnel; furthermore, the introduction of the *Paulette* tax in 1604 led to the sale of more offices as buyers were assured of their hereditary rights and permanent possession.[5] By the 1640's the Paris sovereign courts had unchallenged prestige as judicial bodies and political forums. The Crown's definitive grant of legal ennoblement to these various offices in 1644 and 1645, and during the crisis of the Fronde further enhanced their attractiveness, which the courts' ultimate defeat did not tarnish.[6] Parisian magistrates might be reduced to political silence during the high years of Louis XIV's reign, but judgeships in the capital retained their professional and social appeal and provincials still arrived during the last quarter of the century to purchase these charges. They came seeking other positions in the government as well. The monarchy's increased responsibilities and functions in a more regulated society required an enlarged administrative network; at the same time, war and fiscal necessity further forced the Crown to multiply government offices.

Again, during the last years of the seventeenth century and the first two decades of the eighteenth, high profits and rapid gain lured provincials to the capital. Colbert's policies en-

[5] Cf. Mousnier, *La vénalité des offices,* 241–43, 266, 278.
[6] Cf. Ford, 63.

couraged a resurgence of business activity which the wars did not undo.[7] Particularly during the War of the Spanish Succession men with sharp eyes and quick minds could make immediate fortunes selling supplies to the army and lending money to the government. In the years afterward, the mania set off by the Law "system" created riches overnight for the lucky or the shrewd who speculated at the right moment in inflated stocks and depreciating currency. With large amounts of cash in hand these newly rich could easily buy any office that would enhance their prestige and endow them with nobility—an ambition they were anxious to achieve. Professional considerations and social aspirations, rather than direct profit motives, explain the influx of provincials in the mid-eighteenth century. All but one of the twelve who came to Paris between the 1740's and 1760's were the first members of their families to settle in the capital; and all sought careers in government—each of them becoming a provincial intendant.

The questions of where these families originated, when they settled in Paris, and why they moved to the capital are preludes to the fundamental problem of social analysis. The significant questions regarding the origins of these intendants and the evolution of their families yet remain. Who were their ancestors? What were the major changes in profession and status of these families from the time of the forebears to the intendants' day?

II

Age distinguished families in the *ancien régime*. Whether noble, bourgeois, or peasant, the more generations a family could trace back in its history the more pride it had in itself

[7] François Crouzet, "Angleterre et France au XVIIIᵉ siècle: Essai d'analyse comparée de deux croissances économiques," *Annales: Sociétés, Économies, Civilisations,* 21ᵉ année, no. 2 (Mar.–Apr. 1966), 257, and Pierre Léon, "La crise de l'économie française à la fin du règne de Louis XIV (1685–1715)," *L'Information Historique,* 18ᵉ année (Sept.–Oct. 1956), 133 ff.

and the greater standing it had in the community. But a determination of the age of a family depends on several contingencies, now as well as centuries ago. Memory and verbal testimony might prove family descent among neighbors in town and countryside in the *ancien régime*, but for some of the exigent royal commissioners and genealogists, as well as for historians, documentary proof alone attested to filiation. Even by the eighteenth century the passage of time, war, accident, and disaster had caused the disappearance or loss of genealogical documents; pillaging during the Revolution created further lacunae. In the present day, remaining evidence may be held by surviving relatives, hidden in parish records, or jealously guarded by notaries succeeding to the practice of their centuries-old predecessors. Hence these proofs lie unknown or inaccessible to the historian. He cannot turn confidently to published genealogies, particularly to discover the earliest ancestors, since many of these were devised merely to exalt family egos. He can accept only those secondary accounts which show a scrupulous regard for historical truth; but for the most part he must limit himself to the documentary evidence available to him. For this analysis of the family histories of the ninety-four intendants—one of them remaining unknown—I have relied on the information provided by the collective volumes in the Cabinet des Titres of the Bibliothèque Nationale, aided by critical genealogical studies, the most noteworthy being François Bluche's genealogical dictionary, *L'origine des magistrats du Parlement de Paris au XVIIIe siècle (1715–1771)*.

For some among the intendants, their family lineage can be traced back nine, ten, even twelve generations; for others we known nothing about the family prior to the father or even the intendant himself. Three to five generations of proven ancestry is the average among most of the ninety-three intendants. In general we may presume that the older a family was the more noted it was. High social rank might guarantee that more people would know its history over a longer period of time and that members of the family would proudly guard their records from one generation to the next. This is true of some of the intendants' families, notably Turgot and La Bourdonnaye, who could list a minimum of eight and ten generations respectively of proven ancestry by the eighteenth century. Yet age was not always synonymous with honored rank. At the end of the eighteenth century the Terray family included an intendant, a high-court magistrate, and a minister of finance, but seven generations before, in the early sixteenth century, its first known ancestor was a simple peasant.[8] Thus, how old a family was and how many generations it had of proven ancestry are alone not significant in the historian's dossier. The important facts to determine at the start in studying the intendants' family histories are the occupation, profession, and social rank of their first known ancestors.

Whether the first ancestor was recent or ancient, information is often meager and a certain amount of guesswork is necessary to ascertain his social or economic standing. This is particularly true in a society such as early modern France, where men assumed higher rank than was theirs legally. What was the status of an ancestor who is known to us merely as *"sieur de"* or even as *"seigneur de"; or as "écuyer,"* or *"chevalier"?* Was he a nobleman? Was he a commoner pretending to be a gentleman? And the ancestor whose name is preceded by the quality *"noble homme"?* Was he in social and legal fact a nobleman? Evidently not, according to the best authorities.[9] A forebear who had enough money to pur-

---

[8] Abbé Merle, "Les Terray à Boen, notes généalogiques sur les ascendants de l'abbé Terray," *Bulletin de la Diana,* XXIV (1931–1934), 301–10.

[9] For an incisive discussion of all aspects of this problem see L. N. H. Chérin, *Abrégé chronologique d'édits, déclarations, règlements, arrêts et lettres patentes des rois de France concernant le fait de noblesse,* in *Dictionnaire héraldique,* Charles Grandmaison (Paris, 1852), 837–52; and Jacques Marie Joseph, Vicomte de Marsay, *De l'âge des privilèges au temps des vanités: Essai sur l'origine et la valeur des prétentions nobiliaires* (Paris, 1946).

chase an estate, however large or small, had sufficient pretext to imitate the mode of life and assume the nomenclature of a nobleman. To resolve this dilemma the historian may use a rule that is somewhat arbitrary but nevertheless based upon historic fact. For the greater part of France it was approximately in the sixteenth century that noble lands came on the market in large quantity. Indigent noblemen needed money, and wealthy commoners desired landed estates and the panoply of the noble way of life. The exchange of land for cash was made. Then gradually commoners also acquired the habit of titling themselves *écuyer, chevalier,* or *seigneur.* Thus, all such titles are accepted as indications of actual noble status for the period before the sixteenth century; afterward, they may merely denote men who were "bourgeois living nobly." On the other hand, since men in the *ancien régime* often included their profession after their family name, the most skeletal reference to a forebear in a document sometimes provides such concrete details which make the ancestor's status more certain.

The careers or status of eighty-nine first ancestors are documented, and three more appear in genealogical accounts without documents to confirm their rank or profession. (The existence of one first ancestor is documented but with no references indicating his social position or occupation.) We may classify these earliest forebears of the intendants, ranging from their fathers to ancestors twelve generations earlier, into two groups: public officials and private persons. Fifty-eight of them, plus the three whose careers are probable, were officials; their posts provided their main occupations and their rank in society. The remaining thirty-one had occupations and social standing independent of government service.[10]

---

[10] Among these 31, I include 4 who were royal doctors and one the royal surgeon; although they served the king, their basic functions involved medicine and not tasks of government.

If by "origin" Saint-Simon, Boulainvilliers, and Tocqueville referred solely to the first ancestors of the intendants, there would be some justice to their remarks. Only four of the ninety-two known first ancestors of the intendants were provincial *seigneurs,* though in fact these were only two, since one was the common ancestor for three of the intendants. The latter, La Bourdonnaye of Brittany, was the sole feudal knight and nobleman. He appears in history by the mid-fifteenth century as a fiefholder called to arms to fight in the service of the duke of Brittany.[11] The other ancestor, who lived as late as the mid-seventeenth century, appears in the records fleetingly and dimly. Known only by his titles of "chevalier, seigneur de la Tour, vicomte de Glené," he seems to have been a country nobleman, yet how he attained this status and what his antecedents were remain unknown.

In contrast, ten first ancestors may be classified as bourgeois. But what does this term signify? Certainly not middle-class according to income, as in modern usage. Nor is it simply the opposite of noble. Men in the *ancien régime* had another word for commoner—*roturier,* referring to all non-nobles. The word "bourgeois" had strict application in the *ancien régime.* According to social custom, a "bourgeois" was a man who no longer actively engaged in work or business but lived off his inherited wealth, savings, or interest from investments or loans; he might also have acquired a rural estate, and thus be "living nobly." In modern terms, he would be an urban *rentier* or a country landowner. According to legal definition, a "bourgeois" was a townsman who lived in the town the required number of years and earned enough money or paid enough taxes to meet the financial requirements for enjoying the rights and privileges of the town *bourgeoisie.* He would then be able to vote for the town government or to be a member of it; he might be exempt from certain taxes and tolls, and from the onerous

[11] PO 465, "Bourdonnaye," fs. 48–50.

and expensive duty of quartering soldiers; and his legal disputes might be settled in the courts more swiftly.[12] In the original sense of the word, then, these 10 bourgeois first ancestors included 5 known simply as "bourgeois" of a town (3 in this count being the same man, ancestor of the 3 Chaumonts who were intendants); 3 bourgeois "living nobly," entitled *sieur* of the lands they possessed; and 2 bourgeois fiefholders ennobled by their possessions (in historical fact one man, the common ancestor of the Turgot family).

The documents reveal the occupations of the remaining seventeen nonofficials, ranging from farming and business to the professions. Those engaged solely in business numbered six. With the exception of one, they were small merchants or shopkeepers: a druggist, three clothiers, and one whose trade is unknown. The single exception, Dupleix, was a tax farmer and director of the French Indies Company, obviously engaged in larger financial ventures, which undoubtedly enabled him to obtain the honorific post of "equerry in the Great Stable of the King." Two of these first ancestors were peasants, undoubtedly of the peasant *bourgeoisie* and well off: one was virtual proprietor of his lands—a *laboureur*—and even became a local tax-agent. The remaining nine were professionals. Five were in medicine, two as surgeons (actually one man, the ancestor of the two intendants La Porte de Meslay) and three as physicians, and all of them served the king or distinguished court nobles, which easily explains the future distinction of their descendants. The last four were lawyers (in fact only three, since one of these men was the common ancestor of the two intendants Chauvelin); all four had lived in the sixteenth century, when lawyers and their sons entered government service in greater numbers and the legal profession ranked immediately beneath officialdom.

[12] See Chérin, 867, for some of the royal proclamations regarding rights of bourgeois.

The transformation from private person to public officer was profound. A commoner who acquired an office acquired special legal rights and higher social standing. The law exempted him henceforth from numerous duties, from military conscription to payment of taxes, and conferred upon him definite privileges, such as speedier adjudication of his legal disputes or personal or hereditary nobility. His former peers now deferred to him as he walked at the head of a public procession or sat in one of the front pews in the parish church. The number and character of these rights and privileges depended upon the rank of the office; yet every office, however subordinate and insignificant, in some way separated and elevated its holder in society. It is therefore no wonder that men who had the education and means aimed at becoming government officials.[13]

The presence of fifty-eight, perhaps sixty-one, officers among the ninety-two first ancestors of the intendants testifies to the predominance of public officials in the society of the *ancien régime.* The men in this group held varied posts, at different levels of government; often they held different posts at different times in their lives or held several offices at the same time. How, then, may we classify them? In either of two ways: by the office that they held for the longest time or that was most important in their careers, or by the office in which they ended their careers. Offices also ranged within a more clear-cut double hierarchy of administrative rank and legal and social status: the former is determined by the functions attributed to the office, the unit of government to which it was responsible, and the size of the area within its jurisdiction; the latter, by the rights and privileges attached to the office.

Only three or four of the sixty-one officeholders did not

[13] Cf. J. R. Bloch, "L'anoblissement en France au temps de François 1ᵉʳ," *passim,* and Pierre Goubert, "Les officiers royaux des présidiaux, bailliages et elections dans la société française du XVIIᵉ siècle," *Bulletin de la Société d'Étude du XVIIᵉ siècle,* Nos. 42–43 (Paris, 1959), 55.

serve within the regular structure of the monarchical government. Two of them, one only a probable ancestor, were councilors to princes or dukes who ruled provinces, namely Burgundy and Dombes, before the French Crown annexed them. The remaining two held offices within the royal household: one had a merely honorific post without function but conferring privileges and status; the other (Auget) was the king's music master, whose descendant became the sovereign's provincial intendant.

Forty-six, perhaps forty-eight, of the intendants' first ancestors passed their entire careers as officers of the Crown, holding various posts in the monarchical government from minor local offices to the most important offices in the sovereign courts and on the Royal Council. One among them even served in the king's army as a military engineer; the rest were civil functionaries. They administered laws, settled legal disputes, wrote and registered contracts and decrees, collected taxes, and maintained civil order as officials in villages, towns, or cities, in one or several provinces, or in the central offices of the royal bureaucracy in Paris and Versailles. We may classify these men into the following groups: local officeholders, including municipal officials, having judicial, administrative, or financial functions; officeholders in the central administration, including the *secrétaires du roi* and the financial magistrates (i.e., the treasurers-general and receivers-general in the provinces) ; sovereign-court magistrates; and members of the Royal Council.

Local officeholders among the first ancestors numbered eleven, including two who were notaries. Two of the eleven held other offices later in life or for shorter periods of time: one became a *secrétaire du roi,* a purely honorific and expensive post by the late seventeenth century coveted because it conferred immediate hereditary nobility; and the other became the second in command (*subdélégué-général*) to the intendant in his province, as well as *secrétaire du roi.* Slightly fewer first ancestors held posts within the central administration: nine, plus one probable ancestor. Among them were four *secrétaires du roi,* three of these dating from the sixteenth century, when the offices were few in number and consequently held greater importance in the royal government. One of the four *secrétaires du roi* apparently held no other post while three did for shorter periods in their careers, two as financial magistrates and one as a sovereign-court magistrate. A total of four were mainly financial magistrates, three of whom also acquired other offices during their professional lives: two (actually one, the single ancestor of the two intendants La Briffe) were personal secretaries to Louis XIII's finance minister and *secrétaires du roi;* and the other (Le Fèvre d'Ormesson) became a member both of a sovereign court and the Royal Council. The last two were primarily administrative functionaries in the central bureaucracy. One of them, whose existence and career is not documented, was a secretary in the war ministry as well as a *secrétaire du roi.* The other had a remarkable career: he was first, presumably, a merchant, then became a mail carrier, advanced to become chief of the royal postal service, and finally, after acquiring much wealth, became a tax farmer or financier to the king and an ennobled *secrétaire du roi.*

The largest single group of officeholders among the intendants' first ancestors were magistrates of the sovereign courts in Paris and in the provinces: they totaled eighteen (plus one probable ancestor) —almost one-fifth of the total group of first ancestors. Except for three or perhaps four who were parlementary presidents and an *avocat-général,* they were all simple councilors in the courts. Four among them held other offices before or after becoming magistrates: Amelot (de Chaillou) previously had been mayor of Orléans; Le Pelletier (de la Houssaye) had been a local fiscal officer and became a *secrétaire du roi;* Trudaine was also a financial magistrate and a *secrétaire du roi;* and Boucher (d'Orsay), living in the late fourteenth century, had been the king's valet and treasurer before entering the court.

Officers at the summit of the administrative hierarchy were fewest in number among the intendants' first ancestors: only seven were members of the Royal Council, five as councilors of state (actually four, including the ancestor of the two intendants Lamoignon, father and son), one as ambassador and *maître des requêtes,* and one as chancellor of France and minister of state. In addition, all of them had been magistrates in the sovereign courts before advancing to the Royal Council.

Nine of the first ancestors included among the sixty-one officeholders combined both private and public careers in their lifetime. Except for one, they were tradesmen, large businessmen, or financiers before turning to public office. What were their business occupations, and what were their official careers?

Small merchants numbered five but in fact were only three, since two were common ancestors of four intendants. The offices they acquired, mainly secondary in importance and prestige, indicate their limited wealth. Two of them (but a single common ancestor) became treasurers for the Paris Parlement, receiving the court fees and distributing the salaries and emoluments to the judges; two others (again one common ancestor) became collectors of an emergency war tax, probably a special and temporary post; and the last became a provincial supervisor of gunpowder supplies but later purchased the expensive, ennobling office of *secrétaire du roi.*

The business and administrative careers of the remaining four are more complex and varied. One started out as a local retail merchant and then became a town judge and mayor before directing his attention and money elsewhere; he later became a royal financier and ended his career as *secrétaire du roi.* Two engaged in various business, financial, or speculative affairs before acquiring several offices and entering government service, one becoming a financial and judicial magistrate and *secrétaire du roi,* the other becoming a director of the French Indies Company and a member of a provincial sovereign court and of the Royal Council. The last in this group began his career not in business but as a minor functionary, first in a provincial postal bureau and then as secretary to the provincial intendant, when he began to speculate in the grain trade and became wealthy; with his new fortune he was able to purchase several offices, each of greater standing, from local to provincial fiscal agent to *secrétaire du roi,* and he continued to increase his riches as a tax farmer.

If we could go back one, two, or more generations in the family histories of these ninety-three intendants, would we find significant or striking changes in the professions and social status of their ancestors? Undocumented references to earlier forebears than the first known permit us to delve deeper into the ancestry of forty-nine of the intendants to see what their families perhaps were at an earlier time.

Only three of the earlier, probable ancestors had the same social and professional status as the documented first ancestors of their families: they were a sovereign-court magistrate, a bourgeois, and a merchant (though the latter may have been in a smaller business and so less wealthy). In the total group of ninety-three proven and presumed first ancestors, there were the same number of country *seigneurs,* peasants, financial magistrates, and royal commensal officers as among the documented first ancestors. Yet on the whole there were more proven and presumed first ancestors engaged in private affairs (16) and fewer of them who were public officers (15) than among the documented first ancestors. In contrast to the latter, consisting of 31 private persons and 58 officeholders, the first ancestors proven and presumed included 47 private persons and 46 public officers. In what groups were these changes concentrated? (See Table 4.) Significantly, more of the earlier, probable first ancestors were tradesmen and local public officers: 11 and 12 more respectively. Although, by going back in time, we might expect more lawyers

113

in this group, only 3 more appear. In contrast, there were 3 fewer ancestors who combined business and office, and only one less who was a *secrétaire du roi*. But among these earlier ancestors there was a considerable decrease among those who were sovereign-court magistrates and members of the Royal Council, 15 and 6 fewer, respectively, making a total of only

Table 4. Changes in social-professional status between the documented first ancestors and the proven and presumed first ancestors *

Documented first ancestors		Proven and presumed first ancestors	
Private persons	31	Private persons	47
Business	6	Business	17
Lawyers	4	Lawyers	7
Business and office	9	Business and office	6
Public officers	49	Public officers	40
Local	11	Local	23
Secrétaire du roi	4	*Secrétaire du roi*	3
Sovereign courts	18	Sovereign courts	3
Royal Council	7	Royal Council	1

* The figures indicated under the headings "private persons" and "public officers" do not represent the totals within each group, but only the numbers for each category where changes in profession and in social status were concentrated or significant.

3 magistrates and one royal councilor among the earlier probable first ancestors.

Two conclusions may be drawn. By tracing the intendants' ancestry farther back to the earliest ancestors, whether documented or not, we see that the family origins of almost all of them were more modest and ordinary—or, as Saint-Simon contemptuously stated, vile. But if we compare the earliest probable ancestors with the earliest proven ancestors one or more generations later, we anticipate the future transformation of these families: already they had begun to change their professional and social status; this early in their histories they were moving up in the social hierarchy of the *ancien régime*.

III

Contemporaries of the intendants and of their ancestors viewed each other from different perspectives. To a duke and peer of the realm, few were above him in society and almost all men were beneath him. Yet a man who was a councilor in a sovereign court, a treasurer-general in a province, even a lesser provincial or municipal officer, believed that he too ranked high professionally and socially, though never did he consider himself the equal of a duke and peer. Artisans and merchants, even lawyers or bourgeois *rentiers*, acknowledged these governing officials as their superiors; and country peasants in the *ancien régime* even looked upon townsmen as privileged beings. Whose view was closer to reality?

As society in the *ancien régime* had many ranks, each group viewing the other from its own place in the hierarchy, so the origins of the intendants' families were diverse and their place in the social order relative to those above or below them. The intendants' first ancestors were from many professions and occupations, from several rungs in the social hierarchy. More than one-third of the intendants (34 out of 93) sprang from councilors of state, sovereign-court judges, financial magistrates, and provincial *seigneurs*. Can the entire group then be blanketed as socially base? Roughly two-thirds of them could trace their roots to ancestors who were prestigious officeholders throughout or at some time in their careers (61 out of 93), or to esteemed lawyers, privileged bourgeois, and lifelong professional officers (61 out of 93). Were these many families not in the upper orders of society —some even in the highest—from their beginnings? Yet, only 3 percent of the families were noble since their first appearance in history, with perhaps 9 percent more whose families were questionably noble from their origins.[14] Thus the overwhelming proportion of the intendants' first ancestors were commoners—97 percent in all. And about one-third of these forebears were in or had just emerged from the lower orders of society, or were in the middle orders, where men might still labor for their livelihood: they were peasants, tradesmen, businessmen, and also town bourgeois. Certainly the corps of intendants in the eighteenth century was not a closed caste if it included men with such antecedents.

Through the family origins of the intendants we see a microcosm of French society in the *ancien régime:* a privileged, traditional, and hierarchical society, yet one in flux. Men of high standing could more easily obtain important positions of power and prestige, yet men with ambition, ability, and perseverance could work, become wealthy, obtain government posts, and ultimately raise their social status—for themselves and for their families. Members of the intendants' families in the generations following the first ancestors continued these efforts and advanced further, professionally and socially, or passed on the advantages they already had inherited.

[14] The family La Bourdonnaye, counting three intendants in the corps, had always been noble; 8 other families—Beauharnois, Bertier de Sauvigny (father and son), Chazerat, Cluzel, Gallois de la Tour de Glené, Guignard de Saint-Priest, Maignard, and De Pont de Monderoux—claimed but could not prove nobility from their families' origins. Other families did the same, but evidence definitely disproves such claims. For an analysis of the noble origins of the intendants' families see Chapter 6 below.

Nobility, Robe, and Pen: The Rise of the Intendants' Families

Before the generation of intendants appeared, almost all the families passed through two decisive stages and some entered upon a third. All became noble; almost all entered the high magistracy; and half were members of the high administration. Those families whose first ancestors were noblemen, magistrates, or royal functionaries maintained their position or even improved it during the succeeding generations; other families underwent a profound social transformation in the period that separated the first ancestor from the eighteenth-century intendant.

I

Noble status was not new for these families. Of the 92 families whose nobility is known,[1] only 18 or 19 were second-generation nobility; another 2 were either second- or

---

[1] The noble origins of two intendants are unknown, although both were nonetheless noble. There are no genealogical data for Etienne Louis Journet, intendant of Auch and Bayonne (1767–1776), but since he himself was a *maître des requêtes* that post would legally ennoble him. Charles Jean Baptiste des Gallois de la Tour, intendant in Provence (1744–1771 and 1775–1790), was the son of Jean Baptiste des Gallois, who was himself a magistrate, *maître des requêtes,* and three times intendant, including the intendancy of Aix immediately before it was assumed by the son; therefore the family Gallois de la Tour was undoubtedly noble, either through sovereign-court office or possibly of earlier but unknown provincial noble origins (see p. 107 above).

third-generation nobility; and only 2 intendants became noble themselves. Thus 68 or 69 of these families, roughly three-quarters of the total, were noble for three or more generations. According to social custom and jurisprudence in the *ancien régime,* a family with nobility for three to four generations was no longer disparaged as *anobli,* newly ennobled, but was esteemed as a member of the *ancienne noblesse.* The grandfather might have been common, but his grandson was considered a *gentilhomme.*[2] While 29 of the intendants were third-generation nobles and were themselves being assimilated into the old nobility, 39 or 40 of them—approximately 40 percent of the entire group—were fourth-generation nobility or older; the latter were incontestably in the ranks of the *ancienne noblesse.*

Nobility was a birthright: all the children of a noble father were themselves noble. Yet commoners could also become noble. Despite the persistence of the popular myth, few noblemen in the eighteenth century were direct descendants of valorous knights, who, in the dim past, fought on horseback for their suzerain and received fiefs for their reward and sustenance. Among the group of ninety-two intendants, only three could prove such descent, and they were all of the same family, sprung from a single feudal ancestor in the fifteenth century.

Knighthood introduced the order of nobility in feudal Europe, but in France after a time it ceased to be the sole means for acquiring nobility. As early as the thirteenth century other forms arose: royal letters patent conferred nobility upon payment of a fee; and purchase of a fief, together with payment of a tax, endowed the new proprietor with personal nobility, which became hereditary after three generations of

[2] See Ford, 61–63; Mousnier, *La vénalité des offices,* 502; and François Bluche, *L'origine des magistrats du Parlement de Paris au XVIIIe siècle (1715–1771) : Dictionnaire généalogique* (Paris, 1956), 22 (except where another title is given, following page references to Bluche are to be found in this work).

fiefholding.[3] By the end of the sixteenth century, the Crown and its subjects had devised various methods, accepted first in custom and later in law, for transforming a commoner into a nobleman; events in the seventeenth century accelerated and crystallized this development.

The monarchy desperately needed money, particularly to wage the numerous, almost unceasing wars in these two centuries; it had to gain political allies among its subjects to buttress itself against rebellious princes and dukes who were demanding greater powers for themselves or, in the least, more posts and pensions; and in the mid-seventeenth century it had to pacify those already in office, magistrates and tax agents, discontented by their loss of administrative autonomy and quick to rise in protest.[4] Men with newly gained wealth had the money to buy offices; those who had lower offices sought higher ones; and ambitious Frenchmen, enamored with the exalted status and legal privileges that nobility conferred, undauntedly sought ennoblement. The interests of Crown and subjects thus overlapped and resulted in mutual benefit: both national needs and personal desires could be satisfied. More offices, therefore, were exchanged for money during the seventeenth century; and increasingly officeholders assumed noble status and were accepted as nobles until, by the middle of the seventeenth century, royal statute recognized and defined ennoblement through office.

Magistracies in the Paris sovereign courts were the first offices to obtain in law the right of ennoblement; in the

[3] Chérin, 841, 855; Marsay, 38 ff.; and Philippe du Puy de Clinchamps, *La noblesse* (Paris, 1959), 23. The second method, variously known as "anoblissement par les fiefs," "noblesse inféodée," and "noblesse à la tierce-foi," was formally prohibited in law following the meeting of the Estates of Blois in 1579; cf. Chérin, 882, for the text of this ordinance.

[4] J. R. Bloch, *passim;* Ford, 63–64; and Roland Mousnier, "Recherches sur les syndicats d'officiers pendant la Fronde: Trésoriers généraux de France et élus pendant la Révolution," *Bulletin de la Société d'Étude du XVIIᵉ siècle,* Nos. 42–43 (Paris, 1959), 76–117.

following decades various decrees extended this right to offices in the provincial sovereign courts.[5] The law granted ennoblement not only to judicial magistracies but to other offices as well, ranging from the Royal Council to municipal governments. Henceforth, holders of these many offices, and even their entire families and all their descendants, were transformed into nobles. In addition, the Crown at times conferred nobility on holders of nonennobling offices, presumably as rewards for their service and loyalty, perhaps also for a fee. Even individual claims and pretensions to nobility were accepted by the government to betoken royal favor or to solicit political support. Ennoblement, in short, was rampant at the end of the seventeenth century: as it became systematic within the ranks of the royal government, so it indelibly marked French society. Much of the nobility in the eighteenth century, like the intendants in this study, were descended from ennobled commoners. (See Table 5 below for the classification of the noble origins of the intendants' families.)

Eighty-nine of the 92 intendants were from families ennobled at specific times by specific acts, rather than immemorially noble through knighthood as national mythology prescribed. All but sixteen acquired their nobility through officeholding, signifying that government service was the most frequent means for acquiring nobility in the *ancien régime*. Only one ancestor was *noblesse de cloche*—ennobled through municipal office both as *échevin* of Paris and *capitoul* of Toulouse. Six families were ennobled by virtue of the office of treasurer-general of finance in the provinces. The nobility of nineteen families can be traced back to sovereign-court offices; and eleven families were originally ennobled by serving on the Royal Council as *maîtres des requêtes* or councilors of state. Among these seventy-three families ennobled by office, the largest single group consists of thirty-

[5] Ford, *loc. cit.;* see also pp. 124–125 below.

four, perhaps thirty-five, families whose ancestors first acquired nobility by becoming *secrétaires du roi,* an office with few important functions but one that conferred immediate nobility; thus this *savonette à vilain* removed the taint of common origins for over one-third of the intendants' families.[6] The last ancestor included in this category is a questionable figure. He was a simple country landowner whose probable antecedents were non-noble; presumably with the favor of his cousin through marriage, Chancellor Séguier, he obtained an honorific charge in the royal household as *maître d'Hôtel ordinaire du Roy,* which was generally reserved for men of proven, even old nobility. This example seems to indicate that royal household service, prestigious though powerless, was employed as early as the seventeenth century to mask or legitimize ennoblement. Neither law nor honored traditions remained immune before social pretensions, individual ambition, and changing customs.

By what legal process and social practice did a commoner who had acquired an ennobling office become transformed into a nobleman?[7] Public offices that conferred nobility on their possessors were divided into two groups: those that ennobled in the first degree (or generation), and those that ennobled in the second degree. Offices with first-degree ennoblement were the most coveted, for their holders obtained, in the language of the *ancien régime,* "perfect nobility." Upon receiving his charge, the officer immediately obtained for himself and his wife all the privileges of nobility; after twenty years of service, or upon death while in office, this nobility was transmitted to all his sons and daughters and henceforth became hereditary in his family. Qualifications

---

[6] Three of these *secrétaires du roi,* however, acquired their offices in the sixteenth century when this post still had important functions and its status had not been debased by excessive numbers.

[7] The following discussion is based on Guyot, II, 219, and IV, 21, 289–90; J. R. Bloch, 75 ff.; Ford, 59 ff.; Puy de Clinchamps, 20–32; and Bluche, 23 ff.

and short cuts soon abounded. If the individual held two ennobling offices, his years of simultaneous service might be added together to fulfill the twenty-year requirement. Furthermore, he might receive dispensation from the full twenty years and satisfy the requirement earlier, receiving his *lettre de vétérance* which certified his nobility after perhaps only fifteen years in office.

First-degree ennoblement, which provided the most rapid means for becoming noble, was attached to the most important and highest offices in the royal government. From earliest times the Great Offices of the Crown, including that of chancellor, and the several secretaries of state conferred first-degree ennoblement. So too did those offices attached to the Royal Council: councilors of state and *maîtres des requêtes,* as well as the presidents of the sovereign courts so long as the latter actively participated in the Council. The office of *secrétaire du roi* also provided first-degree ennoblement after the famous edict issued by Charles VIII in February 1484. Originally these officers were responsible for placing the seal on and dispatching royal orders, functions that gave this post importance in the work of the Council. Moreover, in the Middle Ages and through the fifteenth century, there were few *notaires et secrétaires du roi, maison et couronne de France,* and their small numbers augmented their prestige and importance. By the mid-seventeenth century and later, however, there were several hundred *secrétaires du roi* created by financial need and filled by social craving; since these officers merely had to be able to read and write to qualify, the newly rich *bourgeoisie* flocked to purchase this charge and thereby acquire nobility for themselves and all their family within twenty years or less.

Offices with second-degree ennoblement conferred, in the words of contemporaries, "gradual nobility." The first member of the family who held this charge acquired personal privileges of nobility, but not transmissible hereditary nobility for his family. Only if two succeeding generations in the same family possessed the ennobling office and each exercised its functions for twenty years, or died in office, could personal nobility become transformed into hereditary nobility for all members of the family living and in the future. In practice this meant that the first two generations of officers lived as nobles but died as commoners, their property and wealth being divided among their heirs according to the legal provisions for commoners; only in the third generation, if the descendant still held an ennobling office, did he both live and die a nobleman, dividing his property among his children according to the custom of nobles.[8] Yet short cuts and exceptions speeded up the process of ennoblement for second-degree ennobling offices as for those with first-degree ennoblement. Moreover, once the family acquired transmissible hereditary nobility for all its members, the date of its original ennoblement was made retroactive to the time when the first member of the family had obtained an ennobling office. With its noble lineage extended back in time, the family's nobility became more ancient and honored—an arrangement designed to satisfy family pride and to qualify its members for high honors at court or prestigious positions in the army and in religious orders nominally reserved for the oldest nobility.

Gradual nobility, obtained more slowly, was attached to offices lower in the government hierarchy. This practice had been customary before it was authorized in law. Almost from the beginnings of the sovereign courts in Paris and in the provinces, various magistrates enjoyed some of the privileges and exemptions allowed the nobility so long as they remained in office; once they completed twenty years of service,

---

[8] In terms of the custom of Paris, noble division of property differed only with regard to the inheritance of noble fiefs: if there were only two children, the eldest son had to receive two-thirds of the noble lands; if there were three or more children, the eldest son had to receive half of the noble lands, the remaining half being divided equally among the other children, daughters included.

they and their wives continued to enjoy these rights even after they resigned the office. In 1519 Francis I extended this practice to the provincial treasurers-general. During his reign a host of judicial and financial officers who were commoners demanded, usurped, and had legitimized their personal nobility.

As one group of officers after another became ennobled, so the personal rights of nobility which these officers assumed were transferred to their families and inherited by succeeding generations. In the course of the sixteenth century this practice became widespread, and despite the protests of commoners, ennobled officers, particularly sovereign-court magistrates, doggedly insisted on preserving their privileges for their children. The Crown, weakened by recurrent civil wars, ultimately capitulated. In 1578 the Royal Council resolved a dispute which the Third Estate of Dauphiné lodged against the privileged officers of the province; by decree it reconfirmed the officers' rights of nobility and tacitly approved their claim to transmit these privileges to their children. Thus a legal precedent was set that other privileged officers throughout the country used to justify their own claims to hereditary nobility. By 1613 Charles Loyseau, in his *Traité des ordres et simple dignités,* defined what was already a common and accepted practice: an officer, whose father and grandfather were also officers, had acquired perpetual nobility for his posterity.[9]

Throughout the remaining two centuries of the *ancien régime,* offices of financial magistrates, with few exceptions, retained ennoblement in the second degree.[10] Offices in the

[9] J. R. Bloch, 77–81.

[10] These exceptions are the following: the presidents and treasurers-general of the Bureau of Finance of Grenoble became ennobling offices in the first degree after 1639; and all the officers of the Bureau of Finance of Paris were ennobled in the first degree from 1705 to 1715, and again from 1720 and after. Cf. Puy de Clinchamps, 31.

sovereign courts, however, had greater fortune. Discord between the Crown and its various opponents during the minority of Louis XIV induced the government in 1644 to barter first-degree ennoblement for the political support of the Paris parlementarians; this was repeated in 1645 for the judges in the Grand Conseil and the Chambre des Comptes of Paris. By 1719 all the Parisian magistrates enjoyed perfect nobility; their colleagues in Grenoble had acquired this privilege as early as 1639. Within five years after the death of Louis XIV, specific laws confirmed hereditary nobility for all the holders of judicial offices in all the sovereign courts of the realm, gradual nobility for most but for some, immediate nobility. With the exception of two of these courts, it was the awesome Sun King himself who granted these many and important favors to his quarrelsome magistrates.[11] Under his successors, the nobility of sovereign-court judges remained unquestioned: their legal and social rank assimilated them into the highest order of society and associated them with the most important persons in the realm working directly with the sovereign in his Council or his court. Thus the reign of Louis XIV, the period in which the sovereign courts suffered total political defeat and submitted absolutely to the will of the monarch, was also the time when the magistrates entrenched and fortified themselves for future battle against their sovereign. Along with their personal privileged status in society, they gained the secure legal base and permanent title for their nobility which made them the Crown's most formidable adversaries in the eighteenth century.

[11] For a listing of the sovereign courts and the years in which they acquired first-degree or second-degree ennoblement see Ford, 63–64; Puy de Clinchamps, 29–32; and especially François Bluche and Pierre Durye, *L'anoblissement par charges avant 1789* (2 vols.; La Roche-sur-Yon, 1962), II, 15–32. The latter is a definitive study which lists all the ennobling offices in France, the laws that conferred ennoblement and their dates, and the type of nobility that these offices bestowed.

Originally ennoblement was justified, in the rhetoric of royal letters patent, as the reward for able and loyal service. At first the office did not ennoble the officer, just as in French feudal law the land did not ennoble the fiefholder: the sovereign specially and deliberately raised his servitor into the privileged and exalted order of nobility in recognition of the officer's work, as of the knight's valor. Custom soon eroded legal theory. Beginning in the sixteenth century not the king's choice but purchase and possession actually made the officer noble, even though the same letters patent repeated old phrases. Moreover, since the officer originally enjoyed personal privileges of nobility so long as he held the office, in law nobility adhered to the charge and not to the person; but once the law recognized hereditary nobility for officeholders this distinction between the person and the office disappeared, and in fact the family was and remained noble regardless of public office. Thus, ennoblement was automatic and perpetual for members of the Royal Council, judicial and financial magistrates, *secrétaires du roi,* and some municipal officers once they had fulfilled the legal requirements attached to their charge. With regard to these officers the Crown lost its sovereign prerogative to raise its subjects into the nobility. Yet other offices lower in the governing hierarchy and with less power and responsibility did not carry ennoblement—whether hereditary or personal, whether immediate or gradual. Some subjects who were not public officers might render personal services to the king which he chose to reward—such as his doctor or banker. For the lesser officer or the favored subject the sovereign could still exercise his original right to make men noble and on occasion did so: ostensibly, in rhetoric, to honor service and loyalty; practically, in fact, to court favor or make money. The king conferred royal letters patent, and the commoner became a nobleman. In these instances ennoblement was extraordinary—the willful act of the sovereign and not the automatic appurtenance of office; and nobility belonged to the individual, not to the public charge. The end result, however, was the same: henceforth not only one person but his entire posterity were noble.

Among the ninety-two intendants, seven sprang from ancestors who had acquired their nobility by royal letters patent as rewards for their services.[12] The earliest among them, first-known ancestor of the intendant Boucher d'Orsay who served Louis XIV, was ennobled in 1397. In an age when the royal household and the royal government were not strictly separated, Arnoul Boucher d'Orsay could advance from the post of valet to the king to that of royal treasurer and financial officer, and be rewarded with letters patent of nobility; he then culminated his career as a magistrate in the Paris Chambre des Comptes. Such a *cursus honorum* is unique; the other forebears ennobled by letters patent had more prosaic careers that gained them their nobility. Four, including the common ancestor of two intendants, were minor provincial officers in the mid-seventeenth century: a judge in Poitiers, a municipal officer and member of the Third Estate in Burgundy, and a collector of the war tax in Normandy. Undoubtedly their services in such subordinate posts could not attract the attention of a government dignitary or alone merit nobility. They may have been able and loyal, but the words in the letters patent were standard. One of the ancestors who was a provincial officer, the judge, became a nobleman when the Crown bestowed letters patent upon several subjects in the kingdom in celebration of the birth of Louis XIV; the other two, we may safely assume, paid the necessary fees and became transformed. The remaining two ancestors ennobled by royal letters patent were not officers in any branch of the royal government. They were doctors—one serving in the army, the other the personal physician of the king and members of the royal family. For their medical services they received letters patent conferring hereditary

---

[12] In effect this represents six distinct forebears, since one was the common ancestor for two intendants who were father and son.

nobility on themselves and their descendants, the former in 1574 and the latter as late as 1720.[13]

Before the French Crown assumed sovereign authority throughout the realm, feudal rulers also had the power to raise subjects into the noble order; thus within the French nobility there were families descended from officials of feudal princes and dukes. Their members, however, were few among the intendants in the eighteenth century. Only two ancestors acquired nobility in this manner: one in 1620 from the ruling princess of Dombes; the other, whose existence is undocumented, as early as 1464 from Philip the Good, Duke of Burgundy.[14]

Seven ancestors remain whose ennoblement was gratuitous, not remotely related to service to the Crown: they gained their status by favor or fortune. Personal connections enabled one forebear to acquire his nobility. In March 1700 royal commissioners confirmed the nobility of Melchior de Blair, a tax farmer and grandfather of Louis Guillaume de Blair de Boismont, intendant of La Rochelle from 1749 to 1754. Nothing indicates that the former was noble by birth or through office, even though his brothers were presidents in the Parlement of Metz—a court noted for its many parvenus, which fact underscores the "newness" of the family. Why had De Blair won this favorable judgment? Ostensibly because Madame de Maintenon, his protectress, supported his claim and one of the royal commissioners conducting the investigation, Le Fèvre de Caumartin, was related by marriage to his family.[15]

Wealth invested in landed estates produced nobility for

[13] Carrés d'Hozier 254, "Ferrand," f. 61; and DB 237, "Dodart."

[14] Eudoxe de Lombardon-Montézan, *Notes et souvenirs d'ancienne principauté de Dombes et son Parlement: la famille Cachet de Montézan, des comtes de Garnerans* (Marseilles, 1885), 43; and Nouveau d'Hozier 3, "d'Agay," fs. 14, 55.

[15] Chérin 27, "de Blair de Boisemont"; Nouveau d'Hozier, "de Blair de Boisemont," fs. 10ᵛ, 11; and Bluche, 94.

six of the intendants' ancestors. Ennoblement through the purchase and possession of fiefs was not extensive in France during the Middle Ages; although tolerated in custom, it was rarely embodied in law. The one major exception was in Normandy, the most prosperous province in France, where, at an early date, large numbers of wealthy bourgeois were able to purchase feudal domains and thereby insinuate themselves into the ranks of landed *seigneurs*. So insistent were these new nobles about their status that they refused to pay the *franc-fief* which the Crown levied on commoners possessing noble lands. Louis XI, equally determined to gain their active support in his wars against the powerful feudatories, conceded their claims and in November 1470 issued a charter ennobling all *roturier* fiefholders in Normandy. This undoubtedly set a precedent in the province for the future ennobling of bourgeois owners of fiefs. On the basis of this Charter of 1470, Jean Turgot, *écuyer, seigneur de Touraille*, the common ancestor of two of Louis XIV's intendants—and the forebear as well of Louis XVI's famous minister—paid 10 écus in 1470 and again 48 sous 9 deniers the following year to obtain formal ennoblement.[16] Two other Norman families represented among these intendants became noble in a similar fashion. The documented filiation of one and the probable filiation of the other begin with ancestors who were possessors of feudal lands in the last quarter of the fifteenth century and entitled *écuyer* and *seigneur;* within two to three generations both families were able to obtain legal confirmations of their nobility.[17]

The law later interceded and formally changed this practice. Henceforth, in the words of the ordinance of Blois of 1579, no commoner who purchased a noble fief could

---

[16] For the Charter of 1470 see J. R. Bloch, 42–44; for the ennoblement of the Turgot family, see Chérin 200, "Turgot," fs. 2ᵛ, 15, 16, 19.

[17] For Jubert de Bouville see: PO 1596, f. 164ᵛ, marriage contract of 9 Feb. 1499, and Carrés d'Hozier 358, especially f. 368. For Maignard de Bernières see Chérin 127, f. 3.

thereby become ennobled; this rule applied to the entire kingdom. Jurists repeated the admonition. But, as a contemporary of the intendants in the eighteenth century wrote, the empire of manners supersedes that of laws. Technically, ennoblement by fiefholding remained prohibited; theoretically, according to French jurisprudence, nobility was not prescriptive; [18] in practice, both rules were ignored.

The family of two intendants, Bernard Chauvelin and his son Jacques Bernard, was confirmed as noble in 1699 by royal commissioners; indeed Bernard himself was named in this certification. Nothing in the family's direct lineage indicates that any ancestor was ennobled, and certainly their professions reveal them as non-nobles. It even seems likely that Bernard's father was fined 2,000 livres in 1668 for usurpation of nobility. What occurred between 1668 and 1699 to substantiate the family's nobility? Its relations by descent or marriage to many prominent parlementary and ministerial families—among them the elder Chauvelin branch, Le Tellier-Louvois, and Le Peletier—may have prompted royal investigators to be indulgent. But another explanation exists apart from presumptions of influence. The certificate states that the family's nobility descended from the great-grandfather of Bernard Chauvelin. From the great-grandfather to the intendant four generations of the family possessed seigneurial lands; perhaps only the grandfather, who had no title of *seigneur,* held no feudal property. According to contemporary mores and regardless of the word of the law, a commoner who purchased a fief acquired personal and temporary nobility, and a non-noble family that retained its feudal landholdings for three generations assumed complete, hereditary nobility. Thus Bernard Chauvelin, the fourth-generation fiefholder, had unquestioned prescriptive rights to noble status whereas his father's nobility was still tenuous. Families whose nobility derived from fiefholding

---

[18] Chérin, 845 and 881.

were not considered *anoblis,* as were ennobled officers and others, but *agrégés*—joined to the nobility over the course of time by the exercise of seigneurial rights and by their way of life.[19]

In several ways commoners could become noble in the *ancien régime.* To avail themselves of these opportunities they had to be educated to carry out judicial, administrative, or financial tasks; they had to demonstrate ability in their work; and finally, they needed sufficient wealth to purchase an ennobling office, a noble fief, or even letters patent of nobility. Society was not frozen: men could advance through the acquisition of wealth and by professional achievement. The family histories of the intendants bear witness. These noblemen of the eighteenth century were almost all the progeny of men who had been commoners, the span of time separating the intendants from their *roture* origins ranging from as little as one generation to as much as two centuries. But their ancestors had become noble at one time, and thereafter they were radically transformed.

Once noble, a man ceased to be a commoner and was separated permanently and fundamentally from his former equals in all ways—legally, socially, and psychologically. He no longer bore the legal and fiscal burdens of commoners; he removed himself from social gatherings or marriage alliances with them and sought company and marriage with others among the nobility; he lived in aristocratic luxury and behaved with aristocratic formality; and he believed, and society acknowledged, that he was a different person, superior to his peers of yesterday. If he was a new-noble, the older ones would look upon him with disdain and he might feel deeply uncomfortable among them. Within time, however, his family too would become "ancient," his sons or grandsons would have a more secure and respected place within the

---

[19] PO 722, "Chauvelin," f. 230, and Nouveau d'Hozier 95, "Chauvelin," f. 14, certificate of nobility 23 May 1699. See also Bluche, 25–26.

nobility, and they in turn would scorn the newer members of their order.

II

Entrance and absorption into the high robe further

Table 5. Noble origins of the intendants' families *

Origin	Louis XIV 1710–1712	Louis XV 1749–1751	Louis XVI 1774–1776
Feudal	1	2	—
Prescription †	5	1	—
Royal letters patent	3	3	1
Official favor	—	1	—
Ducal services	—	—	2 ‡
Royal office:			
Sovereign court	6	6	7
Royal Council	6	4	1
Secrétaire du roi	8	12	16 ‡
Financial magistracy	—	1	4
Commensal office	1	—	—
Municipal office	—	1	—

* The noble origins of only 92 of the intendants' families are known.

† Prescriptive nobility refers to ennoblement obtained after three generations of fief-holding.

‡ The nobility of one of these families is undocumented.

marked the large majority of the intendants' families. Ninety-one of the families belonged to the sovereign courts. From local office in town or province, where they served as judges, tax collectors, or administrative agents; from provincial estates, where bourgeois lived nobly or noble *seigneurs,* after generations of military service, tranquilly tended their lands or turned to civil occupations as lawyers, mayors, or judges; from the law or from medicine; from honorific charges as *secrétaires du roi* or in the royal household; from higher office as treasurers-general and receivers-general in the provinces, the forebears of the intendants pursued their ambitions and purchased charges in the provincial or Parisian courts. Rarely did a member of these families advance from local commerce or larger business and finance directly into the sovereign courts. Usually a generation elapsed, or several years in the life of one man, during which time the family cleansed itself of its identification with business and enhanced its standing by obtaining an ennobling charge or even a simple yet prestigious public office. Only one of the intendants came from a family where the father moved directly from business and speculation into the magistracy; and this did not impede the son's career, since he became not only a provincial intendant but also controller-general and minister of state. For more than half the families—a total of fifty—whose nobility antedated their admission into the sovereign courts, obtaining a magistracy nevertheless signified an even greater professional advance and rise in status.

Few of the families were new members of the courts: only 18 of the intendants were first-generation magistrates, the first members of their families to hold sovereign-court office. Thus 73 families in all belonged to the high robe for varying numbers of generations: one family for as long as nine generations; 2 families for seven generations; 6 families each for five and six generations; 12 or 13 families for four generations; and 15 families for three generations.[20] The largest single group of intendants, numbering 30 or one-third of the total, were of families with two generations in the high robe (28 of whose fathers were magistrates, plus 2 whose uncles were magistrates). We may look at this group of intendants in yet other ways. Forty-two of the 91 were both sons and grandsons of sovereign-court judges; and 40 or 41 of the total were of families that had succeeded each other into the high courts, in direct line and without break, for three or more generations. Thus, the dominant profession of almost all the

[20] One of the 15 families in the last group did not serve in the courts for three successive generations: the grandfather and the grandson (i.e., the intendant) were sovereign-court magistrates, but not the father.

families placed the intendants in the highest ranks of the government hierarchy. Their families' extended service in the high robe gave to almost half of them superior and honored status in society which few among their contemporaries could outrank.

Yet this was not all. Many of the 93 intendants whose antecedents are known were from families belonging to the governing elite of the kingdom—the members of the Royal Council who advised and acted for the king, representing him throughout the realm and in foreign lands. Almost half of the intendants, a total of 44, were descendants of *maîtres des requêtes,* councilors of state, provincial intendants, intendants of commerce or finance, ambassadors, and even of a chancellor and a secretary and minister of state (while 50 of the total group of 94 intendants were the first of their families to enter the Royal Council) . Furthermore, these 44 families served for long periods in the high administration: one family passed eight generations on the Council; 4 families had six generations of service; 4 (or 5) families had five generations; 7 families had four generations; and 9 families had three generations of service. The largest single group consisted of 18 families who had served for two generations on the Council. An even larger number of these intendants, 27 (almost one-third of the total of 94) , were preceded by both their fathers and grandfathers in the select and small body, the nobility of the pen.

III

Let us focus now on the two immediate ancestors of the intendants. From the grandfather to the father to the son, within this span of three generations, the changing or fixed fortunes of the intendants' families are telescoped. Moreover, the father's status determined the son's status as the latter began his career. (See Table 6, which compares the social and professional status of three groups of the intendants' forebears.)

Who were the intendants' grandfathers, and what was their place in society? The careers of eighty-eight of them are known (including 5 probable grandfathers whose careers are not documented), while those of 6 remain unknown. Thirteen of the grandfathers plus 2 probable ones engaged in private business or professional affairs. In comparison to the first ancestors, slightly fewer were ordinary provincial *seigneurs*, lawyers, or doctors; more significantly, many fewer were simple bourgeois or local merchants. For the intendants' families to rise in society in the generations between the first ancestor and the grandfather meant above all to leave forever the world of business and the *bourgeoisie*.

These commoners turned from commerce and became officers of state. In contrast to their first ancestors, many more of the intendants' immediate forebears entered the ranks of government office, the means and the symbol of social elevation in the *ancien régime*. Seventy grandfathers plus three probable ones held public office; these included seven who combined careers in business and government.[21] Among them were three officers in the royal household, one ducal official, and even one military officer. The number of local officers among the intendants' grandfathers, as well as those who were financial magistrates or simply *secrétaires du roi*, remained approximately the same. A new group, however, appeared in this generation: some of the grandfathers were large businessmen and financiers, as well as tax farmers. The largest and most significant increases were in three other groups. Many more grandfathers started as businessmen or financiers and later obtained some government office—

---

[21] Whereas 13 or 15 grandfathers were private persons and 70 or 73 were public officers, the analogous figures for the first ancestors are 23 private persons and 36 or 37 public officers—this does not include the 23 grandfathers and 8 fathers who were also the earliest known ancestors. In sum, there was approximately a 20 percent decrease in private persons and a 20 percent increase in public officers among the grandfathers.

indeed, even the grandfather who was a peasant, though to be sure a wealthy *laboureur,* also became the local tax agent. An even larger number of grandfathers passed their lives as magistrates in the sovereign courts or culminated their careers as members of the Royal Council. We may compare the documented careers of 88 of the intendants' fathers to those of their 88 grandfathers whose careers are known or presumed in order to see how their families' status in society changed from the one generation to the next. Few of the intendants' fathers retained the modest social position or professional rank of the grandfathers: only 5 to be exact. Two were local officers, one a financial officer in the royal household, one a court physician, and the last a lawyer and provincial *seigneur* (whereas the grandfather had been a country gentleman and held an honorific post in the royal household). Another father of an intendant also remained in the same profession as the grandfather, but one more prestigious and lucrative: tax farming. Many of the fathers continued the family's advance. A total of 38, by acquiring offices of greater prestige or importance than those held by the grandfathers, or by gaining even greater wealth in finance or business, enhanced their own place in society. Several of these fathers (9, including the single father of the two intendants Chaumont), originally of moderate status as sons of non-officers or minor officers, first became wealthy in business or finance to begin their rise and then, to cap their success, purchased prominent offices: 7 as *secrétaires du roi* and even two as magistrates. Another large number of fathers (40) came from families already in the highest ranks as members of the sovereign courts or of the Royal Council, and they continued this family tradition through their own careers.

Only in exceptional cases did the social or professional status of the intendants' fathers decline. One father was a financier and tax farmer in contrast to the grandfather, who had been a sovereign-court magistrate; undoubtedly the lure of great profits accounts for this rare reverse move from the magistracy to finance. The father of another intendant remained a simple magistrate, yet the grandfather had served in the court and on the Council; within the world of the robe and pen the father certainly lost rank, yet to society at large the family's honored status in the high robe remained untouched. Two other families seem to have fallen some rungs in the hierarchy: the grandfathers had been sovereign-court magistrates, but one father remained a country *seigneur* without office and the other chose a career in the army. Perhaps both fathers had less public power than if they had entered the magistracy, and undoubtedly the cavalry captain earned less than a sovereign-court judge; but to their more traditional contemporaries steeped in older social values, the *seigneur* and the captain were even more esteemed than the magistrate.

The exact professions of the intendants' fathers indicate the latter's social status and, consequently, the intendants' status at the outset of their careers. Of the total group of ninety-two fathers whose careers are known, plus one whose career is probable, only seven engaged in private affairs throughout their lives. A total of eighty-five (or eighty-six) held public office, including twelve who were in business or finance before becoming government officers. None of the intendants' fathers were simple bourgeois or local merchants; in contrast, those in finance or business, the same number as among the grandfathers, were all tax farmers. Some doctors—all court physicians—and a lawyer still appear, and also a military officer. Far fewer fathers than grandfathers were local officers; about the same number were financial magistrates; and slightly more held varied positions in the central administration, including the royal postal service. Most of the fathers, like most of the grandfathers, either combined business or financial affairs with officeholding, were magistrates in the sovereign courts, or served the king on the Royal Council. Indeed the largest increase in num-

137

Table 6. The family origins and social evolution of the total group of
intendants sampled *

Status	First ancestor †	Grandfather	Father
Private persons			
Provincial *seigneur*	3	2	1
Bourgeois	8	3	0
Commerce	4	1	0
Finance and large business	0	3	3
Peasants	1	1	0
Medicine	3	1 (2)	2
Law	4	2 (3)	1
Business and office	3 ‡	7 ‡	12 ‡
Public officers			
Local office	8	9 (10)	3
Financial magistrate	3	4	3
Sovereign courts	10	20 (22)	26
Royal Council	6	21	37
Secrétaire du roi	3	3	0
Royal administration	1	1	2 (3)
Royal household	1	3	1
Military	0	1	1
Ducal office	1 (2)	1	0
Total	59 (60)	83 (88)	92 (93)

* The figures in parentheses include probable forebears as well.

† The figures for the first ancestors in this table include only those forebears of the generations before the grandfathers and fathers of the intendants; the analysis on pp. 106–114 is based on the figures for all the
earliest known ancestors, including 23 who were also grandfathers and 8
who were the intendants' fathers.

‡ These 3 first ancestors all held local office; of these 7 grandfathers, 2
held local office, 3 were *secrétaires du roi*, one held local office and was a
secrétaire du roi, and one was a financial magistrate; of these 12 fathers, one
was a local financial officer and functionary in the royal administration,
6 were *secrétaires du roi*, 2 were both *secrétaires du roi* and financial magistrates,
one was a sovereign-court magistrate, and 2 were royal councilors.

bers was among those fathers serving in the Council—sixteen more than among the grandfathers. Moreover, in this single generation immediately before the intendants and for the first time in their histories, many more of the families were nobility of the pen than simply nobility of the robe.

Thus, from the generation of their grandfathers to their own generation, approximately forty of the intendants' families moved up in society as they gained higher office, while approximately another forty had already attained and remained in high positions in government and in society.

IV

Purists and peers may dispute the pedigree of the royal intendants, but the elevated status of the latter during their lifetime was an irrefutable, unqualified fact that few contemporaries would contest. From beginnings that differed in rank and prestige, during a few or many generations, their forebears passed through varied occupations, professions, and offices until the descendants in the corps of intendants shared the same honored place in society. All were noble, and all were of the robe and pen. Those who forged their own careers and were the first to enter the upper hierarchy were fewest: only two were first-generation nobles and eighteen were first-generation magistrates, while fifty were first-generation administrators. And for more than two-thirds of the intendants, their immediate origins were untainted: their fathers practiced no professions and held no offices lower than that of sovereign-court magistrate or royal councilor. Moreover, through their brothers, uncles, or cousins, many of the intendants were also linked with the nobility of the sword.[22] Within each family the play of ambition and

---

[22] Cf. Bluche, *op. cit., passim,* and *Les magistrats du Parlement de Paris,* 305–307; Ford, 138, 143–44; André Corvisier, *L'armée française de la fin du XVII* siècle au ministère de Choiseul: le soldat* (2 vols.; Paris, 1964), I, 131; and Mousnier, . . . *Chancelier Séguier,* I, 61–63. The latter provides evidence of the family links between the nobilities

ability, wealth and prestige, loyalty and personal contacts had wrought this major transformation. Thus, the group of royal intendants combined noble status and membership in the robe, pen, and even sword; the resulting fusion of professional esteem with privileged rank and high standing distinguished them among their countrymen.

In France, no Peter the Great had to establish in law a nobility of service for his high functionaries; one already existed. A nobility that governed was embodied in the administrators who were noble. These men were creatures of long-standing laws and traditional mores of the *ancien régime;* within the structure of aristocratic society and monarchical government they formed a single governing nobility united by function and status. The same society and government that had spawned noble intendants continued to foster their growth. Thus administrative and social practices did not become reactionary in the eighteenth century, as some historians claim.[23] Nobles did not pre-empt places in the high administration during the reigns of Louis XV and Louis XVI, excluding commoners who presumably had served under Louis XIV, because the latter were noble as well: all of the royal intendants who served the three kings were noblemen. To rise in society required that men obtain office, wealth, and nobility: the indissoluble trinity that signified social aspiration and conferred social esteem in the *ancien*

---

of the sword and of the robe even in the first half of the seventeenth century. Documentation for this relationship among many of the 94 families of intendants studied may also be found in the relevant volumes of the Cabinet des Titres in the Bibliothèque Nationale listed in the bibliography below.

[23] Cf. Georges Lefebvre, *The Coming of the French Revolution,* trans. by R. R. Palmer (New York, 1958), 15–16, 41–42; and R. R. Palmer, *The Age of the Democratic Revolution:* I, *The Challenge* (2 vols.; Princeton, N.J., 1959), 459. See Chapter 8, second section, below for an analysis of the changing pattern of recruitment in the corps of intendants during the eighteenth century that provides a statistical refutation of the argument for an "aristocratic reaction" in the high administration.

régime. All the royal intendants in the eighteenth century, and their families in earlier times, shared this common experience: they pursued the same ambitions and gained these same rewards.

Without a new law, without a change in custom, the provincial intendants formed a professional and social elite: they represented the royal sovereignty and they belonged to the nobility.

CHAPTER 7

Rank and Prestige within the Administrative Nobility: The Family Histories of Several Intendants

The nobility formed one order, according to legal theory in the *ancien régime;* but according to social fact it formed several groups within the single order. This was true of the nobility of the pen as it was true of the nobility as a whole. All the ninety-four intendants had the same legal rights and privileges as noblemen. All had the same status and prestige as royal functionaries, but all did not share exactly the same rank within the noble order and in relation to their colleagues within the administration. The antiquity of their families and of their noble lineage, the years or generations their forebears served the Crown, the importance of the offices the latter held, and the marriage alliances and wealth of their families distinguished the individual intendants and determined their place in the ruling elite. Not one of these factors outweighed the others as the single or dominant key to social rank. They were, rather, a basic but changing ensemble, marking different intendants to different degrees, and reflecting the ways in which their families rose in society.

I

Foremost in rank among the intendants were those whose families served for many generations both in the courts and on the Council: families of the high robe and the pen. Among them sons succeeded fathers, grandfathers, and even earlier ancestors in office, nephews succeeded uncles and cousins, each family forming a dynasty of magistrates and administrators. But most important, these were the families engrossed, generation after generation, in the work of the Council rather than of the courts: they were bred in the tradition of dedicated service to the Crown, commitment to royal interests, and deep loyalty to their sovereign against nobles and magistrates alike. Understandably, the kings trusted such men and favored their families with offices and power.

Some of these families were familiar names in the *ancien régime:* Lamoignon de Basville and Lamoignon de Courson, father and son; Turgot de Soumons and Turgot de Saint-Clair, first cousins, and respectively grandfather and first cousin twice removed of Louis XVI's famous minister; Le Fèvre d'Ormesson; Le Bret; Le Peletier de Morfontaine; Amelot de Chaillou; D'Aligre de Boislandry; Barentin; and Le Fèvre de Caumartin, among others. These families, and a few others, had been in the courts and on the Council for three or more generations preceding the intendants included in this study.

Other families identified with both the sovereign courts and the high administration were newcomers in this exalted rank, only one or two ancestors having preceded our intendants as magistrates and royal agents. Among them were Gallois de la Tour, Creil de Bournezeau, and Rouillé d'Orfeuil. Also included in this latter group were those intendants whose families recently had risen through lesser offices and already had passed one or two generations in the courts and on the Council. Bertier de Sauvigny, last intendant of Paris, Barberie de Saint-Contest de la Chataîgneraye, and La Briffe des Ferrières were among their representatives.

The family of Charles Boucher d'Orsay, intendant of Limoges (1710–1719), was one of the oldest in noble lineage,

143

had the longest record of service in the robe and the pen, and was the earliest to originate in Paris. In 1397 the first ancestor of the family, Arnoul Boucher, received royal letters patent of nobility for his services to Charles VI as royal valet and treasurer. Two years later he entered the Paris Chambre des Comptes to begin his family's tradition of service in the sovereign courts, a tradition that lasted until the first half of the eighteenth century. From the early fifteenth century, beginning with the son of Arnoul, until the death of Louis XIV's intendant, each generation of the Boucher d'Orsay family—a total of seven generations—served uninterruptedly on the Royal Council as *maîtres des requêtes* or councilors of state, the father of Charles Boucher also filling the office of *prévôt des marchands* of Paris from 1700 to 1709. Other families might surpass the Boucher d'Orsay in the importance of their offices and accomplishments, or in the splendor of their name and alliances, but none could equal them in their unique combination of ancient origin and nobility, and length of continuous service to the Crown.

Of almost equal age and nobility, but not equal in service, was the Turgot family, whose two branches were represented among the intendants serving Louis XIV: Marc-Antoine Turgot de Saint-Clair, intendant in Auvergne (1708–1713), and Jacques Etienne Turgot de Soumons, intendant of Moulins (1709–1713). Their common first ancestor, Jean Turgot, became the *seigneur* of Tourailles in Normandy, evidently by marrying the heiress to the fief. Despite his claim in 1463 of descent from an old and renowned Breton noble family, which thirteen witnesses supported, Jean nevertheless was declared non-noble and had to pay the *taille*. Only in 1470, benefiting from the Charter which Louis XI granted in November of that year to gain the allegiance of the wealthy landed *bourgeoisie* of Normandy, did royal commissioners declare Jean Turgot noble by possession of a fief and upon payment of a sum for his ennoblement.[1] The following four

[1] Chérin 200, "Turgot," fs. 2ᵛ, 15, 16, 19; DB 650, "Turgot," f. 1.

generations of Turgots passed their lives as provincial *seigneurs* on their country estates; the last two became interested in local judicial affairs, one acquiring a judgeship in Caen and the other presumably becoming a lawyer in the Parlement of Rouen. Not until the sixth generation, in the early seventeenth century, did a Turgot become a magistrate in a sovereign court; and the immediate success of that ancestor, the grandfather of Louis XIV's two intendants, transformed the family fortunes in government and in society.

Jacques Turgot became a councilor in the Parlement of Rouen in 1615 and within three years entered the Royal Council as a *maître des requêtes*. In 1619 he married the daughter of Jacques Favier du Boullay, a councilor of state; undoubtedly his prominent father-in-law aided his career. Shortly after his marriage he became one of Louis XIII's new intendants, empowered at times to regulate justice and police, at other times to supervise the army; first he was sent to Picardy in 1622, then to Berry in 1623, to Orléans, and in 1632 to his native province, Normandy. Eleven years later Jacques Turgot obtained a place as *conseiller d'état ordinaire*, serving on the Royal Council throughout the year; and in 1657, two years before his death, he became President of the Parlement of Rouen, no doubt assigned the important task of bringing his turbulent native province and its sovereign court under the control of the Crown.

The ability and loyalty in royal service demonstrated by Jacques Turgot assured the future of his three sons: the two youngest, the fathers of Louis XIV's two intendants, were both Parisian magistrâtes in the Parlement and the Grand Conseil, *maîtres des requêtes*, and councilors of state, and one was also a provincial intendant; his eldest son succeeded him as President of the Parlement of Rouen. Thus Marc-Antoine Turgot de Saint-Clair and Jacques Etienne Turgot de Soumons represent a family with seven previous generations of noble lineage, mainly as provincial *seigneurs*, and with but two preceding generations as magistrates and royal agents: they were relatively new in the courts and on the Council, but entrenched and respected in the place that their grandfather and fathers had secured.

The classic family of the high robe and pen was originally of the provincial *bourgeoisie,* holding some lower office as local judge, municipal officer, or even financial magistrate; in the late sixteenth century or early seventeenth century one of its members entered the Parisian sovereign courts and within a short time also acceded to the Royal Council. The family began to serve in the judiciary and the administration during the reigns of the last Valois kings or of Henry IV and Louis XIII. This was the time when the courts were increasingly engaged in governing the country, and its members were acceding to the nobility, thus becoming more politically powerful and socially prestigious; these were also the turbulent and decisive years when the Crown was tentatively creating its bureaucracy to centralize and strengthen royal authority. In the courts and on the Council the average family of the high robe and pen remained for between one hundred and two hundred years, executing their sovereign's policies and ensuring their own status.

Antoine Louis François Le Fèvre de Caumartin, intendant in Flanders and Artois from 1756 to 1778, came from such a family. His earliest ancestor, whose existence and filiation remain uncertain, was Jean Le Fèvre, a *procureur* in Abbeville in the province of Picardy during the last half of the fifteenth century. Jean, presumably, had a son also called Jean, whose professional and social ascent was rather rapid: in 1555 he was a treasurer-general of finance in his native province and was already known as *écuyer, seigneur de Caumartin.* The family's definite and direct descent begins with the Jean Le Fèvre who was treasurer-general of Picardy and living in Amiens in 1564; he probably was the son of the preceding Jean Le Fèvre, acquiring his office after his father's death. He then seems to have risen in the hierarchy of financial magistrates, probably becoming treasurer-general of Champagne in 1566 and of Paris in 1570; by 1576 he was residing permanently in Paris.

The family entered the sovereign-court magistracy and the royal administration in the succeeding generation: one of Jean's sons, Louis, became a councilor in the Paris Parlement in 1578 and was admitted into the Council as a *maître des requêtes* in 1585. His varied and important career as the king's trusted agent during the critical decades that followed, until his death in 1623, assured his descendants the Crown's favor. President of the Grand Conseil in 1587, in the following year he began his noted career as special royal emissary to different provinces. His first assignment was as intendant of justice in the army in Poitou; following the assassination of the Duc de Guise he was dispatched to Touraine, Brittany, and other neighboring provinces to prevent insurrections by supporters of the Catholic League. In 1590 Henry IV chose him as intendant of his native province, Picardy, since his family acquaintances there would facilitate his task of dissociating the province from the League and winning it over to the royal cause. In 1596 he was able to leave Picardy, his mission successfully completed, and as reward he obtained the honorific intendancy of that province in perpetuity, which his son occupied after him. Other critical and short assignments quickly followed: to restore order in the finances of Lyon, Berry, and Auvergne (1596–1597); to assist in the defense of Picardy against Spain (1597); to negotiate with the English government (1597 or 1598); to regulate the finances and aid in the defense of Normandy (1598). In 1599 he was given the difficult mission of negotiating Henry IV's divorce from Marguerite of Valois; and in the same year he went to Auvergne and Bourbonnais to enforce tax collections, at the same time suppressing a tax revolt in Auvergne. In the following years he was dispatched on several diplomatic missions to pacify dissident French nobles and to negotiate with foreign powers. Following Henry IV's assassination, Louis Le Fèvre became a member of the Council of

Regency, assisting the *garde des sceaux* Duc de Luynes and representing the Crown before provincial estates. He continued to serve Louis XIII when the latter assumed sovereign power: as royal commissioner in 1617 he suppressed a revolt in Champagne, and in 1622 he obtained the important and honored post of *garde des sceaux,* only to die shortly thereafter.

Henceforth, the family's fortunes were fixed: the place that Louis Le Fèvre de Caumartin had attained was preserved by succeeding generations from his son to his great-great-grandson, all of whom benefited from royal favor and proved their merits through personal service. Four generations of descendants served in the sovereign courts of Paris, either in the Parlement or the Grand Conseil; all were *maîtres des requêtes;* and all were councilors of state. Furthermore, each of them held other important offices as well. Louis Le Fèvre's son was twice intendant in Picardy, twice ambassador to Venice, and also President in the Chamber of Requests of the Paris Parlement. His grandson was intendant in Champagne, royal commissioner to the Estates of Brittany, and keeper of the seals for the investigating commission in Auvergne in 1660. The great-grandson, grandfather of Louis XVI's intendant, also served as intendant of commerce on the Royal Council; and the great-great-grandson, father of Louis XVI's intendant, was also twice President of the Grand Conseil. A long and distinguished line of magistrates and royal administrators: such was the heritage which gave Antoine Louis François Le Fèvre de Caumartin esteemed membership in the high robe and pen, placing him in the highest ranks in the corps of intendants.[2]

[2] In addition to genealogical sources in the bibliography, see Bluche, *L'origine des magistrats,* 258; Edmond Esmonin, "Le Fèvre de Caumartin, intendant de Picardie pendant trente-deux ans," *Revue d'Histoire Moderne,* nouvelle série, no. 3 (May–June 1932), 272–83; and Fernand Le Fèvre du Grosriez, "L'origine de la famille Le Fèvre de Caumartin," *Cabinet Historique d'Artois et de la Picardie* (Nov. 1886).

These families with members in the sovereign courts and royal administration for many generations set the pattern of continued service to the Crown which they felt as a duty and cherished for its prestige. After them newer families sought to emulate their achievements. In the late seventeenth and early eighteenth centuries, as in the preceding century and a half, new families continued to enter the courts and the Council and to succeed one another in these offices from one generation to the next, forming younger dynasties of royal agents. Thus again an ancestor fewer generations removed from the intendant entered the king's service and rose from low office and status to power and eminence; and his descendants continued to serve in the highest posts of the royal government.

Gaspard Louis Rouillé d'Orfeuil, intendant in Champagne for an unusually long period from 1764 to 1790, represents such a family. The origins of the Rouillé family and its ascent begin with the great-grandfather in the last few decades of the seventeenth century. Louis Rouillé's achievements were indeed remarkable. His own family, presumably, were carters and ferrymen in and around Tours, and he himself might have begun his career as a merchant in that city. His documented career began as a mail carrier, first in Tours and then in Paris; the Marquis de Louvois, in charge of the royal postal service, seems to have given him this job since his family was already engaged in conveying private messages. Thereafter Louis Rouillé advanced his career through the postal service: he became a clerk in a local bureau, then head of the provincial mail service in Touraine, and finally, in 1679, the director and controller-general of the postal service for the entire kingdom. In that same year, to cap his career and transform his status, he purchased the office of *secrétaire du roi* and thereby he and his family were ennobled. From postman to nobleman in one generation!

With such achievements and advantages, Louis Rouillé's

son could begin his own career in higher office. Starting as a councilor in the Paris Parlement, he entered the Royal Council as a *maître des requêtes* and afterward became a provincial intendant and an intendant of commerce; following the family tradition set by his father, he too became controller-general of the postal service. Once admitted into the court and the Council, the family remained there. The grandson of Louis Rouillé, father of Louis XVI's intendant, followed the customary *cursus honorum* of high functionaries: he was a councilor in the Paris Parlement, *maître des requêtes*, provincial intendant, as well as director of publishing, in charge of censoring and approving all writing in the kingdom. Thus Gaspard Louis Rouillé d'Orfeuil, succeeding his grandfather and father as magistrate and administrator, qualified as a member of the high robe and pen; but with only two generations of forebears preceding him in the court and the Council, his family had less prestige than the eldest families of the magistracy and royal administration and therefore he ranked lower than they in the corps of intendants.[3]

Next in rank to the intendants whose families had served in both the sovereign courts and the royal administration, yet equal in prestige and power in the eyes of their contemporaries, were those intendants whose families had held high offices only in the courts. Their forebears, for two or five generations, had served in the sovereign courts of Paris, sometimes in the provinces as well, rising originally from lower office or from simple bourgeois status. Hence their ancestors made their careers through work in the courts rather than in the royal administration, and the prestige of their families' names arose from their identification as magistrates, not as administrative officers. Jean François Joly de

---

[3] In addition to genealogical sources in the bibliography, see Bluche, 378–79; and Etienne Prévost de Levaud, *Les théories d'intendant Rouillé d'Orfeuil* (Thèse pour le doctorat, la Faculté de droit de l'Université de Poitiers [Rochechouart, 1909]), 9 f.

Fleury de la Valette, intendant in Burgundy from 1749 to 1760 or 1767, was in this group.

The Joly de Fleury family was relatively old and had a varied professional history. Although there is no documentary proof, some of their earliest ancestors presumably lived in Burgundy as far back as the early fourteenth and fifteenth centuries; the first two were simple town residents and then, for five generations, members of the Joly family held various posts as municipal officials, local judges and administrative officers, and councilors to the Duke of Burgundy. The first proven ancestor was a lawyer in Beaune and perhaps in the Burgundian Parlement as well in the early sixteenth century. For the remainder of the century the family remained in Burgundy, the second ancestor also becoming a lawyer and then advancing to the office of chief clerk in the Parlement. In 1595 one member of the large Joly family left his native province and moved to Paris, where he became a famous lawyer active in the Parlement of the capital and in the Grand Conseil. His career advanced notably: within five years he became *maître des requêtes* to the Queen of Navarre, and presumably *avocat-général* in the Grand Conseil and chief of Cardinal Richelieu's council. The son of this first Parisian Joly, who was also the great-grandfather of Louis XV's intendant, became the family's first sovereign-court magistrate whose career is documented: he held the office of councilor first in the Parlement of Brittany and then in the Grand Conseil.

Henceforth the Joly de Fleury family of Paris remained in the sovereign courts. In the two generations immediately preceding the intendant, it continued to rise in the judicial hierarchy. The grandfather began his career where all the young parlementarians saw greatest and most immediate promise: he became *avocat-général* in the Parlement of Metz. Afterward he obtained the office of councilor in the Paris Parlement and ended his career as a magistrate in the elite Grand'chambre of the Parlement. The intendant's father, Guillaume François Joly, did not have to seek his fortune in the provinces; he remained in the capital, where he rose in the ranks of the Parisian magistracy, beginning as *avocat-général* in the Cour des Aides and then acquiring fame as *avocat-général* and lastly *procureur-général* in the Parlement. Both older brothers of the intendant, Guillaume François Louis and Jean Omer, followed their father in the office of *avocat-général,* the former also succeeding him as *procureur-général* and the latter ending his career as *président à mortier* of the Paris Parlement; moreover, both brothers were as esteemed as their father. Thus with three or four generations of predecessors in the sovereign courts, especially in the courts of Paris, and with his father and two brothers as superior officers in the Parlement of the capital, Jean François Joly de Fleury had a secure place in the high robe which afforded him great prestige as a royal functionary.[4]

Sons, grandsons, even great-grandsons of ordinary councilors in the sovereign courts—men from families in the lower ranks of the magistracy in Paris or the provinces—followed next in order of prestige among the intendants. The status of their immediate forebears linked them socially, yet they too reveal different origins ranging from feudal knight to Parisian merchant and represent varying family experiences culminating in accession to sovereign-court offices.

Yves Marie de La Bourdonnaye, who served as intendant of Orléans from 1709 to 1713, was the rare intendant who descended from a Breton knight and fiefholder of the early fifteenth century or possibly fourteenth century. His family was thus among the oldest of the intendants' families and surpassed all the others in noble lineage: Yves Marie was himself a tenth-generation noble in direct descent. The family's name and its nobility came from a fief of the same name in Brittany; whether an ancestor ever held that land is un-

---

[4] In addition to genealogical sources in the bibliography, see Bluche, 220–21; and Bisson de Barthélemy, 15 and 319.

known, but in the eighteenth century Yves Marie was the *seigneur* and *comte* of another estate which originally entered the family patrimony shortly after 1426. His ancestors fought for the Duke of Brittany when the province was still independent: in 1479 one of them, François de La Bourdonnaye, appeared in the muster of Breton nobles as a mounted crossbowman, accompanied by an archer and a page. A century later, in 1598, his great-grandfather was a captain in the army of the Duc de Mercoeur.

For a total of seven generations the La Bourdonnayes remained provincial *seigneurs* and occasional soldiers; in the two generations immediately preceding the intendant the family turned to judicial service. Its entrance into the judiciary was modest: the grandfather, obviously benefiting from his prestige as a nobleman, became a local judge, a *sénéchal*. The intendant's father, however, became a magistrate in the sovereign court and for over forty years served as councilor in the Parlement of Brittany. Yves Marie began his career in the same court, but a successful marriage which made him son-in-law to the councilor of state Antoine de Ribeyre and also allied him to the famous parlementary family Potier de Novion enabled him to establish himself in Paris; indeed his bride's dowry was assigned for the purchase of the office of *maître des requêtes*, a condition that no groom of that time would oppose. Louis François de La Bourdonnaye, the son of Yves Marie, was himself intendant of Rouen from 1732 to 1755, yet he may no longer be ranked among the intendants from ordinary robe families: his father's achievements placed him in the higher ranks in the corps, with those of his colleagues from families in the upper echelons of the magistracy and the royal administration.[5]

A shop in Paris was the original patrimony of the family of César Charles de L'Escalopier, intendant in Champagne

[5] In addition to genealogical sources in the bibliography, see Bluche, 222–23.

from 1711 until 1730. Two centuries earlier, in the 1540's, the first member of his family, known without noble particle simply as "Jean Lescalopier," was a merchant and a member of the Paris *bourgeoisie*. But commerce did not keep him for long. By 1562 he was a financial officer for the Parlement, receiving and distributing the court fees among the magistrates; even earlier, in 1553, he presumably had been a municipal judge. The rise from labor and trade to office and honors had begun for the L'Escalopier family. Jean Lescalopier's son succeeded to his office and advanced further: he too was presumably a municipal judge and then definitely became a provincial treasurer-general, culminating his career as *secrétaire du roi* and possibly also as a member of the Paris Chambre des Comptes. Thus by 1600, within sixty years, the family was definitely ennobled and possibly in the robe as well. In the next generation no doubt remains that the L'Escalopier acceded to the sovereign courts and also to the Royal Council for a short time: the third ancestor, great-grandfather of the intendant, had a full and varied career as a parlementary councilor, *maître des requêtes, secrétaire du roi,* parlementary president, councilor of state, and chancellor to the queen. The grandfather and father of the intendant had less noted careers, but they nevertheless retained their family's place in the Parisian magistracy, both of them passing their lives as councilors in the Parlement. Thus César Charles de L'Escalopier had three, possibly four, generations of ancestors who served in the sovereign courts.[6] Other intendants of robe families serving with L'Escalopier in the early eighteenth century or in the two later periods under study had three or only two previous ancestors in the sovereign-courts who had been ordinary judges without gaining higher office: the families of these intendants had acquired the prestige of the magistracy without greater éclat.

[6] In addition to genealogical sources in the bibliography, see *ibid.,* 179.

II

The L'Escalopier family had risen gradually in the social hierarchy for more than three generations. Moreover, they held their magisterial status for at least three generations before the intendant's appearance. In contrast, other families represented among the intendants had ascended gradually but more recently, and still others had transformed their status with remarkable swiftness. From mere ordinariness and moderate standing in French society, from even menial or obscure beginnings abruptly ended by adventuresome enterprise, they had entered the honored ranks of their society. They were the new families in the upper ranks of the governing hierarchy, and the intendants from these families constituted the "new men" among the king's agents. In social rank they held a modest place beside their other colleagues, yet their careers did not suffer since some became ministers of state—and all succeeded in becoming royal intendants.

Social and political prominence came in more diverse ways to these new families. By the late seventeenth century and during the eighteenth century new forces came into existence in French society and increased in strength. New means of achievement appeared, and new channels of mobility opened. Economic activity intensified: business and financial ventures offered more numerous and more lucrative opportunities for success. Government broadened its responsibilities, and the expanding royal bureaucracy required more recruits for a greater variety of administrative tasks. Thus the traditional mode of ascension through office no longer remained the sole way to rise in society and attain the highest offices in government. Families continued to advance through the regular hierarchy of public office, but larger numbers engaged in various businesses or in financial affairs before entering office—some even while they held their charges or afterward; and a few advanced from administrative posts in the central bureaucracy to older, prestigious offices. In short, the traditional structure of society was being recast, yet its ethos remained the same: new and rising families adopted customary values, and they too desired time-honored offices and noble status.

Following in the tradition that the older families set were those new families who promoted their social fortune by advancing from lower to higher office; some even had entered the sovereign courts, but only recently, the intendant's father being the first magistrate in the family. Such was the case with Charles Alexandre de Calonne, intendant of Metz from 1768 to 1778, and later famous as controller-general and minister. Calonne's father became a councilor in the Parlement of Flanders in 1726, and rose to be *procureur-général* and twice president. Nothing precise is known about earlier generations of the family except that they were *bourgeois* in Tournai in the seventeenth century and that the intendant's great-grandfather was a tax clerk. Obviously, Calonne's family was new, having just entered the high magistracy.[7]

The family Pineau de Lucé had a relatively longer history—a slow but persistent rise through public office and, finally, accession into the upper hierarchy. Jacques Pineau de Lucé, intendant of Hainaut-Maubeuge from 1745 to 1752, was the fifth generation of a family that was originally from Poitou and had settled in Paris in the late seventeenth century. His great-great-grandfather, who begins the family's history, was a judicial officer in the *bailliage* of Partenai; the latter's son in turn became a *présidial* judge, the next higher rank in the judiciary, in the provincial capital of Poitiers and ended his career as dean of his company. The family

[7] For the Calonne family, see Michaud, VI, 424–27; Paul Ardascheff, *Les intendants de province sous Louis XVI*, trans. by Louis Jousserandot (Paris, 1909), 34, 40, 43; Jolly, 7; and Lacour-Gayet, 12–13. There is, surprisingly, no information about Calonne and his family in the genealogical collection of the Bibliothèque Nationale (except for one meager and insignificant reference).

became noble when the great-grandfather, the *présidial* judge, obtained one of the letters patent that the Crown distributed in 1638 in celebration of Louis XIV's birth. The intendant's grandfather moved to Paris to promote his career, but he remained simply a lawyer attached to the Paris Parlement; the father, however, became a magistrate—a councilor in the Parlement—in 1709, and at the end of his career he was dean of one of the chambers. Thus in each generation the Pineau family doggedly advanced: one after another they sought higher office in the province and in the capital, and each member in succession achieved moderate success until the status and titles attached to the nobility, the magistracy, and the high administration embellished the family name.[8]

The path from the world of business to the world of public office was increasingly well trodden, and families took several different routes to arrive at the single goal. The classic circuit began with commerce and ended in the courts and the Council. The great-grandfather or grandfather had stood behind the counter of his shop in Paris or in a provincial town where he sold his wares; in the third or fourth generation a member of the family appeared at the bar of a sovereign court as magistrate and decided the law of the land; and one generation later a descendant carried out the sovereign's will as royal intendant.

The family of Jean Louis Moreau de Beaumont, intendant of Poitiers from 1747 to 1750, had made this ascent. The great-grandfather, originally perhaps from Lorraine, settled in Paris in the mid-seventeenth century and opened a shop on the Rue Saint-Denis where he sold cloth. Drapers were the patricians of the merchant class in this era, and the family's fortunes undoubtedly prospered; the great-grandfather himself, although not a native Parisian, already was enrolled among the merchant *bourgeoisie* of the capital.

[8] In addition to genealogical sources in the bibliography, see Bluche, 348.

His two sons inherited the family business, and they gained greater profits and prestige. France was then engaged in the War of the Spanish Succession, and the king's troops required provisions, for which the Crown paid large sums of money. The Moreau brothers obtained a government contract and supplied their clothing to the royal army. Much wealth now came to them: as early as 1706 the older brother had purchased the expensive office of *secrétaire du roi* as well as numerous estates, and in 1708 the younger brother, the intendant's grandfather, also became a *secrétaire du roi* and thereby ennobled himself and all his heirs. During the remaining years of his life the grandfather continued his ascent: he became treasurer-general of the Invalides, the army hospital in Paris which Louis XIV had established; and he purchased a country estate, becoming not only a landowner but a *seigneur* as well. The ties of the Moreau family with commerce and with commoners were now definitely broken.

The intendant's father began and ended his career in the sovereign court. He entered the Paris Parlement in 1709, one year after his own father's ennoblement, as a *substitut;* he became a councilor in 1711; and as early as 1713 he became the president of the first Chamber of Requests, holding this position for thirty-seven years until his retirement in 1750. This was not the full extent of the family's ascent. The Moreaus had many members and branches, and all prospered, gaining wealth, office, and honors; of all the descendants of the two brothers who owned the shop on the Rue Saint-Denis, the career of one close relative of the intendant warrants mention. An uncle, the younger brother of the intendant's father, was Jean Moreau de Séchelles. The latter followed his elder brother into the Paris Parlement and preceded his nephew as *maître des requêtes* and intendant, serving in Lille from 1743 to 1754, when he capped the family's fortunes by becoming minister of state. The next year, 1755, he obtained the important office of controller-general of finance. Thus, the history of the Moreau family illustrates not only the rise from merchant to magistrate in three generations; in this time as well it rose from merchant to minister and journeyed from the shop on the Rue Saint-Denis to the Royal Council in the palace of Versailles.[9]

Increasingly by the late seventeenth century the business world expanded to include finance as well as commerce, and the most prominent and wealthy among the financiers, as well as the ones with the most effective connections in high government circles, were the tax farmers. By contracting to collect the various indirect and excise taxes, paying the Crown a flat fee and then squeezing even larger sums from the taxpayers, they gained enormous profits that made them among the wealthiest men in France. Closely allied with them in the quest for riches were the *affairistes* or *traitants*. These were the men who lent money to their king at almost astronomical rates of interest: men such as Samuel Bernard and Turcaret, in life and in drama, who grew fat on their king's hunger for money. But with their wealth they could buy offices, and with offices they could remove the stain from their lucre and further raise their status and enhance their prestige.

Such was the history of the Dupleix family. Provincial in origin, with several generations of presumed ancestors as merchants and landowners, René François Dupleix, the first known ancestor, settled in the early eighteenth century in Paris, where he became a tax farmer, investing in the returns of the tobacco tax. Other financial ventures followed: John Law having set up the French Indies Company to promote French trade overseas, René François Dupleix contributed his share, which was undoubtedly a large portion since he also became director of the company. The final acquisition of his career was a purely honorific post, exalting to his ego but devoid of practical function or power: he

---

[9] In addition to genealogical sources in the bibliography, see *ibid.*, 319–21.

became an ordinary equerry in the king's Great Stable. His two sons shared his financial and business interests. The younger one, Joseph François Dupleix, promoted French commercial activities in India and became famous as the governor of Pondichéry, in charge of the French colony and trading outposts in the East. The elder son followed his father's career and became a tax farmer as well as Director-General of the French Indies Company. And he advanced one step further, for in 1734 he purchased the office of *secrétaire du roi* and entered the order of nobility. Guillaume Joseph Dupleix de Bacquencourt, intendant in Burgundy from 1774 to 1780, was the grandson of the first tax farmer and son of the second. His career was entirely in the magistracy and high administration. In 1752 he obtained his first office as councilor in the Grand Conseil, entered the Royal Council in 1756 as a *maître des requêtes,* and served as president of the Grand Conseil in 1762. In 1765 he began his fifteen years of service as a provincial intendant, culminating his government career in 1780 as councilor of state.[10]

The world of finance was magnetic. The profits it offered and the opportunities that great riches promised increasingly drew officeholders into its sphere. The process became dual: office preceded finance often as much as finance led to office. After a period of time engaged in financial ventures, an individual would use his augmented wealth to obtain an even more prestigious office for himself or for his son. Thus for a family formerly or actually identified with public office, tax farming was an interlude, a breathing spell designed to replenish its fortune before it forged ahead.

---

[10] In addition to genealogical sources in the bibliography, see Michaud, XII, 12–19; P. Louis Laîné, *Dictionnaire véridique des origines des maisons nobles ou anoblies du royaume de France* (2 vols.; Paris, 1828–50), I, 688; Bluche, 162–63; Fréville, II, 347; and Charles Victor Émile, Baron de Boyer de Sainte-Suzanne, *Les intendants de la généralité d'Amiens* (Paris, 1865), 209.

Louis Thiroux de Crosne, intendant of Rouen from 1768 to 1785, was of such a family. The Thiroux originated in Burgundy in the early sixteenth century. For four generations, from the last half of the sixteenth until the early eighteenth century, each of the intendant's ancestors was a lawyer and officeholder, filling various local charges such as municipal tax agent and magistrate, and deputy to the provincial estates. As reward for the family's long period of service, the intendant's great-great-grandfather obtained royal letters patent of ennoblement in 1659. The last ancestor to hold local office was the first to enter the world of finance. Lazare Louis Thiroux, the great-grandfather, was a lawyer in the Parlement of Burgundy and a councilor in the Burgundian Estates; at the turn of the century he moved to Paris and in 1709 became a tax farmer, engaging in financial affairs for ten years. As a new Parisian on the rise, seeking to make himself known, he also obtained the minor post of administrator of the capital's oldest hospital, the Hôtel-Dieu. Lazare Louis' son began and ended his career in finance. In 1712 he was engaged in farming the salt tax in Berry,[11] and at his death in 1742 he was the farmer-general for all the indirect taxes levied in Lorraine and Barrois. In the interim he also held other posts, performing administrative tasks as treasurer-general of the royal household and grandmaster of the royal post. This stage in his career illustrates another significant development: the expanding royal bureaucracy, set apart from the traditional hierarchy of venal charges, now offered additional opportunities to new families. But ultimate prestige flowed from a single source, venal offices in the magistracy. And so Lazare Louis' son, father of the intendant Louis Thiroux de Crosne, served his full career as a judge in the sovereign court, entering as a councilor and

---

[11] The official title of Jean Louis Thiroux de Lailly in 1712 was "receveur-général des fermes des gabelles de Berri."

ending as a president. The next phase in the rise of the Thiroux family occurred during the lifetime of the intendant, who combined both robe and pen in his career.[12]

These "new men" in the corps of intendants—Calonne, Pineau de Lucé, Moreau de Beaumont, Dupleix de Bacquencourt and Thiroux de Crosne—were of families that recently had attained the highest ranks in government and society, through the personal achievements of the intendants or of their fathers. Yet each of these families had gained success gradually. Each had raised itself in the course of several generations, as one member after another scaled the rungs of the professional and social hierarchy, passing from an inferior position to a relatively superior one. Other "new families" represented in the corps, however, had ascended rapidly. Following several generations of an unchanging modest place in society, suddenly one member gained astonishing success and catapulted the family into honored rank: he became a magistrate and a royal intendant. In other instances, the family's history is almost totally unknown before the generation of the intendant's father who, from humble or even menial position, with daring and luck gained great wealth and important office, climbing several rungs at once and emerging in high place in government and society. Efforts otherwise spread over several generations, achievements otherwise garnered by one ancestor after another, were here telescoped in the lifetime of one man—magistrate, intendant, sometimes councilor of state and minister—who consummated the family's fortune.

Charles François Hyacinthe Esmangart, intendant of Bordeaux from 1770 to 1775, and then intendant of Caen until 1783, represented one of these "new families." For about two hundred years, from the early sixteenth century until the eighteenth, his family resided first in Pierrefonds and then in Compiègne. Their history was inauspicious. Generation

[12] In addition to genealogical sources in the bibliography, see Bluche, 397–98.

after generation four of his six forebears were administrative and judicial officers in their local region, while one of the non-officers was a simple squire—in other words, a bourgeois "living nobly." From the great-great-great-grandfather until the father, five generations, the family's professional status changed but little. The former was a captain in the chateau of Pierrefonds and an officer in charge of the adjoining forest; the great-grandfather was keeper of the royal seals in Compiègne; the grandfather was a lawyer attached to the Paris Parlement, steward for a local abbey, royal judicial officer, and then municipal judge in Compiègne; and the father was a royal tax agent in several districts bordering Paris. The family seemed ensconced in minor, local office. Its legal status, however, had changed in an important way: the grandfather, by purchasing the office of *secrétaire du roi* in 1722, had made his children and all his posterity noble. Yet the family's nobility was merely a façade for prestige and a shield against tax collection; no Esmangart gained increased fortune or higher status for over thirty years. Then in 1758 or shortly before, Charles François Hyacinthe went to Paris, the first of his family to settle in the capital, and soon he was inscribed as an advocate in the Paris Parlement. His career now developed rapidly: on May 12 of the same year he became a councilor in the Grand Conseil, three years later a *maître des requêtes*, within ten years President of the Grand Conseil, and by the twelfth year, in 1770, a royal intendant. After more than two hundred years as ordinary subjects of the king, within little more than a decade a member of the Esmangart family became a trusted servant of the Crown, standing close to the summit in the hierarchies of government and society.

The rise of the Peirenc family, represented by François Marie Peirenc de Moras, intendant of Riom from 1750 until 1752, was even more meteoric and certainly more colorful. The intendant's father is the first in the family whose career is known and documented; before him the family's history is conjectural, grossly distorted by contemporary gossipmongers. The Peirencs were probably natives of the Cévennes, the Huguenot region of Languedoc, in the seventeenth century, and were themselves Protestant as well as members of the town *bourgeoisie* and minor officeholders. The intendant's grandfather was perhaps a master surgeon in an age when surgeons were partly barbers. This enabled eighteenth-century pamphleteers to label the grandfather a barber and to spread the rumor that François Marie's father also had been a barber in his youth.

Abraham Peirenc, the father, came to Paris at the turn of the century when he was still young. There he obtained employment as a clerk to the wealthy *munitionnaire* Fargès. The latter had a young daughter, and an amorous adventure ensued which founded the fortune of the Peirenc family. While still a clerk to Fargès, Abraham Peirenc seduced Anne Marie Josephe Fargès and the two fled France; the irate father managed to bring them back and had them married. The young, ambitious clerk probably needed little inducement to marry the daughter of his rich employer. So contemporary gossips related the tale, perhaps exaggerating the incidents that led to this unusual marriage of a clerk and an heiress in order to besmirch the Peirenc name. Whatever the exact truth may be, in 1713 Abraham Peirenc married the heiress to the Fargès industrial fortune. The War of the Spanish Succession was still in progress, and the new son-in-law made his first great profits as the associate of Fargès in supplying the royal armies with war matériel. The Law "system" then succeeded the war as a source of riches, and Peirenc made a second, even greater fortune through timely and lucky speculations and by shrewd investments in the French Indies Company, one of whose directors he became. Having already accumulated riches through business and investments, he now proceeded to add to his wealth more safely and securely by becoming a private banker. He also began to enrich his mind: his aspirations did not cease once he made his fortune but enlarged to include officeholding, for public office brought ennoblement and dignity. But the magistracy required knowledge, and so the wealthy businessman educated himself, above all learning Latin quickly in order to qualify for a university degree. With this last endowment he was prepared to obtain a judicial office, for which he could easily pay the price.

His professional career was as rapidly successful as his business career: in 1720 he was a councilor in the Parlement of Metz, and two years later he entered the Royal Council as a *maître des requêtes*. Peirenc became a nobleman not through lowly office, but by means of the most honored and important charges in the realm. His last position added a further touch of prestige to a man who lusted after eminence: he was chief of the council of the Duchesse de Bourbon. Thus by the 1720's, two decades after his arrival in Paris, Peirenc was one of the foremost parvenu noblemen in France. Country estates came into his possession one after another, bedecking his family name with seigneurial titles. On the Rue de Varennes in Paris, the capital's new aristocratic quarter, he built his new home; Gabriel, the famed architect, constructed the classically elegant *hôtel* as a miniature palace of Versailles, complete with beautiful formal garden and sculptured fountains beyond the doors of the salon. Paris preserves Peirenc's monument to his wealth and success, the building known today as the Rodin Museum.

François Marie Peirenc's career and place in society were assured despite his father's early death, and he entered directly into the magistracy. Moreover, the intendant scaled even greater heights: not only was he twice provincial intendant and intendant of finance, but in 1756 he became a councilor of state and obtained the pre-eminent post of controller-general of finance, which he exchanged the following year for that of minister of state of the marine. Thus in social status and official position Peirenc de Moras became the equal, even the superior, of the most renowned among the

French nobility. Luck, wealth, and some talent had drawn the family out of its modest place into the highest ranks of society. Although lowly origins did not preclude the achievements of father and son, the memory remained to provide wits with material for barbs and jingles: the minister became the butt of jokes about the barber.[13]

III

Joined in a single corps, linked in the same social order, the intendants in the nobility of the pen did not, however, constitute a uniform group. They came from diverse sections of French society, became colleagues in government, and stood in rank to one another according to their family's history and social standing. Yet the differences in the origins and evolution of their families were not all in some remote, indeterminate past. For many among them the family "past"—the time before it acquired standing and honor—was actually or almost in the present. Whether those intendants numbered one or two centuries of ancestors, or merely one or two generations, nobility and high office, wealth and prestige, were recent family attainments. Success and status came to his grandfather shortly before the intendant's birth, to his father during his lifetime, or in the course of his own career. These were the "new men" in the corps— fresh arrivals at the summit of the governing and social hierarchies. The way had been open to them to move up. Their presence in the upper ranks of royal government testifies to the possibilities for social mobility in the *ancien régime*.

[13] In addition to genealogical sources in the bibliography, see C. Boy, "Les Peirenc de Moras," *Bulletin de la Diana*, XXIV (1931–1934), 154–61; and Bluche, 341–42.

CHAPTER 8

Social Mobility and "Aristocratic Reaction" within the High Administration in the Eighteenth Century

I

What is the gauge for social mobility in a society? No social structure remains forever unchanged; if we search into the history of any community we may discern some movement among individuals and families from group to group up and down the social hierarchy. If we compare the intendants with their first recorded ancestors we find that only ten or eleven of the latter held positions approximately equal to those of their descendants; in short, out of ninety-three families of intendants whose history is known, eighty-two or eighty-three families bear witness to upward mobility. But how significant is such mobility if it occurred five generations back, and if thereafter the family's status remained fixed? And for whom was it significant? The problem is both statistical and psychological.

A society where ruling elite owed their fortune or status to the archievements of ancestors five generations previous would not offer its people the hope or possibility of professional or social advancement. If, however, some of the governing families acquired their wealth and rank within the lifetime of contemporaries, rose socially and professionally within the memory of men, then their success might inspire others. Sufficient examples offer a promise, if not yet a myth. What might strike men as a measure of success are the accomplishments and comparative standing of a family within the span of three generations, from the grandfather to the grandson. Individuals build for the future of their immediate posterity and may live to take joy in the achievements of their sons and grandchildren; moreover, sons and grandsons, whatever their success, still bear the memory and social imprint of their immediate origins. So from the points of view of the members of an elite and their contemporaries, a family's achievements from the generation of the grandfather to the generation of the grandson is a measure of social mobility.

The "new men" in the crops of intendants—Calonne, Pineau de Lucé, Moreau de Beaumont, Dupleix de Bacquencourt, Thiroux de Crosne, Esmangart, and Peirenc de Moras—were all of families that had risen professionally and socially within one to three generations, from the grandfather to the intendant. There were others as well in this category. Of the ninety-four intendants included in this study, forty-five were from "new families" which had begun to move up in society beginning in the generation of the grandfather, the father, or even of the intendant.[1]

The patterns of mobility as well as the rates of mobility of the families of these forty-five intendants varied. Within the larger group of "new men" we may distinguish three different types. Eight of these intendants were "self-made" men. Their fathers' professions did not foreshadow the successful careers that awaited the sons, for the fathers did not have positions in society giving them sufficient prestige or power to assure the places the sons would later occupy. Two fathers

---

[1] This figure of 45 includes one intendant whose father's career is not proven by documentary evidence, and one whose family history is unknown and presumably without renown; it also includes 5 intendants from only 2 families: 3 from the Chaumont family and 2 from the Moreau family.

were minor officeholders, and one presumably a minor functionary in the central bureaucracy; one was a textile merchant; one a country gentleman and lawyer; one a commensal officer; one an officer in the army and royal household; and the career of one remains unknown and presumably not outstanding.[2] Hence we may assume that these intendants made their way on their own; the history of Charles François Hyacinthe Esmangart, the seventh generation of a family of minor local officers who nevertheless rose to become an intendant in the royal government, is one such example, as we have seen. One of these eight, however, was an exception, for his way evidently was made *for* him.

Bernard Chauvelin, intendant of Tours from 1709 to 1718, was the youngest son of Louis Chauvelin, an officer in the royal household (controller-general of the treasurers of the royal household), Parisian *rentier,* and private banker to the upper nobility and magistracy of the capital; his grandfather also had been a commensal officer, the treasurer of the royal stables. The family "lived nobly": the father possessed country estates and assumed noble titles, but twice, in 1666 and 1668, he was fined for usurping the status of nobility. Moreover, Louis Chauvelin died when his son was merely ten years old, leaving Bernard's future still undecided. But the latter, though fatherless, counted among his brood of cousins some of the foremost members of the high administration and high robe. There was his father's namesake, Louis Chauvelin, representing the elder branch of the Chauvelin family, a provincial intendant, *maître des requêtes,* and councilor of state; Michel Le Tellier, Marquis de Louvois, Louis XIV's minister and secretary of state for war, and his son the Marquis de Barbézieux, also councilor

---

[2] The grandfather of the intendant whose father was an officer in the army and in the royal household had been a sovereign-court judge, and so the family had some standing in society and government. Moreover, two of the grandfathers and two of the fathers of the eight intendants above had been *secrétaires du roi.*

and secretary of state; the several members of the Le Peletier family: Claude, minister of state, controller-general of finance, and *prévôt des marchands,* his son Louis, president in the Paris Parlement, his brothers Jerome, councilor of state, and Michel, intendant of finance and councilor of state, and the latter's son, who was also a councilor of state and intendant of finance; and Guy and Michel Chamillart, father and son, both *maîtres des requêtes* and provincial intendants, the latter yet to become councilor of state and controller-general. Undoubtedly these powerfully placed relatives helped their young cousin to enter the sovereign court and to advance in the royal administration. So Bernard Chauvelin, a first-generation nobleman whose status was legally recognized only in 1699, became the first member of his immediate family to enter the sovereign courts and the royal administration.

Other "new men" among the intendants—twenty of the forty-five, or 44 percent—were of families whose fortune and prestige came in the preceding generation, through the achievements of their fathers.[3] For half of the twenty, the father's success marked a radical change in the family's status. Wealth, rapidly accumulated through business, speculation, or tax farming, changed the destinies of eight of these fathers, providing them with the means for purchasing offices and acquiring nobility: six became *secrétaires du roi,* one of them later becoming president in a provincial sovereign court; one became a parlementary magistrate and then entered the Royal Council as a *maître des requêtes;* and the last used his riches to advance his son's career in the court and on the Council. The father of the ninth intendant, the famed administrator and writer Sénac de Meilhan, was Louis XV's physician and so acquired close connections with members of the court and the government which aided his

[3] This figure and those that follow represent the fathers of individual intendants; the father of the brothers Chaumont de la Galaizière and Chaumont de la Millière is therefore counted twice.

son's advancement. The father of the tenth intendant, Louis de Bernage, made his success through marriage: in one year, 1645, he married into the famed family Voyer de Paulny d'Argenson and also acquired the office of councilor in the Grand Conseil. Having the keeper of the seals as first cousin undoubtedly eased the intendant's career as well.

For the remaining ten families in this group of twenty, the father's career continued the family's gradual and persistent rise in society yet also marked a breakthrough into higher and more prestigious ranks. Seven of the fathers entered the sovereign courts and two also served on the Royal Council. Finance transformed the fates of the three other fathers: one became a tax farmer and the intimate of royal ministers; one became a treasurer-general in his native province; and the third, through tax farming, acquired wealth which he then used to obtain the offices of *secrétaire du roi* and receiver-general, thereby becoming ennobled.

The third group among the "new men" in the corps of intendants came from families whose social ascension was still more gradual, resulting from the cumulative achievements of their fathers and grandfathers. These intendants numbered seventeen of the forty-five—38 percent of the total group of "new men." [4] As third-generation members of parvenu families, they were in the process of being assimilated into the ranks of the older, established families of the governing nobility, and their children would be counted among the latter. Yet they still bore the last imprint of their families' origins—which they acknowledged or disguised, and which members of high society disdained or ignored.

Each of these seventeen families, whether its history antedated or began with the generation of the grandfather, made its decisive entrance into the society of men of influence and

[4] Two of these intendants were of families included as well in the preceding group: Antoine Chaumont de la Galaizière, son of Antoine Martin, and Jean Louis Moreau de Beaumont, nephew of Jean Moreau de Séchelles.

prestige as a result of the grandfather's successful career. The means for this breakthrough conformed to a pattern already familiar: local administrative or judicial office, or the financial magistracy; business, finance, or tax farming; purchase of the quickly ennobling office of *secrétaire du roi*. In short, each grandfather had one of these careers or a combination of several of them.[5]

Most of these seventeen families continued their ascent during the father's lifetime. Only two fathers remained in the grandfathers' profession and social rank as tax farmers, one of these two also continuing as director of the French Indies Company. Three families made only slow progress up the social ladder. The grandfathers had been primarily municipal or local officers; in contrast, one father became a financial magistrate, the other two tax farmers and financial agents in the central administration, and one of the latter also an investor and director in the French Indies Company.[6] The social standing of the remaining twelve families advanced considerably through the fathers' achievements: five fathers became sovereign-court magistrates, and six combined careers in the court and on the Council. By their success they carved out places in the high ranks of the judicial magistracy and the royal bureaucracy which their sons succeeded to as they would to newly gained family legacies.

From the "self-made" man to the heir of a place in the robe and the pen, all were "new men" in the corps since all were from "new families"—families that were socially mobile within the immediately preceding three generations.

[5] There is one exception to the above. The grandafther of the intendant Denis Dodart was the royal physician and so was the father. As in the case of Sénac de Meilhan's father, their service in the court enabled them to make contacts with members of the royal family, courtiers, and government officials which undoubtedly helped to advance Dodart's administrative career.

[6] With each of these three families ennoblement came in the grandfather's generation, through municipal office for one and through the charge of *secrétaire du roi* for the other two.

In the *ancien régime* the family was foremost, subsuming the individual and stamping its identity upon its members. The individual then assumed the place in society which the family held, and embodied its history and achievements; and each member in turn served the interests of the family, his accomplishments designed to promote its fortune, enhance its social position, and bring honor to its name.[7]

II

None of these intendants and few of their families went from poverty to riches; the road to the top did not begin at the bottom.[8] Indeed, the base from which social mobility began was located in the middle of the social hierarchy—and above it. Even to start off from this upper half and rise to the top required certain advantages in society.

One needed office, for only those who had passed through the courts and had served on the Council, who had acquired judicial and administrative experience, could become intendants. One wanted office, for office provided the means for honor, professional service, and ennoblement. And to obtain an office one had to have sufficient wealth to make the purchase: the higher the office in power, status, and prestige, the higher the price. Moreover, to qualify for office one had to be educated. Universities and secondary schools provided free education to many poor, lower-class students in the eighteenth century, so poverty was not a direct barrier; yet lack of wealth had indirect consequences which served to bar the

[7] Cf. Bernard Barber, *Social Stratification: A Comparative Analysis of Structure and Process* (New York, 1957), 359–66.

[8] This was true not only in eighteenth-century France but also in nineteenth- and early twentieth-century America, however more egalitarian and flexible American society was. For accounts of the latest studies disproving the American myth of "rags-to-riches" see *ibid.*, 427–69; Stephan Thernstrom, *Poverty and Progress: Social Mobility in a Nineteenth-Century City* (Cambridge, Mass., 1964); and S. H. Aronson, *Status and Kinship in the Higher Civil Service* (Cambridge, Mass., 1964).

way for many or to leave it open for only a few. Families might not have to provide funds for tuition, and poorer students might be able to work in their schools or for wealthier fellow students to obtain money for their daily upkeep; yet all too often fathers would withdraw their sons after a short period of schooling to bring them back into the family trade or shop. What would keep these poorer boys persevering through the long years of study but the hope of a higher profession and a better life, represented for many by a government post. So again they had to have some money with which, eventually, they might buy an office and justify their years spent in the *collège* and the university. With less money, however, they could obtain only minor office and thus climb only a small way up the social ladder. In short, with little or moderate wealth one could only begin to rise in society; with great wealth one could consummate this rise by entering the nobility, the robe, and the pen.[9]

Wealth, then, was a prime requirement for social advance in the *ancien régime:* to complete higher education, to gain office, and thus to rise in society. Riches might not directly buy one's way to the top in this aristocratic and hierarchical society, but certainly did provide the means for making the ascent. Wealth alone enabled one to take the final surge upward and complete the image of the *arriviste.* With money one could buy landed estates and provide bountiful dowries

[9] For an analysis of the financing and social character of education in eighteenth-century France, see Ariès, 306 ff.; Shelby T. McCloy, *Government Assistance in Eighteenth-Century France* (Durham, N.C., 1946), ch. 17; Georges Snyders, *La pédagogie en France aux XVIIe et XVIIIe siècles* (Paris, 1965), 346; and especially P. François de Dainville, "Effectifs des collèges et scolarité aux XVIIe et XVIIIe siècles dans le Nord-Est de la France," *Population*, No. 3 (1955), 479–88, where the author states that in the secondary schools of Champagne, owing to the practice of free tuition, 48–62 percent of the students during the years 1618–1736 were "enfants du peuple et de la petite bourgeoisie," avid to learn Latin in order to obtain minor office and thereby raise themselves in society.

to marry into prominent aristocratic families, and thereby assume the total guise of the contemporary social model, the nobleman.[10]

Legally as well as financially, families that were socially mobile were already in the top half of society before they attained the highest ranks. The "new men" in the corps had to be wealthy as a precondition for moving further up in society; moreover, they had to be noble as a consequence of their social ascension. Once their families began to rise, and having come so far, they could not fail to obtain nobility.

All of the 45 "new men" among the intendants were noble, ranging from first-generation to fifth-generation nobility.[11] The overwhelming majority of them (86 percent) were second- and third-generation noblemen, 19 and 20 respectively (42 percent and 44 percent); only 2 each were first-generation and fourth-generation nobility (4 percent) and one was a fifth-generation nobleman (2 percent). Some

[10] Cf. Mousnier, *La vénalité des offices,* 501 ff., 520–21, and 532 for his similar conclusions regarding the magistrates of the Parlement of Rouen in the early seventeenth century. Sénac de Meilhan, writing during the Revolution to refute the argument that the monarchy had been tyrannical and that aristocratic society had denied opportunities for social advancement, testifies to the role of money as a force for social mobility in the *ancien régime.* The following quotations are from Sénac de Meilhan, *Du gouvernement, des moeurs, et des conditions en France:* "Let us suppose, and this supposition is the exact history of one thousand individuals, that the son of a peasant [*laboureur*] had acquired by his efforts 50,000 écus [= 150,000 livres]. His son then increases these savings and doubles it; he acquires nobility, and the grandson is a magistrate or army officer. The fourth generation raises itself to even more eminent positions, and if the following generation equally applies itself, or if luck falls its way—which may happen to any class, if marked success attracts public attention—there is no military or civil employ to which it cannot aspire" (pp. 91–92). "All these means to become wealthy, to raise oneself, to marry into the greatest families, to be admitted into the highest circles, do not exist in other countries" (p. 105).

[11] The generations of nobility of one intendant, Etienne Louis Journet, intendant of Auch and Bayonne (1767–1776), remain uncertain.

of their families were even further up in the hierarchy: 5 of the fathers were already magistrates and 6 others were in both the sovereign courts and the royal administration. Their families wanted offices to advance themselves and had the wealth to purchase them; and by virtue of these offices almost all of these families became noble. The sovereign courts provided ennoblement for some of them—10 in all; and offices in the financial magistracy, municipal government, and royal household ennobled a few others. Yet the most expensive charge of *secrétaire du roi* ennobled half of these families, a total of 22 or 23. The nobility of the 6 remaining families came indirectly as a result of their wealth: through payments for royal letters patent (4) and long-standing possession of a fief (one); and for the last, a tax farmer and money lender, through favor with a member of the royal family (as well as family ties with a high administrator). And so the circle was completed, linking money, office, and nobility in the process of social mobility in the *ancien régime*.

The fact that these "new men" were also noblemen does not mean that social advancement was impossible for commoners, but that it was limited to those who could afford to become noble, as the histories of these families attest. To be sure, nobility set one apart in French society; but on the other hand nobility was not the exclusive privilege of a set, unchanging, and very limited few.

Nobility was comparatively widespread in France, with almost two nobles to every hundred commoners; this placed France in the middle ranks of the European nations, with an aristocracy in proportion to the total population smaller than in Poland and Hungary but larger than in England.[12]

[12] According to Georges Lefebvre (*The Coming of the French Revolution*, 7), in 1789 there was a total of 400,000 nobles out of a population probably numbering 23,000,000, or 1.7 percent. This was the same proportion as the nobility of Russia, calculated in the 1760's, although much less than the Hungarian nobility, which constituted 5 percent of the population, and the Polish nobility, which numbered 725,000 (8%) in the eighteenth century. On the other hand, it was

Moreover, many of the 400,000 nobles at the end of the eighteenth century had this status because they, their fathers, husbands, grandfathers, or earlier forebears held ennobling office, purchased letters patent of nobility, or became proprietors of seigneurial estates.

The eighteenth century witnessed a marked increase in the numbers and proportion of the nobility in France: in 1715 there were 190,000 nobles out of a population of 20,000,000 (0.9 percent) ; by 1789 there were 400,000 among a total of 23,000,000 (1.8 percent). While the entire population increased by 15 percent, the nobility increased by 100 percent. We might expect a higher rate of natural increase for the nobility than for the rest of the population, because nobles could obtain more and better food and lived under healthier sanitary conditions. Nevertheless, even assuming a natural increase of 20 percent, this would add only 38,000 to the nobility, bringing the total to about 230,000 by 1789. Yet the aggregate increase was in fact 210,000, and the actual total was 400,000. In short, approximately 170,000 additional people became noble, apart from the natural population growth of the nobility, between 1715 and 1789—an estimated increase of 74 percent through ennoblement.[13] Of-

---

almost three times the proportion of the Swedish nobility, which was 0.6 percent, the latter figure however referring to the population of Sweden in 1718. For the population and social character of the various European nobilities see A. Goodwin, ed., *The European Nobility in the Eighteenth Century: Studies of the Nobilities of the Major European States in the Pre-Reform Era* (London, 1953), 123, 139, 165, 176. Similar figures are found in Palmer, I, 389, 413, 440. In stark contrast with the French nobility in the eighteenth century was the English aristocracy of that period. The number of *individual* peers before 1784 has been variously estimated at 160–170 and even as high as 250–350, and the number of gentry *families* is calculated at 8,000–20,000; with a population about 7,500,000 before 1785, this means that 0.1 percent to 0.3 percent consisted of aristocratic families—in a land where primogeniture strictly prevailed. Cf. G. E. Mingay, *English Landed Society in the Eighteenth Century* (London, 1964), 6.

[13] The figures for 1715, total population and nobility, come from Ford, 31, and those for 1789 may be found in Lefebvre, 7. Various other

fice alone accounted for the original noble status of many among the nobility. There were 4,300 venal charges in the eighteenth century which carried various degrees of nobility; projecting this figure back to 1600, and taking into account the fact that nobility for the officeholder brought nobility in most cases and within time to his entire family as well— though sons, grandsons, and later descendants might be in the army and hence assumed to be *noblesse d'épée*—one may calculate an approximate total of over 150,000 nobles, about 38 percent of the nobility in 1789, whose noble status derived from office.[14]

---

estimates set the general population in 1715 at 19 million, and in 1789 between 24 and 26 million. With these figures as bases, the increase between 1715 and 1789 in the number of nobles, apart from natural population growth, is an estimated 130,000, or a 50 percent increase through ennoblement.

[14] The number of ennobling offices may be found in Ford, 53–54, and in Henri Carré, *La noblesse de France et l'opinion publique au XVIII* *siècle* (Paris, 1920), 7–9. Ford gives a somewhat higher figure for the sovereign courts than does Carré, so that the total, based on his sources, comes to 4,300, and on Carré, 4,020. Carré bases his figures on those provided by Necker; the latter, in his *De l'administration des finances de la France* (3 vols.; [1785]), III, 101–102, gives the totals for each group of ennobling offices: Parlements—1,100 (1,250 according to Ford); Chambre des Comptes and Cour des Aides—900 (800 and 150 respectively according to Ford) ; Cour des Monnaies—30 (70–80 according to Ford) ; Grand Conseil—70 (63 according to Ford) ; *secrétaires du roi*— 900; Châtelet—80; commissioned officers in the courts of Nancy, Colmar, and Arras—220; *bureaux des finances*—740; *grands baillis, sénéchaux, gouverneurs,* and *lieutenants-généraux d'épée*—50. Necker states that he does not include the second-rank offices in the Council, chancellery, *tribunaux de la table de marbre,* as well as others. I have also excluded from this count the posts of councilor of state and *maître des requêtes,* for although these were ennobling in law it is improbable that anyone holding such a position was not already noble. Necker also excludes from his count the ennobling municipal offices and ennobled military officers. According to the calculations made by Bluche and Durye, *L'anoblissement par charges avant 1789,* I, 23–38, there were 41 ennobling municipal offices during the eighteenth century, making a total of approximately 600 individuals so ennobled during the course of the century; there was an even larger total of ennobling municipal offices in

Mathematical estimates for the *ancien régime* are calculated risks, yet they may still serve as guides. Thus an estimate based on the number of ennobling offices and on demographic statistics indicates that approximately 38 percent to 74 percent of the nobility in 1789 originally acquired their status through ennoblement. So high and broad a range need

the seventeenth century, 165, some however eliminated by mid-century, which would produce a total of 800–2,400 individuals whose noble status derived from those offices. The ennoblement of some military officers through service in the army before 1634 and after 1750 is discussed in *ibid.*, II, 35–43. These authors also list all the ennobling offices in the French government at all levels, the laws that created them, and the dates during which they conferred nobility; unfortunately they do not always state the numbers for each of these ennobling offices.

For the offices of *secrétaires du roi* and those following in the list above drawn from Necker, a total of 1,900, given their nature I have assumed they ennobled 100 percent of their holders for a total of eight and a half generations from 1600 to 1789. For the parlementary offices, 42 percent ennobled their holders in the late eighteenth century (cf. Ford, 146, and Jean Egret, "L'aristocratie parlementaire française à la fin de l'Ancien Régime," *Revue Historique,* CCVII [July–Sept. 1952], 1–11), a proportion more or less true probably since the later seventeenth century. The other sovereign courts, having less prestige, received more commoners, so I increased their proportion of ennoblement to 50 percent. For the period 1600–1650 I have assumed 100 percent ennoblement for all the holders of sovereign-court offices. One may argue that the latter may be too high a percentage for the first half of the seventeenth century and that there were fewer ennobling offices in the seventeenth century than in the eighteenth century; but since the total number of ennobling offices, as indicated above, does not include municipal offices and others of second rank as well as ennobled military officers these differences may balance off in the end. Moreover, although the number of offices is multiplied by five to include the entire family of the officeholder, this would account for only one—the immediate—generation and not succeeding generations; to include later generations in the male line of the descendants of ennobled officeholders would further swell the total. My thanks go to Mr. Dirk Houben, Research Assistant in the Office of Institutional Research, Hunter College, City University of New York, for helping me make some statistical sense of all these various figures and arrive at, hopefully, a valid estimate of the proportion of the nobility in 1789 originating from ennoblement.

not be considered excessive. The French historian Henri Carré claims that there might well have been more nobles by usurpation than by letters patent or even by ennobling offices, though their exact number may never be known; and Louis XVI's minister Necker estimated that nearly half of the nobility in 1789 had acquired their status during the preceding two centuries.[15]

Nobility, in eighteenth-century France, was and remained accessible to newcomers precisely because commoners with sufficient wealth and education could—and did—obtain ennobling offices, buy estates, or purchase letters patent. Any family and any individual who rose to the top at some time and in some way would become noble: even Figaro's creator, Beaumarchais, ended up as a nobleman.

The social history of the *ancien régime* was complex and paradoxical, and words often belie reality. Society was not closed and fixed; the high administration was not a self-perpetuating aristocratic preserve. Both the upper echelons of government, and hence the upper ranks of society, were open to new recruits and to those moving up in society. Yet those who newly entered had assumed noble status and were in the process of adopting aristocratic mores. Their transformation was total. The magic wand was golden, for money had wrought the change. Thus the aristocratic mold remained, enlarged and made more flexible by the addition of riches. In sum, the governing class and the socially dominant class in eighteenth-century France was an aristocracy embodying a plutocracy.

III

A considerable proportion of "new men" had reached the top in government and in society in the eighteenth century.

[15] Carré, 13; Norman Hampson, *A Social History of the French Revolution* (London, 1963), 11, refers to Necker's estimate. For a summary of information about the proportion of nobility in France and of ennobled nobles, see Appendix III below.

Behind them, were there others still seeking admission? And since some had been successful, could other men duplicate this success? Or were opportunities diminishing in the last half of the eighteenth century, as the *ancien régime* was drawing to a close? Was there, in short, an "aristocratic reaction" reaching into the upper ranks of the government as, historians claim, it reached into the farmlands of the countryside, the royal army, and the sovereign courts? We must try to see whether fewer "new men" entered the upper administration or, instead, whether the older and higher nobility increasingly monopolized top positions in the royal government—whether those already in the pen entrenched and perpetuated themselves—thereby preventing newcomers and outsiders from advancing.

Until now we have looked at the intendants as a bloc, without citing the differences among the three groups chosen for this study. To answer the question whether or not there was an "aristocratic reaction" in the high administration in the later eighteenth century we must now focus on each of the three groups—the intendants for the years 1710–1712, 1749–1751, and 1774–1776—which together provide a span of the entire century and separately present concrete examples for the early, middle, and late years of the century.[16] Do

---

[16] Of the 32 intendants for the years 1774–1776, 25 continued to serve into the 1780's; also 3 intendants who are included in the second group and served in the mid-seventies as well, functioned in the last decade of the monarchy. Among the intendants during the 1780's were 2 sons of intendants included in the third group—Amelot de Chaillou and Le Fèvre de Caumartin. Thus a majority of intendants who served in the last five years of the *ancien régime* are of families included in this study whose histories are known; only 18 of the intendants from 1784 through 1789 are men not included in this study. (Cf. *Almanach Royal*, volumes for the years 1785–1789.) In short, the conclusions that follow regarding an "aristocratic reaction" in the later eighteenth century, based on an analysis of the 32 intendants for the years 1774–1776 plus the 3 intendants from the years 1749–1751, also apply in the main to the final decade of the *ancien régime*.

the different traits of each group provide evidence to substantiate the theory of an "aristocratic reaction"?

The intendants from families of provincial origin predominated throughout the century. Their proportions, however, varied substantially in each of the three periods: Louis XIV, 23 out of 30 (14 definite, 9 probable—77 percent) ; Louis XV, 28 out of 32 (16 definite, 12 probable—87.5 percent) ; and Louis XVI, 28 out of 31 (26 definite, 2 probable—90 percent).[17] Even more significant is the length of time these families, originally provincial, had been in Paris (see Table 7).

Table 7. The comparative proportions of "new Parisians" among the three groups of intendants

Reign	First-generation Parisians	Families in Paris fifty years	Total of "new Parisians"
Louis XIV	3 (10%)	1 or 2 (3.3%–6.6%)	4 or 5 (13%–17%)
Louis XV	2 (6%)	7 (22%)	9 (28%)
Louis XVI	10 (32%)	5 (16%)	15 (48%)

As we can see then from the preceding statistics, toward the end of the century not only were there more intendants who came to Paris directly from the provinces, but more of them came from families settled in Paris within approximately two generations. As the eighteenth century progressed, more—not fewer—provincials were in the corps of intendants, and more recent Parisians were among them as well. Indeed, the latter composed almost half the corps in the last quarter of the century. It seems obvious, then, that the move to Paris was part of an effort the intendants or their families made to advance professionally and rise socially. Yet they and their families were comparatively less established and

[17] The geographical origins of the family of one intendant in the last group remains unknown.

entrenched in the upper circles of influence, power, and prestige in the royal government and in Parisian society than families with longer residence in the capital. Still they had succeeded in entering the high administration.

More important and more revealing than geographic origin and mobility are social origin and mobility. How do the eighteenth-century intendants compare in terms of family roots and fortune at the time of their families' entry in history four generations and more before the intendants? (See Table 8.)

For 10 of the intendants under Louis XIV, their families first appear in history already in the high ranks of government and society: of 23 known first ancestors, 6 were magistrates in the sovereign courts and 4 had careers in the courts and on the Royal Council.[18] In contrast, of 18 known first ancestors among Louis XV's intendants, only 2 were sovereign-court magistrates and 2 more held positions in both the robe and the pen. Even more striking in contrast are the family origins of Louis XVI's intendants: of the 19 first ancestors who are known, 2 alone were sovereign-court judges and none were in the courts and the high administration.[19] The distance in time between these intendants and their first ancestors in the courts and the Council varies but without undue significance, especially since high status for four generations or more anchored a place in society for most of them. In the first group, four, five, and six generations

[18] These ten first ancestors represent nine families, since the two intendants, Lamoignon de Basville and Lamoignon de Courson, father and son, had a single progenitor.

[19] One of Louis XVI's intendants (Nicolas Dupré de Saint-Maur, intendant of Bourges, 1767–1776) was descended from a first ancestor who was a *secrétaire du roi* (in which group he is categorized) and also a sovereign-court magistrate for a shorter period of time; for three succeeding generations, however, until the time of the grandfather, the family did not occupy judicial office. If we nevertheless include this one additional intendant in the count for the third group, the figures change to three sovereign-court judges (16 percent in the tabulation below).

separate the first ancestors from the intendants, nine generations being the exception for one among them; the same range of four to six generations applies to the second group; and for the last there is an increase to six and seven generations between the first ancestors and the intendants. However, one of the two first ancestors in this last group (also one of the two first ancestors in the second group) held a high position in the robe which the family did not maintain for several generations.[20] In contrast, the nine families represented by Louis XIV's ten intendants succeeded to positions in the courts and on the Council similar to those their first ancestors acquired, thus maintaining their high status from their beginnings four to nine generations earlier.[21] Let these figures for the first ancestors highlight the differences from the beginning to the end of the century: [22]

> 1710–1712: 26 percent robe
> 17 percent robe and pen
> 43 percent total

[20] The common ancestor for the two intendants in the second and third groups launched the family Caze de la Bove (Gaspard Henri de Caze de la Bove, intendant in Champagne, 1749–1750, and his son Gaspard Louis, intendant in Brittany, 1775–1785); during four generations before the appearance of these intendants the family remained as financial magistrates. The remaining four families in the last two groups are: 1749–1751—D'Aligre de Boislandry, Bernage de Vaux, and Camus de Pontcarré; and 1774–1776—Amelot de Chaillou.

[21] The nine families represented by these ten intendants of Louis XIV who retained their high position from the time of the first ancestors are: Barrillon d'Armoncourt, Bauyn d'Angervilliers (except that the intendant's father turned to tax farming as well), Boucher d'Orsay, Le Bret, Doujat, Foullé de Martargis, Lamoignon de Basville and Lamoignon de Courson, Le Pelletier de la Houssaye (whose first ancestor was a local tax official before entering a sovereign court), and Maignard de Bernières.

[22] These percentages are calculated in terms of the known first ancestors: 23 out of 30 for the first group, 18 out of 32 for the second group, and 19 out of 32 for the third.

1749–1751: 11 percent robe
            11 percent robe and pen
            22 percent total
1774–1776: 10.5 percent robe
            no member of the robe and pen
            10.5 percent total.

Clearly, fewer intendants in the last half of the eighteenth century and even fewer in the last quarter of the century came from families who, from their beginnings one hundred to more than two hundred years earlier, were at the top of the professional and social hierarchies.

An inverse development is also true. The evidence is limited but nevertheless instructive. In contrast to Louis XIV's intendants, slightly more intendants of Louis XV, and less removed in time, sprang from local officers, and some few more of Louis XVI's intendants one and two generations more distant had similar origins. These are the figures for the intendants in the three groups: one first ancestor of Louis XIV's intendants was a local officer seven generations back; three first ancestors of Louis XV's intendants were local officers four and five generations earlier; and four first ancestors of Louis XVI's intendants were local officers five to seven generations removed (one of them also the forebear of an intendant in the second group, the common ancestor of the Bertier de Sauvigny family). Thus as the eighteenth century progressed there were more royal intendants in the corps whose families' social and professional status was more modest in origin four to seven generations back, and whose histories began at a lower rung in the hierarchy.

All of the intendants' families did ultimately rise in society. Nevertheless, as we draw closer to the generation of the intendants, do significant differences appear in the status of their immediate predecessors which yield evidence of an "aristocratic reaction" in the later eighteenth century? Let us

Table 8. Comparative status of the first ancestors of the eighteenth-century intendants sampled

Periods	Total known	Sovereign courts	Sovereign courts and Royal Council	Total in courts and Council	Distance in generations	Local officers	Distance in generations
1710–1712	23	6 (26%)	4 (17%)	10 (43%)	4–9	1 (4%)	7
1749–1751	18	2 (11%)	2 (11%)	4 (22%)	4–6	3 (17%)	4–5
1774–1776	19 *	2 (10.5%) †	0	2 (10.5%) †	6–7	4 (21%)	5–7

* One presumed ancestor is included in this count.

† In the third period one first ancestor who was initially a *secrétaire du roi* and is categorized in that group, also became a sovereign-court judge; with this addition, the figures change to 3 (16%).

first compare the grandfathers of the intendants and then their fathers.

To be sure, more of the intendants' grandfathers were sovereign-court judges and members of the robe and pen in each of the three groups. But the totals, although larger, vary considerably.

Table 9. Comparative status of the grandfathers of the eighteenth-century intendants sampled

Periods	Total known	Sovereign courts	Sovereign courts and Royal Council	Total in courts and Council
1710–1712	29	9 (31%)	10 (34%)	19 (65%)
1749–1751	31 *	8 † (25.8%)	7 (22.5%)	15 † (48%)
1774–1776	27 †	5 † (18%) ‡	4 (15%)	9 † (33%) ‡

* Three presumed grandfathers are included in this count.

† One presumed grandfather is included in this figure.

‡ In the third period one grandfather who is categorized as a financial officer also became a magistrate; with this addition, the figures change to: 6 (22%) and a total of 10 (37%).

As Table 9 clearly indicates, throughout the century there was a constant decline in the numbers and proportion of intendants whose grandfathers were judges and high administrators. The greatest decrease was among the intendants of Louis XVI.

In contrast, the grandsons of men connected with finance—private businessmen, financial officers in the government, or businessmen transformed into government officers—entered the corps at a constantly increasing rate: 1710–1712, five (17 percent); 1749–1751, seven (22.5 percent); and 1774–1776, nine (33 percent, including one who became a sovereign-court judge). The last quarter of the century also witnessed a marked increase among the grandsons of local officers whose numbers had been minimal in the two earlier periods: 1710–1712, two (7 percent); 1749–1751, one (3.3 percent);[23] and 1774–1776, six (22 percent). Taken together, the total of intendants whose grandfathers were either in private or public financial affairs or in local office falls in the following order: 1710–1712, seven (24 percent); 1749–1751, eight (25.8 percent); and 1774–1776, fifteen (55 percent). The conclusion is clear. Among the royal intendants in the last half of the century, above all in the final two decades of the *ancien régime,* there were continually more men from families of recent moderate status still rising in society than from families long established and entrenched in the upper ranks.

Perhaps, however, the "aristocratic reaction" took the form of fathers passing on office and rank to their sons in increasing numbers. In other words, social and professional status was perpetuated within a limited span of two generations. So let us now compare the intendants' fathers in each of the three groups.

On the whole we may expect an increase of fathers in high positions. But again the relative differences from one period

[23] One grandfather in this second group was presumably a municipal official; with him included the percentage becomes 6.

to the next reveal significant changes in the recruiting patterns through the century—not, however, according to the favored assumptions of historians.

Table 10. Comparative status of the fathers of the eighteenth-century intendants sampled

Periods	Total known	Sovereign courts	Sovereign courts and Royal Council	Total in courts and Council
1710–1712	30	10 (33%)	16 (53%)	26 (86%)
1749–1751	32	8 (25%) *	12 (37%) *	20 (62%) *
1774–1776	31 †	8 (26%) ‡	9 (29%)	17 (55%) ‡

* In the second period three fathers who were in business and office, and are so categorized, held judgeships during their varied careers; with these included, the figures change to: 9 (28%) and 14 (43%), totaling 23 (71%).

† One presumed father is included in this count.

‡ In the third period one father who is categorized as a financial officer also held judicial office; with this addition, the figures change to: 9 (29%) and a total of 18 (58%).

Two conclusions may be drawn from this comparison of the intendants' fathers, as shown in Table 10. First, in each of the three periods more of the fathers of the intendants were magistrates and royal administrators than were their grandfathers. In short, there was greater co-optation within a span of two generations than over three generations. Yet this is no surprise. Second, despite these increases, the total numbers and percentages of intendants whose fathers were in the sovereign courts and especially on the Royal Council declined as the century advanced: there were fewer in the second period than in the first, and comparatively still fewer in the third period than in the second. Hence rather than tightening their grip on offices in the upper echelons of government, the high aristocracy of the robe and pen relaxed their hold, and their representation diminished in the second half of the eighteenth century, particularly during the final two decades of the *ancien régime.*

An inverse process also took place, similar to that which statistics revealed for the grandfathers. More of the intendants of Louis XV and of Louis XVI, in contrast to the intendants of Louis XIV, were sons of men who were identified with the world of finance as private businessmen, financial officers, or businessmen turned into public officers: 1710–1712, two (6.6 percent), one of whom, however, was from a long established robe family; 1749–1751, eleven (34 percent), one of whom acquired a high judicial office and two of whom entered both the courts and the Council; and 1774–1776, eight (26 percent), one of whom became a magistrate.[24]

Examination of the antecedents of the intendants—their first ancestors, grandfathers, and fathers—thus yields evidence of a gradual decrease in the course of the century in the recruitment of men from long-established families in high rank, and a gradual increase of men from newly rising families. Only in one respect do these statistics show a slight shift in the overall, predominant pattern. Among the intendants for the years 1774–1776, there was a relative increase of sons whose fathers served in the courts and in the Council, a relatively greater incidence of co-optation between fathers and sons. Among Louis XIV's intendants, there were eight more who succeeded their fathers as judges or high administrators than those who succeeded both their grandfathers and their fathers into these posts, an increase of 26 percent; there were five more among Louis XV's intendants, an increase of 15 percent; yet among Louis XVI's intendants there were ten more who followed their fathers into the sovereign courts or the royal bureaucracy than those who followed both their fathers and grandfathers into the two corps, an increase of 32 percent.[24] So far this is the sole

[24] These figures vary slightly from those that would result from comparing the figures in Tables 9 and 10. For the first period, 18 of the

evidence to corroborate the theory of an "aristocratic reaction" in the ranks of the high administration. But as shown above (Tables 8, 9, and 10), recruitment of intendants whose fathers, grandfathers, and first ancestors were magistrates and royal councilors declined absolutely both in numbers and in percentages in the second half of the century. A single contrary statistic is a slim reed with which to weave a tableau of social change and revolution in eighteenth-century France. (See Table 11 for a comparison of the origins and evolution of the families.)

Status, however, might still be perpetuated in another direction within the span of two generations (as may be seen in Table 12). The intendants as fathers might pass on their social and professional rank to their own sons, thereby forming and preserving an aristocratic elite. This did occur in the eighteenth century. Certainly social mores in the *ancien régime* encouraged and sanctioned the practice of sons succeeding to the fathers' professions as they would inherit name and wealth. Families holding government posts considered these a part of their patrimony equally as much as real property—which was true in law of venal charges although not of royal commissions—and as indispensable in maintaining their prestige and standing. And the intendants were men of their times. Since their sons could not legally inherit their positions, the fathers could groom them by educating them, setting an example for them to follow, and providing them with practical training; and they could easily obtain appointments for them with the contacts and influence they had in the administration. Hence the same names frequently recur throughout the century among the intendants. But more frequently, or less frequently?

----

19 grandfathers were succeeded as magistrates and administrators by the intendants' fathers; for the second period, the 15 grandfathers listed were all followed by the intendants' fathers into these posts; and for the third period, 7 of the 9 grandfathers were succeeded by the intendants' fathers.

Table II. A comparison of the social origins and evolution of the intendants' families in each of the three periods

Status	LOUIS XIV (1710-1712)			LOUIS XV (1749-1751)			LOUIS XVI (1774-1776)		
	First ancestor (23)	Grand-father (30)*	Father (30)	First ancestor (18)	Grand-father (31)†	Father (32)	First ancestor (19)‡	Grand-father (27)*	Father (31)§
Private persons:									
Provincial *seigneur*	1			2	2				1
Bourgeois	4			1	2		3	1	
Commerce	2			1	1		1	2	1
Finance and large business			1		1	1		2	
Peasant	1			1	2*		1	1	
Medicine	1			2	1	1	1		1
Law	1	2*	1	2	3	9	1		
Finance, business and office	1	1	1					3	3
Public officers:									
Municipal				1	1*			1	
Local judicial and administrative	1	2	1	2	1		4	2	
Local financial	1	1		1			1	3	2
Financial magistracy	6	9	10	2	8*		2	3	3
Sovereign courts						8		5*	8
Sovereign court and Royal Council	4	10	16	2	7	12	1	4	9
Secrétaire du roi									
Administrative		2		1	1	1	1	1	2§
Royal household		2	1						
Provincial or military								1	1
Ducal, princely, or royal family		1					2‡		

* One presumed grandfather.
† Three presumed grandfathers.
‡ One presumed first ancestor.
§ One presumed father.

Among the thirty intendants from 1710 to 1712, fifteen had sons who entered the royal bureaucracy; of the thirty intendants in the period 1749–1751, nine had sons who served on the Royal Council; and of the thirty-two intendants serving from 1774 to 1776, only six had sons who became high administrators. Thus, in the early eighteenth century 50 percent of the intendants were followed into administrative service by their sons; in mid-century, 28 percent; [25] and by late century, only 19 percent brought their sons into the royal administration.[26] The progression is clearly downward. Since fewer sons of intendants who were in the service in the two later periods assumed the same careers as their fathers, the high administration obviously recruited less within its own ranks.[27]

[25] If we include in the second group Moreau de Séchelles, whose nephew Moreau de Beaumont was also an intendant in that same period, the figures for the years 1749–1751 change to 10 out of 32, or 31 percent.

[26] If we include in this third group the three intendants who served during the two periods 1749–1751 and 1774–1776, and whose sons also became intendants (Bertier de Sauvigny, La Bourdonnaye de Blossac, and Guignard de Saint-Priest), then we have a proportion of 9 out of 35, or 25.7 percent, still considerably below the percentage for the first group although almost the same percentage as for the second group.

[27] A few of the intendants in these three groups had more than one son who entered administrative service. Thus the 15 intendants in the first group had a total of 18 sons in the high administration, and the 9 intendants in the second group had 10 sons; in the third group there were 6 fathers with 6 sons in the high administration (or, including the 3 intendants with sons in the high administration who served in both the second and third periods, 9 fathers with 9 sons). Moreover, although all of these sons were members of the Royal Council, served in the high administration, and belonged to the nobility of the pen, some of them rose higher than the post of provincial intendant and some of them did not rise above the rank of *maître des requêtes*. In the first group, one son became an intendant of finance, two became *prévots des marchands* in Paris, and 3 remained as *maîtres des requêtes*. In the second group, one son became the king's chancellor and keeper of the royal seals, one became an intendant of bridges and highways and

What made it appear differently, perhaps to contemporaries and to historians as well, was the more frequent practice in the second half of the century of attaching sons to their fathers' posts where they assisted as *intendants adjoints* (sometimes called *sous-intendants*). None of the sons of Louis XIV's intendants held such positions, nor did any succeed directly to their fathers' intendancies. In contrast, five of the sons of Louis XV's intendants became *intendants adjoints,* four succeeding directly as intendants to their fathers' posts; and four (or seven) sons of Louis XVI's intendants were *adjoints,* one (or four) assuming the same intendancy following their fathers, and three more probably would have had not the Revolution removed both the fathers and sons from these offices.[28] (See Table 12.)

This new post of *intendant adjoint* served a double and complementary purpose. On the one hand it was administrative: it provided direct apprenticeship in the field, in the same region where these young men were to become intendants; some indeed, though few in number, became *intendants adjoints* even in the absence of family ties to intendants in office.[29] Family interests, however, were undoubtedly the overriding reason for this innovation: a son who became his father's assistant not only gained practical training but virtually pre-empted succession to the post. Consequently the older custom of inheritance of positions in the high adminis-

---

intendant of finance, and one was a *maître des requêtes* for only one year before he died. In the third group, 3 (or 6) became provincial intendants, 3 remained with their fathers as *intendants adjoints* until 1790, and understandably, none gained higher posts since the Revolution cut short their careers. Perhaps as well the Revolution prevented more sons of the intendants in the last group from entering government service as high administrators, but this will remain forever unknown.

[28] The figures in parentheses include the sons of the 3 intendants who served during both periods, 1749–1751 and 1774–1776. In Table 12 these 3 intendants or their sons are included in the figures indicated by brackets in the third line.

[29] See above, Chapter 4.

Table 12. Succession into the high administration of sons of the intendants sampled

Years	Total	Number of intendants with sons in the high administration	Number of sons in the high administration	Sons as *intendants adjoints*	Direct succession of sons to father's intendancy
1710–1712	30	15	18	0	0
1749–1751	32	9	10 *	5	5 †
1774–1776 ‡	32 [35]	6 [9]	6 [9]	4 [7]	1 [4] + 3 §

* One of these sons was a *maîtres des requêtes* for only one year before he died in 1767.

† The son of the intendant Chaumont de la Galaizière served two years in another intendancy before joining his father as *intendant adjoint* of Lorraine and later succeeding him in this post. See above, Chapter 4.

‡ The figures in brackets include the three intendants who served during both the second and third periods, or the sons of those three intendants.

§ This represents three sons who were *adjoints* but whose careers were cut short by the Revolution.

tration became clearer and more regular, with an exact institutional framework provided for family succession. The Crown acquiesced as it had done traditionally for ages, allowing personal interests to use or even to create new administrative procedures; this was still an age when bureaucratic regularity was only being introduced, built into a system where older mores of personal loyalty and family interests still prevailed. Nevertheless, this innovation had limited impact. Within a span of time from the 1750's to 1789 the frequency of family succession in both absolute numbers and relative proportions declined slightly or remained stable; and in comparison to the early years of the century, the incidence of sons succeeding fathers in the high administration actually decreased. Although new dynasties of the pen were still forming, even more new recruits continued to be admitted. In short, the upper echelons of royal government were relatively more accessible as the monarchy drew to its end.

IV

That all the intendants were noble, and that many of them were from families in the robe and pen, should be no surprise. But do the three groups differ with regard to the antiquity of their noble lineage and the length of their families' service in the courts and on the Council? Do we find more older nobles, more older robe and pen families, among the intendants in the two later periods?

One to ten generations of noble lineage marked Louis XIV's intendants. Only one was a tenth-generation nobleman, while one was first-generation nobility; 2 intendants were second-generation nobles. The largest single group consisted of third-generation nobles, who numbered 12, followed by fourth-generation nobles numbering 5. A span of two to twelve generations of nobility characterized Louis XV's intendants. None of the intendants was himself ennobled, and only one was twelfth-generation nobility.[30] Again the largest numbers were third- and fourth-generation noblemen, between 7 and 9 for the former and 7 for the latter, so that there were some fewer third-generation nobles and slightly more fourth-generation nobles than in the first group. By mid-century many more intendants were second-generation nobles—a total of 8, plus 2 who were either second- or third-generation nobles. Among Louis XVI's intendants, noble lineage varied from one to nine generations. One intendant was himself ennobled and one claimed ninth-generation nobility, although the antiquity of the latter's noble descent remains unverified. Among these intendants in the last quarter of the century the pattern of noble lineage

[30] One was also eleventh-generation nobility in this second group. These 3 intendants in the first and second groups with 10, 11, and 12 generations of nobility were all in the same family, having a common ancestor: La Bourdonnaye.

definitely changed. Only 2 intendants were fourth-generation nobles, while 10 were third-generation nobles and between 7 to 9 were second-generation nobility. Yet in this group there were also more intendants who were fifth-generation nobles: 5 were in this category, as opposed to 3 in the first group and 3 in the second. (See Table 13 for percentages of the generations of nobility in each group.)

Table 13. A comparison of the noble lineage of the intendants in each of the three periods (in percentages)

Number of generations	Louis XIV 1710–1712	Louis XV 1749–1751	Louis XVI 1774–1776
1	3	—	3
2	7	25–32	24–31
3	40	23–29	34
4	17	23	7
5	10	9	17
6	10	6	3
7 or more	13	6	6–10

One constant factor that these figures reveal is the definite increase of second-generation noblemen in the corps: their representation rose approximately 20 percent by mid-century, and until the end of the century they continued to constitute about one quarter of the corps. The proportion of third-generation nobles among the intendants decreased 6 percent from the beginning of the century to the end, although there was an increase of 5 to 10 percent between the second and third periods. The changes among the fourth- and fifth-generation noble intendants fluctuated. There were fewer fourth-generation nobles in the corps in the last quarter of the century, although considerably more of them in the second period than in the first or third periods. As for the fifth-generation nobles, more were in the corps at the end of the century than at the beginning or in the middle of the century.

What is the sum of the evidence for believing there was an "aristocratic reaction" in the corps of intendants later in the century—a resurgence of older noble stock? Merely a 6 percent increase of fourth-generation nobles at mid-century, which was more than wiped out twenty-five years later; another 7 percent increase of fifth-generation nobles among Louis XVI's intendants; and an approximately 8 percent increase of third-generation nobles from mid-century to the end of the century. But these increases are minimal and lose significance in comparison with the approximately 20 percent increase of second-generation nobles, which remained constant, and an overall increase of approximately 10 percent among both second- and third-generation nobles in the corps during the reign of Louis XVI.

Thus under Louis XIV the intendants were predominantly third- and fourth-generation nobility; they were more evenly divided among second-, third-, and fourth-generation nobility under Louis XV; and under Louis XVI more than half of them were second- or third-generation noblemen. In sum, the mean age of their noble lineage dropped from fourth generation at the beginning of the century to third generation in the middle and at the end of the century.

To contemporaries, custom bestowed eminence upon nobles of the fourth generation and older. They were considered ancient nobility, or nobility of race. In this regard the high administration diminished in stature as the eighteenth century advanced, though not completely. From 1710 to 1712 the royal intendants were evenly divided between those who were fourth-generation nobility or more, and those of third-generation nobility or less. During the years 1749–1751, 55 percent of the corps were first- to third-generation nobles. And in the years 1774–1776, between 34 and 35 percent of the intendants had four or more generations of nobility, while 64 to 66 percent of their colleagues had less than four generations of nobility—still without the eminence which age afforded and whim decreed.

Moreover, how one obtained nobility was equally as significant as how old it was; and sometimes the means also revealed the age. Throughout the century nobility through office and service predominated: whether this nobility was attached to the office or conferred through a special grant of royal letters patent, or whether the functions performed were real or illusory. Approximately three-quarters of the families of Louis XIV's intendants had been ennobled by office; a slightly higher proportion prevailed among the families of Louis XV's intendants. Toward the end of the century ennoblement through office was virtually the single means by which the intendants' families had acquired nobility: 87 to 90 percent of the families of Louis XVI's intendants became noble in this way. Increasingly, ennoblement became systematized: more families acquired it by virtue of an ennobling office in the regular government hierarchy, and fewer through special grants honoring personal services in nonennobling posts (7 percent and 6 percent of the latter in the first and second periods, and only 3 percent in the third period). Prescriptive nobility also gradually decreased among the intendants' families. Those in the corps whose families had been able to insinuate themselves into the noble order merely by possessing a fief and living on their estates as *seigneurs* declined from 17 percent in the early part of the century, to 3 percent by mid-century, and none at the end of the century; and most of those families represented in the first and second periods had become noble two or three centuries earlier.

If nobility was acquired increasingly through office, then through which offices? Minor local office, presumably cheaper, was rarely the means for these families: one family in the second group became ennobled in that way. It was through higher office that most of the intendants' families entered the second order. Judgeships in the sovereign courts remained a steady avenue to nobility; one-fifth of the intendants' families in each of the three groups were in origin nobility of the robe, with only slight variations during the century. More than one-third of these families (37 percent) acquired their nobility in the sovereign courts during the eighteenth century—all except one through offices in the courts outside of Paris, and for that single exception the office was not in the Parlement but in the Grand Conseil.[31] Service on the Royal Council brought ennoblement to 20 percent of the families of Louis XIV's intendants. But fewer and fewer families later in the century had been ennobled that way (13 percent in the second group and 3 percent in the third group) and understandably, for such means dated back to the sixteenth and early seventeenth centuries. From the mid-seventeenth century on, the courts were the antechamber to the Council, both for noble status and professional advancement.

The charge of *secrétaire du roi,* so disdained yet desired, was the vehicle of ennoblement for the largest group of families in each period. As the century advanced, first one-quarter, then one-third, and finally almost one-half of the intendants' families removed their taint of common origins with this *savonnette à vilain.*[32] For 40 percent of these intendants, their grandfathers experienced this ritual purifica-

[31] The exception was Sénac de Meilhan, who was himself ennobled by this office. Considering that 6 of these 19 intendants served during the years 1710–1712, it would virtually be impossible for their families to acquire robe nobility in the eighteenth century; thus we may even calculate on the basis of 7 families out of 13 in the second and third groups, which would then yield a proportion higher than one-third for robe families ennobled in the eighteenth century. According to Bluche, *Les magistrats du Parlement de Paris,* 85, there was a constant proportion of 10 percent commoners among the Paris parlementarians. Thus the fathers or grandfathers of these intendants had to seek their ennobling judgeships in those provincial courts that accepted a larger proportion of commoners. See Jean Egret, "L'aristocratie parlementaire française à la fin de l'Ancien Régime," 1–11.

[32] The precise figures are: 26.6 percent of the families in the first group; 37.5 percent in the second; and from 43.7 percent to 50 percent in the last group.

tion; and for 30 percent of them—those who served Louis XV and XVI but not Louis XIV—their fathers were so cleansed. The lure of quick nobility, combined with the lucre they possessed and needed for this charge, spurred them on. Offices as *secrétaires du roi* were almost as numerous as parlementary magistracies—900 as opposed to 1,100.[33] To obtain them required neither education nor nobility, which often were needed in the Parlements, but merely money.[34] Moreover, why should they have to work their way slowly and laboriously into the nobility by becoming financial magistrates, offices which were also expensive and available most likely in a provincial bureau. Hence comparatively few of the intendants' families became noble after twenty years in the financial magistracy: none under Louis XIV, one under Louis XV (3 percent), and four under Louis XVI (13 percent).[35] Why, furthermore, should they be bothered by scorn and epithets when nobility could so easily be gained; and within two or three generations, possibly even one, their progeny would be among the greatest in government and society? Thus from mid-century on, an increasing number of men whose families recently or still were emerging from this vilest of noble origins entered the corps. This clearly indicates no "aristocratic reaction." Instead, the high administration was becoming more accessible to the newly rich who alone could afford to or would want to become *secrétaires du roi.*

Greater corporate exclusiveness is another face to the theory of an "aristocratic reaction." The courts and the bu-

---

[33] Carré, 7–9.

[34] Cf. Bluche, *Les magistrats du Parlement de Paris,* Pt. I, ch. 2.

[35] Two of the four ancestors in the third group who acquired nobility through their offices as financial magistrates dated from the seventeenth century; thus this relatively higher figure in comparison to the two earlier periods for families ennobled through financial magistracies does not indicate that this became a more frequent means of ennoblement in the eighteenth century for the families of the last group of intendants.

reaucracy provided fruitful recruiting grounds for their own members; co-optation had been and continued to be customary, since this satisfied family interests and corporate spirit. Did this increase in the eighteenth century, making the high administration more rigidly exclusive? Did it become increasingly indispensable for candidates to have family membership in the magistracy and the administration—and the older the membership, the more easily one entered the Council?

The oldest lineage in the robe and pen was held by an intendant of Louis XIV: he was the ninth of his family in the courts and the eighth to serve on the Council. For the intendants of Louis XV, none was older than sixth-generation robe and pen. For Louis XVI's intendants, the oldest in the magistracy was seventh generation and in the administration sixth generation. The single evidence for greater recruitment of older robe or pen stock among the intendants later in the eighteenth century was the appearance of two intendants during the years 1774–1776 whose families first entered the sovereign courts seven generations previously; but these two constituted a mere 6.6 percent of the corps.

All other evidence points to the opposite conclusion: in the periods of Louis XV and Louis XVI there was an overall increase of intendants who were first-, second-, and third-generation members of families in the judiciary and the bureaucracy. Specifically, under Louis XIV, 55 percent of the intendants were first- to third-generation members of the robe, and only one of the group was first generation; under Louis XV, 75 percent of the corps were first- to third-generation robe, and 25 percent of the group were first generation; and under Louis XVI, 76 percent were first- to third-generation robe, 30 percent of them being first generation. The balance shifted even more decisively in the two later periods. More than half of the intendants serving Louis XV and two-thirds serving Louis XVI were only the first or second members of their families to be in the magistracy, while one-third who served Louis XIV were first or second generation. As for their lineage in the administrative nobility, similar changes occurred. Intendants who were first- to third-generation members of the pen predominated and increased throughout the century: 70 percent under Louis XIV; 85 percent under Louis XV; and 89 percent under Louis XVI. Most significantly, those who were the first in their families to enter the Council—whose forebears never had served the Crown in the high administration—increased constantly until they alone predominated in the corps: from one-third first-generation administrators at the beginning of the century, to one-half at mid-century, and more than two-thirds at the end of the century.[36] (See Table 14.)

Hence the upper ranks of the royal government were becoming less exclusive, recruiting fewer members of old-stock robe and pen families; they were indeed becoming more accessible as newer members of the robe and the pen increasingly composed the corps of provincial intendants. In sum, as the mean age of nobility among the intendants dropped from fourth generation under Louis XIV to third generation under Louis XV and XVI, so the mean age of robe stock dropped from third generation at the beginning of the century to second generation in the middle and last quarter of the century, and the mean age in the pen dropped from second generation in 1710–1712 to first generation by 1750, where it remained during the last decades of the monarchy.

More new nobles, more newer members of the robe and the pen: in short, more "new men" served the Crown as provincial intendants in the second half of the eighteenth century. Less than one-third (30 percent) of the intendants under Louis XIV came from families that rose in society within one to three generations previously; almost one-half

[36] The exact figures are: 1710–1712, 33 percent; 1749–1751, 53 percent; and 1774–76, 69 percent.

Table 14. A comparison of the intendants' lineage in the nobility, robe, and pen in each of the three periods

Period	Lineage	Generations											
		1	2	3	4	5	6	7	8	9	10	11	12
Louis XIV 1710–1712	Nobility	1	2	12	5	3	3		2	1	1		
	Robe	1	9*	6	6	3	3			1			
	Pen	11	7	4	4	2	1		1				
Louis XV 1749–1751	Nobility†		8 + 2‡	7	7	3	2					1	1
	Robe	8	10	6	3	3	2						
	Pen	17	6	4	1	3§	1						
Louis XVI 1774–1776	Nobility†	1	8 + 1‖	10	2	5	1	2		1#			
	Robe**	9	11*	3††	4‡‡		1	2§§					
	Pen	22	5	1	2		2						

* One of these ancestors was an uncle.
† The noble lineage of one intendant is unknown.
‡ These 2 intendants were either 2nd- or 3rd-generation nobles.
§ One family was not in the high administration for five successive generations.
‖ The noble lineage of one family is undocumented.
The noble lineage of this one family is undocumented.
** The lineage in the robe of one intendant is unknown.
†† Only two successive generations in the robe for one family.
‡‡ The lineage in the robe of one family is undocumented.
§§ These 2 families were not in the robe for 7 successive generations.

(47 percent) of Louis XV's intendants owed their fortune to their fathers or grandfathers; and under Louis XVI almost two-thirds of the corps (from 60 percent to 66 percent) consisted of "new men." (See Table 15.)

Table 15. A comparison of the intendants' family status

Classification	Louis XIV 1710–1712 *	Louis XV 1749–1751	Louis XVI 1774–1776 *
Old families			
High robe and pen:			
3 generations or more	12	3	3
2 generations or less	0	8	4
High robe	1	4	1 †
Medium robe	7	2	2
New families			
Gradual ascension	6	7	14
Rapid ascension	3	8	7 ‡

* One exception to these classifications.
† Undocumented.
‡ One undocumented.

In the early part of the century, few of the "new men" came from families that rose rapidly and through their own efforts; two of these three intendants owed their fortune and their appointments to prominent relatives in the ministry—Chauvelin to his namesake, and Bernage to d'Argenson.[37] The typical "new man" among Louis XIV's intendants was the grandson or great-grandson of a merchant, whose father or grandfather in turn had obtained office and began the family's gradual rise through the ranks of the sovereign courts and the Royal Council. By mid-century the typical "new man" in the corps radically differed. He was the son of a wealthy parvenu who accumulated enormous riches

[37] See pp. 169–170 and p. 171 above for the family histories of these two intendants, Chauvelin and Bernage.

through speculation, tax farming, or supplying government troops, and then proceeded to remove the grossness of his fortune by quickly purchasing an office conferring nobility or even magisterial honor; for only a few of these "new" intendants did the grandfather begin the family's rise. Thus the "new man" who became Louis XV's intendant might have remained a simple shopkeeper, local officer, or even prosperous businessman, as had his father or grandfather before him, had not the War of the Spanish Succession and the subsequent Law "system" presented unparalleled opportunities for riches and success.

Politics, war, and business cycles intervened less to form the typical "new man" among the intendants in the last quarter of the century. Louis XVI had the most "new men" in his corps, but the greater proportion of them were from families that rose gradually and through traditional ways.[38] From comfortable bourgeois circumstances as landowner or local officer, the grandfather obtained an ennobling charge, and he or the father then advanced in the sovereign-court hierarchy. Certainly wealth enabled such a family to raise itself in society, but more than one generation of forebears built up the family's fortune, and one or two generations of officeholders dissimulated their common origins and their new wealth. Still present among these "new men," though less typical in this last period, was the scion of a family made wealthy in business and finance; the grandfather more often than the father then turned to office and nobility, and the grandson entered the high administration.

V

All the evidence concerning the intendants points to a single conclusion: there was no "aristocratic reaction" in the

---

[38] This type constituted about 44 percent of the "new men" in the corps who, during the years 1774–1776, totaled 60 to 66 percent of the intendants.

high administration of the French monarchy in the later eighteenth century. The reverse was true: the highest administrative posts in the royal government were increasingly accessible to men from families of recent modest origin, wealthy, newly ennobled, and new to the courts and the Council.[39] Hence we may reverse the order of Saint-Simon's characterization and current historiographical opinion. At the beginning of the eighteenth century more of Louis XIV's intendants were of older stock in the nobility, the robe, and the pen, with longer-established high standing in society. At the end of the eighteenth century more of Louis XVI's intendants were newer to the nobility and to the robe and pen, and they were still in the process of being assimilated and accepted in the highest ranks of the social hierarchy.

The high administration was an amalgam for older and new families with varying degrees of noble lineage and varying periods in judicial and administrative office; in this society of the *noblesse de la plume* newer recruits mixed with colleagues whose families had older nobility and longer service as sovereign-court magistrates and royal administrators. Service to the king on the Council and in the provinces therefore provided increasing opportunities for social mobility in eighteenth-century France. Status, in the *ancien régime,* was not fixed forever by birth; ability and money enabled men to rise to the top, and more men did so as the end approached for this society and government. It was not yet the era of careers open only to talent—nor was that era born even after Napoleon proclaimed it. But already and

[39] François Bluche, in his article "L'origine sociale du personnel ministériel français au XVIIIe siècle," *Bulletin de la Société d'Histoire Moderne,* 12e série, No. 1 (Jan.–Feb. 1957) , 9–13, also affirms that there was no "aristocratic reaction" within the ranks of royal ministers in the later eighteenth century. However, he does not come to the same conclusion as the above: that more nobles and judges of recent vintage, more "new men," served the king as ministers just as they did as provincial intendants.

increasingly, Guizot's advice to nineteenth-century Frenchmen aspiring to vote would have been appropriate counsel for eighteenth-century Frenchmen seeking nobility and office, aiming ultimately for the highest posts in government and the highest standing in society: "Enrichissez-vous!"

CONCLUSION

Some Thoughts on the *Ancien Régime* and the French Revolution

I

The men who governed the provinces of France in the eighteenth century, the royal intendants, were an elite in a double sense. They were an elite corps within the ranks of the royal administration, and they were an elite group within the hierarchy of French society. Nobility of the pen they were termed: noblemen who were administrative agents, superior moreover as the direct representatives of royal sovereignty.

Royal government in the last century of the *ancien régime* was quasi-bureaucratic.[1] Intendants owed their allegiance to the Crown and served the state and people of France, as much as or more than they gave their loyalty to the person of the king. Although the structure of royal government was a maze of newer and older institutions and offices whose functions and powers often overlapped and sometimes competed, authority and responsibility within the central administration of the monarchy were hierarchically ordered. Jurisdictional confusion and conflicts arose, but they were between the intendants and the parlements or the provincial estates; clashes among ministers and intendants were the result of political rivalries rather than of administrative incoherence. Intendants knew who commanded them, and whom they

---

[1] Cf. H. H. Gerth and C. Wright Mills, eds., *From Max Weber: Essays in Sociology* (New York, 1958), 196–244.

commanded. The king and ministers stood above them and ruled over them within the central administration. In the provinces they were surpassed by no one: within each *généralité* the intendant was the personal embodiment of the monarch's sovereignty and the supreme executor of the Crown's will.[2]

Thus the intendants were near the summit of power in royal government. Men who attained these places had qualified for them: they were tested and proven. True, there were no formal examinations to determine merit; true, as well, personal influence and connections gained preferment; and, equally so, wealth was a *sine qua non* for an administrative system that recruited venal officers. Occasionally ineffectual, mediocre administrators may be sighted at work in the provinces, accomplishing little, merely serving time, even abdicating their functions and authority to aggressive Parlements. Yet one generalization holds true: the intendants were competent men with the abilities and outlook necessary for their administrative tasks, and they fulfilled their responsibility for governing the provinces in the interests of the Crown and with concern for the people who lived there. Formal education at school, family tradition exemplified by forebears in royal service, practical training in the courts, and above all, experience and indoctrination through their work on the Royal Council had prepared them. Wealth and influence without the requisite training and talents could make few men royal intendants, but together they opened the way for entrance into and advancement within the administration. Increasingly in the course of the century, men became intendants even if they did not have the most esteemed origins and the highest standing, because the Crown sought, accepted, and promoted men of talent.

[2] The exceptions to this were the *pays d'états,* where much administrative authority was embodied in the provincial estates; nevertheless, the intendants were still the supreme representatives of royal sovereignty before these estates.

Social esteem capped professional achievement: they were eminent in society because they represented royal sovereignty. For some among them their position as intendant further raised their standing in society, but most enjoyed high status even before becoming intendants; and prior to their tenure in the provinces all were legally noblemen.

By their personal rank and family status, the intendants were of the nobility—some of ancient lineage, others of more recent vintage. Nobility, in short, was not an immutable state, an order fixed in number or a quality determined only by birth.[3] The intendants' ancestors had obtained their nobility through various means, especially through ennobling venal offices which made them sovereign-court magistrates or *secrétaires du roi*. These forebears had been landowners, merchants, minor local officers, before they became prestigious royal officers and privileged noblemen. Thus, professional functions transmitted and elevated social status in the *ancien régime*. In the eighteenth century, wealth more often and more easily promoted social advancement. More commoners amassed great riches from war contracts, tax farming, and speculation or business investments; and with their money they purchased offices and acquired nobility.

Nobility was the goal. Once ennobled, the individual and his family were totally transformed in status, deportment, and outlook. Within three generations his heirs were assimilated, and little distinction remained between them and nobles of older lineage. Thus the legal order of nobility remained constant but its membership was in flux: older families died out, became impecunious, or led leisurely lives, occasionally engaging in public service; newer members with talent, perseverance, and wealth gradually moved up into the noble order. The second estate, in short, was an amalgam where the old and the new ultimately coalesced.

[3] See, for example, Marcel Reinhard, "Elite et noblesse dans la seconde moitié du XVIIIe siècle," *Revue d'Histoire Moderne et Contemporaine*, III (1956), 5–37.

The crucible, at all times, was the royal government. Commoners continued, in the eighteenth century, to buy a variety of offices that conferred nobility, and with an expanding economy providing more opportunities to gain wealth more commoners could obtain ennoblement. Moreover, the central bureaucracy expanded as well: the Crown, assuming more social responsibilities, required a greater number of administrators with specialized knowledge. Thus more men became royal agents, and if they demonstrated sufficient diligence and competence they rose in the service. Eventually, as more recruits entered the government, became noble, and advanced in the administrative and social hierarchies, nobility became not more restricted and exclusive but more widespread; and a greater number of newer nobles held the highest posts under the Crown.

Royal government and nobility therefore nourished each other in the last century of the *ancien régime,* increasingly so as the Bourbon monarchy and aristocratic society drew closer to their end. The position and role of the royal intendants in the eighteenth century exemplify this process. These men formed the governing class, an administrative nobility of newer and older royal servants and noblemen, which was both socially predominant and politically powerful. Yet although they were noble, their primary allegiance was and remained to the Crown: their training, experience, and indoctrination as *maîtres des requêtes* on the Royal Council had so molded them.

II

The French Revolution looms as the Sinai of French history: events and developments that preceded are believed to have led up to this climax, and much that followed stemmed from that dramatic event. So the three fundamental features of the *ancien régime* are viewed as the underlying causes of the Revolution: feudalism, absolutism, and aristocracy. The first of these is not germane to the present study; moreover,

Alfred Cobban has effectively challenged the argument that the Revolution was an attempt by the commercial and industrial *bourgeoisie* to overthrow the encumbering remains of the feudal system, whether seigneurial fees and rights of landholding or economic controls on business activity.[4] The evidence revealed in the present book and the conclusions that may be drawn bear upon the two remaining *bêtes noires:* absolute government and aristocratic society.

The argument that royal absolutism made the Revolution possible, necessary, or inevitable rests upon several points of view. According to one interpretation, Frenchmen rose against despotism in an effort to establish representative, constitutional government and to secure their liberties. How valid is this? Throughout the history of the monarchy every effort at centralization was criticized and opposed by those who lost political or administrative power: feudal vassals, tax agents from the local *élus* to the provincial treasurers- and receivers-general, and sovereign-court magistrates. In the eighteenth century the most popular and evocative political epithet used in reference to the Crown was "ministerial despotism." In one sense the argument that the Revolution was an attack against absolutism is appropriate. As Lefebvre has shown, the Revolution in 1789 had its beginnings in 1787 and 1788 when the nobility, led by the Paris Parlement, launched a final campaign to curtail royal powers—but their explicit purpose was to increase the powers of the sovereign courts or of a reconvened Estates-General where the Second Estate would prevail. In short, their design was to transfer power from the Crown and its agents to the nobility and its institutions.[5]

In other ways as well the interpretation of the Revolution as an attack against absolutism or despotism is overdrawn. Tocqueville provides authority for the view that the strong

[4] Alfred Cobban, *The Social Interpretation of the French Revolution* (Cambridge, Eng., 1964), especially chs. 4–6.
[5] In addition to the general histories of the Revolution by Lefebvre, see also Egret, *La pré-Révolution française, passim.*

control exerted by the central government through the intendants reduced provincial life to silence—to cultural sterility and political impotence.[6] In 1789, therefore, Frenchmen rose to regain former liberties and to assert new rights and principles. Subsequent studies of the intendants and of provincial life, however, reveal a different image: the royal *tutelle* was not total. Provincial organs, the parlements and estates, and municipal governments remained vocal and active, even aggressive and obstructionist, making their ideas, interests, and influence felt although they were no longer fully autonomous. Cultural life beyond Paris remained vigorous; nobles and bourgeois in the provinces engaged in writing, debating, and scientific experimentation, and founded and participated in numerous societies and academies.[7] Moreover, the monarchy had anticipated the desire of the nobles and notables to have representative institutions through which they might play a role in provincial government: beginning in 1787 provincial assemblies were established, and in these final two years of the monarchy the intendants ceded a number of their functions to the new institutions.[8] Yet the question of royal, ministerial, or bureaucratic despotism

[6] Cf. Alexis de Tocqueville, *L'ancien régime et la révolution* (7th ed., 2 vols.; Gallimard, Paris, 1952), I, 112, 118–19, 121–22, 123–26, 132, 135, 180–81, 245.

[7] Cf. Ardascheff, *Les intendants de province sous Louis XVI, passim;* Maurice Bordes, "Les intendants de Louis XV," *Revue Historique,* CCXXIII (Jan.–Mar. 1960), 45–62, and *D'Étigny et l'Administration de l'Intendance d'Auch (1751–1767)* (2 vols.; Auch, 1957), II, 917–36; Charles Dartique-Peyron, *Dupré de Saint-Maur et le problème des corvées; le conflit entre l'intendant de Guyenne el le parlement de Bordeaux, 1776–1785* (Mont-de-Marsan, 1936); François Dumas, *La généralité de Tours au XVIIIe siècle; administration de l'intendant De Cluzel, 1766–1783* (Paris, 1894); Franklin L. Ford, *Strasbourg in Transition, 1648–1789* (Cambridge, Mass., 1958); Robert Forster, *The Nobility of Toulouse in the Eighteenth Century* (Baltimore, Md., 1960); Fréville, *L'Intendance de Bretagne, passim;* Lhéritier, *L'intendant Tourny, passim;* and Temple, "French Towns during the Ancien Régime," 20–23, 25.

[8] Egret, ch. 3.

transcends the limits of this study, since I have not followed the intendants into the provinces to examine their administrative work and political role.

There is truth to the argument of a revolt against absolutism to establish constitutional government, and this is a matter that historians should seek to clarify. Some Frenchmen (their precise status and number remain uncertain, as do their exact motives) held vague ideas of constitutionalism nourished by the ideas of the *philosophes* and by the example of England or America. They wanted the nation, represented in a legislative body, to participate in the actual making of laws; kingship would remain, though sovereignty would be shared, and distinctions of rank would afford merely social pre-eminence without conferring greater political power on any order. The crisis of 1787 and 1788 presented them with an opportunity to realize their program, and it was this more limited group with their equally limited ideas which came to prevail in 1789, carrying the rest of the nation along with them; [9] later on they too would be carried beyond their original goal by the unanticipated pressure of events.

A second interpretation of the Revolution is that the absolute, centralized government of the old monarchy was inefficient, decrepit, in short falling apart: it had to be replaced by something new and better. Consequently the Revolution came about and began the work of reconstruction which Napoleon completed. With the eyes of modern men we may look back to an earlier period, view its medley of overlapping jurisdictions and competing institutions that each age had added to, wonder how this ramshackle structure could ever work, and conclude that all was chaos and that the

[9] See Philippe Sagnac, *La formation de la société française moderne, 1661–1789* (2 vols.; Paris, 1945–46), II, 296–99; Egret, ch. 4 *passim*, 276–78, 325–37, 351–61; and Elizabeth L. Eisenstein, "Who Intervened in 1788? A Commentary on 'The Coming of the French Revolution,'" *American Historical Review*, LXXI (Oct. 1965), 77–103.

government had to be renovated and rationalized.[10] Yet the absence of clearly articulated administrative and judicial units does not mean that the institutions that existed and the men who served them were *ipso facto* bad or ineffectual: we should not mistake the skeleton for the organism. The monarchy had introduced the intendants for the purpose of providing more honest and efficient government, and on the whole their administrative performance was honest and efficient. Moreover, in the course of the eighteenth century and particularly in the last few decades the intendants initiated reforms to improve the quality of government and the conditions of life of the French people.[11] True, inefficiency,

[10] Cf. Lefebvre, 19: "The boundaries of administrative, judicial, financial and ecclesiastical districts overlapped each other in chaos." Albert Soboul, at a later date, viewed the system of royal government even more critically: "L'organisation de l'Etat ne s'est guère ameliorée au cours du XVIII° siècle, Louis XVI gouvernant et administrant à peu de chose près avec les mêmes institutions que son aïeul Louis XIV. . . . Les multiples circonscriptions administratives, fiscales, judiciaires, religieuses se chevauchent en un chaos indescriptible" ("De l'ancien régime à l'Empire: problème national et réalités sociales," *L'Information Historique,* No. 2 [Mar.–Apr. 1960], 60. Within two years Soboul wrote *Précis d'Histoire de la Révolution Française* (Paris, 1962). The same critical tone persists in his general comments on royal government, although his concrete description of its structure and operation reveals a somewhat more subtle appreciation of its work as well as its weaknesses (see ch. 2). This shift in attitude is summed up in a concluding phrase (p. 77): ". . . la complexité et parfois le chaos de l'administration. . . ." To Soboul, now, the monarchy had a complex structure that was only sometimes chaotic; and, as he stated on an earlier page (p. 69), the government even provided some "bienfaits réels."

[11] For a general survey of this aspect of the intendants' administration, see Ardascheff, *passim* and Maurice Bordes, "Les intendants eclairés de la fin de l'ancien régime," *Revue d'Histoire Economique et Sociale,* XXXIX (1961), 57–83. Additional accounts of the accomplishments of royal government in the eighteenth century may be found in special studies of individual intendants or intendancies; see the bibliography for a listing of these works. A more up-to-date and just evaluation of the central royal administration may be found in J. F. Bosher, "French

dishonesty, and selfishness characterized many government officials and their practices, but these faults were least common among the provincial intendants. Further probing of this question, however, would again take us beyond the bounds of this study.

A variation of the argument that the government of the *ancien régime* was incompetent relates to its personnel rather than its institutions. Certain social critics believe that the monarchy's governing elite had degenerated; that more capable rulers lay hidden in the body of French society, unknown or ignored, to be given the opportunity to prove their superiority only during the years of the Revolution and in post-Revolution France.[12] This interpretation may be questioned as it applies to the intendants. To be sure, in any society some individuals who attain and exercise power may not have the most intelligence and talent, or the best understanding of what government requires and the people need. Nevertheless, to run a government efficiently and rationally, and to confront and cope with the problems of a society, require specific abilities that may be acquired through a distinct process of training. The intendants of the eighteenth century who daily exercised the powers of government had undergone such training before assuming office. As *maîtres des requêtes* on the king's Council they had learned the primary functions of government; they had practical experience in performing the tasks of administration, justice, and finance that were necessary to carry out the economic and

Administration and Public Finance in Their European Setting," 565–91, and Douglas Dakin, "The Breakdown of the Old Régime in France," 592–617, in *The New Cambridge Modern History,* VIII (*The American and French Revolutions, 1763–93,* ed. A. Goodwin [Cambridge, Eng., 1965]) , and M. Antoine, "Le Conseil du Roi sous Louis XV," *Congrès Sciences Historiques,* VII (Rome, 1955) , 259–61.

[12] See Ford, *Robe and Sword,* 249–50, for his references to Pareto on this matter, and also the book by a student of Pareto, Marie Kolabinska, *La circulation des élites en France: Étude historique depuis la fin du XIᵉ siècle jusqu'à la Grande Révolution* (Lausanne, 1912) , 109–11.

social programs the Crown undertook during this century. Indeed, individual intendants often initiated policies which were then extended throughout the nation. These men had more than the technical proficiency required for good administration. From their experience on the Royal Council they also acquired a distinct political outlook which enabled them to identify the Crown's interests with the needs of the king's subjects, thereby transcending the narrow outlook and particular interests of any single class, including their own corporate group, the robe, and their own order, the nobility. This working philosophy was indispensable for good governance.[13]

Two criticisms of the aristocracy in eighteenth-century France and of their responsibility for the Revolution are relevant to this study. On the one hand they are accused of being a parasitic group—some living lavishly or languor-

[13] See Cobban, 140, 144, 149, 170, for fleeting and indirect references to this aspect of the *ancien régime* government. See also the titles listed in n. 11 above. That absolute royal government in France in the last century and a half of its existence was *sui generis* is clearly acknowledged by Friedrich Engels in his book *The Origin of the Family, Private Property and the State*, Ernest Untermann, trans. (Chicago, 1902), 108–109: "The state is the result of the desire to keep down class conflicts. But having arisen amid these conflicts, it is as a rule the state of the most powerful economic class that by force of its economic supremacy becomes also the ruling political class and thus acquires new means of subduing and exploiting the oppressed masses. The antique state was, therefore, the state of the slave owners for the purpose of holding the slaves in check. The feudal state was the organ of the nobility for the oppression of the serfs and dependent farmers. The modern representative state is the tool of the capitalist exploiters of wage labor. *At certain periods it occurs exceptionally that the struggling classes balance each other so nearly that the public power gains a certain degree of independence by posing as the mediator between them. The absolute monarchy of the seventeenth and eighteenth century was in such a position, balancing the nobles and the burghers against one another. So was the Bonapartism of the first, and still more of the second, empire, playing the proletariat against the bourgeoisie and vice versa.*" (Italics mine.)

ously, many caught in dire poverty, but all clinging to their privileges and contributing nothing essential or creative to their society, hence deserving to be overthrown. This is a variation of the theme of Pareto's degenerate elite or the Marxists' nonproductive class, although it was given its initial expression by Tocqueville. On the other hand, French society is viewed as becoming increasingly rigid and the government more exclusive as the aristocracy closed itself to newcomers and older nobles pre-empted important public offices: this is the theory of the "aristocratic reaction" in the late eighteenth century.[14] Is either description adequate to characterize the nobility, and by extension to analyze the society of the *ancien régime?* By highlighting what are believed to be key problems of pre-Revolution France, these interpretations implicitly assign some of the causes of the Revolution. Are these arguments valid? Let us examine them.

The image of the parasitic nobleman is the product of a limited view of French history and society. From the time Louis XIV brought the great and wealthy nobles to Versailles, according to this interpretation, the high nobility did nothing but live at court and absorb itself in petty etiquette or palace revels, while in the countryside the *gentilshommes* lived on meager resources, shorn of political power and social prestige, and therefore no longer performed the role of natural leaders.[15] Yet the French nobility was not composed

[14] Although usually presented separately, these two arguments are sometimes joined; cf. Soboul, *Précis*, 22–26. One may question the logical grounds of Soboul's argument. By its nature how may a parasitic group function as government officials or monopolize political power? In short, one should be wary of attributing the traits of smaller groups within the nobility to the entire order, and then using this description to interpret the causes of the Revolution.

[15] In origin this image is found in Tocqueville, I, 39, 178–79. Yet it persists in contemporary histories as well: cf. Soboul, 22–26, and J. O. Lindsay, "The Social Classes and the Foundation of the States," *The New Cambridge Modern History,* VII (*The Old Régime, 1713–63*), ed.

solely of the two extremes: the great court nobility and the impecunious rural *hobereaux.* Louis XV and Louis XVI neither attracted their high nobles nor compelled them to reside under their gaze. Noblemen lived in cities, towns, and on their country estates; they managed their lands and their financial or business investments; [16] they organized and were active in learned societies; and above all they were the high judges, financial officers, superior administrative officials, and royal ministers. To paraphrase John Law, the kingdom of France was ruled by thirty-two noblemen: the provincial intendants, who worked diligently and served responsibly. The French nobility in the *ancien régime* had faults which helped to bring on the Revolution in 1789, but certainly indolence was not one of them. For some, the judges in the Parlements particularly, the reverse was true: they sought to rule too much.

The theory of the "aristocratic reaction" is more modern and fashionable, combining sociology and politics to explain history: an upper class exclusive and grasping, middle and lower classes resentful and demanding provide the archety-

---

J. O. Lindsay (Cambridge, Eng., 1963), 55. Ironically, even Forster, whose aim was to show that not all *gentilshommes campagnards* were indigent but that some were wealthy and businesslike in their financial affairs, nevertheless perpetuates the image of the parasitic noble by contrasting his enterprising and diligent nobles of Toulouse with the "court fops" in Paris and Versailles; cf. his *Nobility of Toulouse,* 152–55.
[16] Cf. Ford, *Robe and Sword,* ch. 8; Bluche, *Les magistrats du Parlement de Paris,* Pt. II; J. McManners, "France," *The European Nobility in the Eighteenth Century,* Goodwin ed., 22–42; Forster, *Nobility of Toulouse, passim,* and "The Provincial Noble: A Reappraisal," *American Historical Review,* LXVIII (Apr. 1963), 681–91; Guy Richard, "Les corporations et la noblesse commerçante en France au XVIII° siècle," *L'Information Historique,* No. 5 (1957), 185–89, and "Un essai d'adaptation sociale à une nouvelle structure économique: La noblesse de France et les sociétés par actions à la fin du XVIII° siècle," *Revue d'Histoire Economique et Sociale,* XLI (1962), 484–523; and George V. Taylor, "Types of Capitalism in Eighteenth-Century France," *English Historical Review,* LXXIX (July 1964), 496–97.

pal conditions for revolution.[17] But does this explain the circumstances in pre-Revolution France? Do facts confirm the theory—any or all of it?

Cobban has provided some evidence that the "feudal reaction" in the countryside was the work not only of noblemen but also of many bourgeois who were profit-making landowners or farmers of seigneurial rents and fees.[18] Moreover, to term all these activities "feudal" is somewhat inaccurate. Nobles and commoners who were landowners, and therefore *seigneurs,* rediscovered and racked up old rents and fees; but also, and increasingly in the later eighteenth century, these same noble and bourgeois landowners introduced new business methods and sought to convert their estates into large-scale enterprises, selling their farm produce, lumber, and mineral deposits on the market for profit.[19] Ironically it was the intrusion of new capitalist methods rather than the resurrection of feudalism that aroused the hostility of the peasantry.

As it applies to the pattern of recruitment for government service, the argument for an "aristocratic reaction" again falls short. François Bluche has studied the secretaries of state of Louis XIV, the royal ministers in the eighteenth

[17] This interpretation is the theme of Elinor G. Barber's *The Bourgeoisie in 18th Century France* (Princeton, N.J., 1955), chs. 6, 7. Within a more rigid Marxist setting this theme pervades not only Soboul's *Précis,* ch. 1, but also Ernest Labrousse's view of pre-Revolution France. Cf. the latter's, "La Société du XVIIIe siècle devant la Révolution," in Roland Mousnier, Ernest Labrousse, and Marc Bouloiseau, *Le XVIIIe Siècle: L'Epoque des 'Lumières' (1715–1815),* Vol. V of *Histoire Générale des Civilisations,* ed. Maurice Crouzet (7 vols.; Paris, 1959), Pt. II, Bk. I, 345–62.

[18] Cf. Cobban, ch. 5.

[19] Cf. *ibid.;* Ford, *Robe and Sword,* 165–69; Forster, *Nobility of Toulouse,* chs. 2–4; Georges Lefebvre, "The French Revolution and the Peasants," in *The Economic Origins of the French Revolution: Poverty or Prosperity?,* ed. Ralph W. Greenlaw (Boston, 1958), 78–83; J. McManners, "France," *passim;* and McManners, *French Ecclesiastical Society under the Ancien Régime* (Manchester, Eng., 1960), 216.

century, and the judges in the Paris Parlement between 1715 and 1771 to determine whether the nobility became more predominant in those offices. He concludes that Louis XIV's secretaries of state were nobles, men from families ennobled in the main through office; that all but three royal ministers between 1718 and 1789 were noblemen; and that all but 10 percent of the Paris parlementarians were noble from the end of Louis XIV's reign to the temporary suppression of the court in 1771.[20] Furthermore, the re-establishment of the courts in 1774 did not inaugurate a new period of greater aristocratic exclusiveness in the magistracy, according to the evidence presented by Jean Egret. Men new to the courts, outside the circle of established parlementary or more broadly judicial families, still gained access to the Parlements: half or more of the new judges in six of the courts, and one-third to one-seventh in four of them, while only five courts accepted very few or no new recruits. Most of these new magistrates, to be sure, were themselves noblemen, but they or their families had been ennobled only recently— during the eighteenth century.[21] Hence, individuals and families were still rising in the social and judicial hierarchies throughout the eighteenth century and during the last decade and a half; yet all during the century as at all times the nobility predominated among the royal ministers and the sovereign-court judges with no increase in their proportion. Thus, without an upsurge of aristocratic representation there could be no "aristocratic reaction" affecting recruitment into these two ranks.

The pattern of recruitment of provincial intendants in the eighteenth century reveals similar yet significantly different features. Again throughout the century noblemen predomi-

---

[20] Cf. Bluche, "L'origine sociale des secrétaires d'état de Louis XIV (1661–1715)," *Bulletin de la Société d'Etude du XVIIᵉ Siècle,* Nos. 42–43 (Paris, 1959), 8–22; "L'origine social du personnel ministériel," 12; and *Les magistrats du Parlement de Paris,* 82–85.

[21] Egret, "L'aristocratie parlementaire française à la fin de l'ancien régime," 1–15, and *La pré-Révolution française,* 206–207.

nated: indeed all the intendants were noble, those serving Louis XIV as well as those serving Louis XVI. But a change did occur. A comparison of the three groups of intendants studied in this book reveals that more new nobles—men from families recently risen in society—were in the corps at mid-century and still more during the reign of the last Bourbon king. Hence the high administration remained aristocratic yet became more open rather than more exclusive.[22]

The army and the Church, as well as the courts and the high administration, are believed also to have become tighter aristocratic enclaves during the eighteenth century, with the famous edict of 1781 requiring four generations of nobility for army officers being the victorious culmination of this policy. Yet misconceptions and exaggerations also characterize these interpretations, and the truth seems to be otherwise according to more recent and more detailed studies. The character of social recruitment into the Church, specifically of bishops, apparently did not change radically from the late seventeenth century to the late eighteenth century. Nobles held most of these high offices throughout; and when ecclesiasts were chosen, the question was less whether they were commoners or nobles than whether they were Jansenists or not, those with pro-Jansenist and anti-Jesuit sympathies being screened out.[23] With the military the problem is more

[22] Unfortunately Bluche does not compare the age of noble lineage among the Paris parlementarians during the years 1715–1771, so whether there were more or fewer older nobles remains unknown. Neither do the figures presented by Egret permit any precise conclusions on this question.

[23] Norman Ravitch, "Robe and Sword in the Recruitment of French Bishops," *Catholic Historical Review* (Jan. 1965), 494–508, and *Sword and Mitre: Government and Episcopate in France and England in the Age of Aristocracy* (Paris, 1966), ch. 2. Ravitch also provides statistical evidence for the increased proportion of nobles of the sword within the overwhelmingly noble French episcopate. As he himself indicates, however, the main reasons for this was the Crown's desire to provide the poorer nobles with a secure livelihood and the Church's suspicion of pro-Jansenism among nobles from parlementary families (see *Sword*

complicated, but certain leading features may be discerned.[24] Even under Louis XIV, nobles of varied lineage overwhelmingly predominated in the officer corps, yet the small proportion of bourgeois officers persisted until the end of the *ancien régime*. Not even the edict of 1781 eliminated those commoners who were already officers or prevented a few others from rising in the ranks. The technical branches, such as the artillery and engineering corps which required specialized skills, remained open to those who met the requirements; and even the infantry and cavalry accepted as officers *roturiers* who had gained military experience in the ranks or were trained in the military schools. The offensive that the government and the lesser military nobility launched seemingly against commoners was not directed at their status but against two other grievances which the *bourgeoisie* only partly embodied. Venality was the evil for the poor country nobility of the sword, and lack of military professionalism, of skills and dedication, was the major abuse in the view of royal ministers, the two problems being connected. The purchase of officers' commissions favored the wealthy—the high *bourgeoisie* and especially the court nobility—who could rise quickly even without sufficient training or experience, or serious application to their military duties. The country no-

and Mitre, 52 and 75–76). One further comment may be in order. His definition of "noble of the sword" is broad and the genealogical works he used (apart from Bluche) are not absolutely reliable (see *ibid.*, 70–71), so that one hesitates to accept all his conclusions as final.

[24] For the following see Carré, 120–24; Alfred Cobban, *A History of Modern France* (London, 1957), I, 105; André Corvisier, "Les généraux de Louis XIV et leur origine sociale," *Bulletin de la Société d'Etude du XVIIe Siècle*, Nos. 42–43 (Paris, 1959), 38–43, and *L'armée française de la fin du XVIIe siècle au ministère du Choiseul: Le soldat*, I, 135–40, 480–84, and II, 955, 982; Egret, *La pré-Révolution française*, 87–94; Emile G. Léonard, *L'armée et ses problèmes au XVIIIe siècle* (Paris, 1958), 163–90, 242–51, 285–90; Hubert Méthivier, *L'ancien régime* (Paris, 1961), 107; and Louis Tuetey, *Les officiers sous l'ancien régime: nobles et roturiers* (Paris, 1908). Historians of the *ancien régime* may hope that this problem will be further illumined when David Bien publishes his study of the royal military schools.

bility therefore pressured the government to grant them preference for promotions in the ranks and for entrance into the military academies in order to help them overcome their handicap of less wealth. The Crown in turn strove to mitigate the effects of venality and raise the fighting quality of the army by imposing requirements designed to recruit officers who would be trained, experienced, and committed to military service, and by promoting such men also to assure itself of a steady inflow of soldiers with equal talent and commitment. Such a policy meant in fact to favor the provincial nobility, traditionally and loyally attached to the army, and secondarily the *roture* career soldiers who by long service gained the requisite knowledge and demonstrated their devotion. Hence, institutional considerations were equally as decisive as, or perhaps even more decisive than, questions of social status in forming the outlook of Church and military men and in determining the monarchy's policies: the political interests of a loyal and obedient Gallican Church, and the professional needs of an army demanding greater military specialization and proficiency.

The social reality underlying these facts of government recruitment seems not to conform to what the theory of "aristocratic reaction" presupposes. Within the traditional framework but with the changing composition of French society, new and rising men could and did gain access to the nobility, could and did associate freely and assimilate with older nobles. As the century advanced, these opportunities increased rather than diminished if the individuals met two requirements: that they have ability for government service, and that they have money to purchase offices and to live in the noble style.[25] Indeed, even able and wealthy commoners were respected and mingled with the aristocracy.

[25] Tocqueville (*L'ancien régime*, I, 153) indeed acknowledged the greater opportunities for ennoblement: "In no other epoch of our history had nobility been as easily acquired as in '89," though he then asserted that bourgeois and noble were never so separated.

The pace and thrust of life in France in the later eighteenth century seemed to be overcoming the legal division between aristocracy and upper *bourgeoisie,* seemed to bring them into closer contact where they were beginning to join in similar pursuits and share common ideas and interests. Nobles were investing in commerce, mining, and industry along with the *bourgeoisie;* the latter in turn were buying country estates and becoming landed proprietors, and both groups, instructed by physiocracy, were applying business acumen to make their domains profitable; and still nobles and bourgeois had the major portion of their wealth in safe and stable government securities *(rentes)* and offices, as well as various forms of real estate. In schools, academies, clubs, Masonic lodges, even in some salons, in the provinces and especially in Paris, bourgeois and nobles new and old met, conversed, exchanged ideas, even formed friendships. As more bourgeois were beginning to "live nobly" on their estates and in their more elegant homes, so more nobles in the latter half of the century were assuming a bourgeois style of dress, wearing black outfits, replacing their swords with canes, and forgoing powdered wigs for their own hair.[26] Marriage was more intractable, unions between the older nobility and the newer nobility or upper *bourgeoisie* being less common; lineage and blood still dictated the choice of mate except when lucrative dowries turned aside the established nobility's aloofness and repugnance toward misalliances. Otherwise, the general line of social, economic, and cultural development was moving in a way we have not hitherto appreciated sufficiently.[27] As one historian who has studied

[26] As described by Mousnier, *Le xviiie siècle,* 183.

[27] The indications above for the continued accession of bourgeois into the nobility, the closer relations between the older and newer nobles and between the nobility and the upper *bourgeoisie,* and the similarity of forms of wealth and economic interests between nobility and *bourgeoisie* may be found in Georges Lefebvre, *Etudes orléanaises: I, Contribution à l'étude des structures sociales à la fin du XVIIIe siècle*

the nobility and *bourgeoisie* in the late eighteenth century concludes: "A patriciate at once noble and commercial is in the process of formation at the end of the eighteenth century, the real importance of which one cannot judge because of the fact that this process was interrupted by the Revolution." [28]

It seems probable, therefore, that in the last decades of the century the *bourgeoisie*, especially the wealthy, upper *bourgeoisie*, were not cut off from relations with those above them nor from professional and social advancement.[29] Indeed

(Paris, 1962), 175–204; Pierre Léon, "Recherches sur la bourgeoisie française de province au XVIII° siècle," *L'Information Historique*, No. 3 (May–June 1958), 101–105; Guy Richard, "Les corporations et la noblesse commerçante en France au XVIII° siècle," 185–89, "La noblesse commerçante à Bordeaux et à Nantes au XVIII° siècle," *L'Information Historique*, No. 5 (Nov.–Dec. 1958), 185–90, "A propos de la noblesse commerçante de Lyon au XVIII° siècle," *L'Information Historique*, No. 4 (Sept.–Oct. 1959), 156–61, and "Un essai d'adaptation sociale à une nouvelle structure économique: La noblesse de France et les sociétés par actions à la fin du XVIII° siècle," 484–523; Daniel Roche, "La diffusion des lumières. Un exemple: l'académie de Châlons-sur-Marne," *Annales: Economies, Sociétés, Civilisations*, Sept.–Oct. 1964, 887–922; P. de Saint-Jacob, *Les paysans de la Bourgogne du nord* (Paris, 1960), 569; Philippe Sagnac, "Les grands courants d'idées et de sentiments en France vers 1789," *Revue d'Histoire Politique et Constitutionnelle*, II (1938), 328; Taylor, "Types of Capitalism in Eighteenth-Century France," 496–97, and "Noncapitalist Wealth and the Origins of the French Revolution," *American Historical Review*, LXXII (Jan. 1967), 469–96; and M. Vovelle and D. Roche, "Bourgeois, Rentiers, and Property Owners: Elements for Defining a Social Category at the End of the Eighteenth Century," *New Perspectives on the French Revolution*, ed. Jeffry Kaplow (New York, 1965), 25–46.

[28] Richard, "A propos de la noblesse commerçante," 161.

[29] Cf. Bluche, *Les magistrats du Parlement de Paris*, 114–17 and 384–85; Egret, "L'aristocratie parlementaire française," 8–10; Forster, *Nobility of Toulouse*, 24–26; McManners, "France," 22–42; and Cobban, *Social Interpretation*, chs. 6, 13, 14.

The articles by Léon ("Recherches sur la bourgeoisie française de province au XVIII° siècle," 101–105) and Richard ("La noblesse commerçante à Bordeaux et à Nantes au XVIII° siècle," 185–90, and "A

the image the *bourgeoisie* impresses upon one of their historians is that of "great activity, enrichment, power, and also frivolity." [30] One may question then whether they were deprived and frustrated, with rebellious consequences. [31] More-

propos de la noblesse commerçante de Lyon au XVIII° siècle," 156–61) provide statistical information on selected groups of provincial bourgeois, thereby presenting a more precise description of the patterns of ennoblement. The two authors summarize evidence for eleven cities and conclude that ennoblement of bourgeois persisted down to the end of the century, sometimes effected through the purchase of letters patent (which diminished in degree) but most often through the acquisition of ennobling offices, especially the office of *secrétaire du roi* and offices in municipal governments; the extent of ennoblement varied in each city, depending on the amount of business activity which would enable men to accumulate large fortunes, and/or the availability of municipal offices that conferred nobility; in all but one of these cities most ennobled businessmen adopted the traditional mode of life of the nobility, leaving business affairs and acquiring lands, titles, and offices, and even wealthy, nonennobled businessmen turned to the land, forgoing commerce to "live nobly." At the end of his article "A propos de la noblesse commerçante de Lyon au XVIII° siècle" (160–61), Richard states, somewhat paradoxically: "Despite the 'aristocratic reaction' at the end of the century, there continued to be an incessant renewal of the nobility by means of the commercial bourgeoisie; . . . in seven provincial cities about a thousand new nobles at least emerged by 1789 from the bourgeoisie in less than one century out of a total which one can estimate for these same cities of approximately five to six thousand nobles."

[30] Léon, "Recherches sur la bourgeoisie," 105.

[31] One may raise this question in particular of the lawyers, local judges, and lesser civil servants who were soon to play prominent roles in the events of the Revolution. Did they, even in the waning years of the *ancien régime,* feel blocked professionally or socially because of their status and so become alienated and revolutionary? Some recent evidence indicates that this was not necessarily the case. Philip Dawson ("The 'Bourgeoisie de robe' in 1789," *French Historical Studies,* IV [Spring 1965], 1–21, especially Tables I and II) analyzed the *cahiers de doléances* of legal corporations in twelve cities; these indicate that the lack of "equal opportunity in the army and Church" was a minimal grievance and that venality—essentially a financial rather than a social problem—was not a significant complaint of most of these corporations,

over, until the very end of the *ancien régime* this same *bourgeoisie* accepted the established hierarchical and aristocratic social order, because it was traditional and sanctioned, and because they feared any change.[32] One may suggest a further reason for this outlook in addition to habit, unquestioned philosophy, and fear. Is it not conceivable that an ambitious French bourgeois in the eighteenth century, surveying the experience of his predecessors and projecting the possibilities before him, might believe that he (or more likely his children) could satisfy his aspirations within the existing society? Status was not unalterable; birth no longer predetermined careers. He could advance along the accepted paths if he had the tools required for success: ability and money. Moreover, he too wanted to become a noble.[33]

---

its abolition being demanded only by (but not the major grievance of) the *avocats*. Egret (*La pré-Révolution française,* 266) describes the sparse support the *avocats* gave to the judicial reforms of May 1788 despite the opportunities for professional advancement these changes offered because, he suggests, the lawyers continued to identify their corporate interests with the parlementary magistrates. The primacy of institutional and political concerns may also be seen in the pre-Revolution career of the future Girondin minister Roland de la Platière. Charles A. Le Guin (*Roland de la Platière, a Public Servant in the Eighteenth Century* ["Transactions of the American Philosophical Society," NS LVI, Pt. VI; Philadelphia, Nov. 1966], 48–49 and 56–69) reveals how Roland's difficulties in rising higher in the bureaucracy were due not to his status as a commoner but rather to policy disagreements and personality clashes with his superiors in the government. In short, not the existing social hierarchy but the authority inherent in an administrative hierarchy halted his career at a rank that was still considerable.

[32] For the former explanation see E. Barber, *Bourgeoisie in 18th Century France,* ch. 4, Forster, *Nobility of Toulouse,* 109, and Palmer, I, 79 and 474–75; for the latter see Cobban, *Social Interpretation,* chs. 12, 13.

[33] Despite her predisposition to accept the theory of "aristocratic reaction," Elinor Barber nevertheless presents evidence to support the point of view expressed above; see chs. 4–6. Lefebvre, describing the *bourgeoisie* of Orléans, also provides evidence for these several facets which made up the bourgeois attitude toward society; see *Etudes orléanaises,* I, 202–04 and 209–10.

The ease of social intercourse between noblemen and upper bourgeois, the similarity of cultural and economic pursuits among them, the accession of talented or wealthy commoners into the nobility, and the ultimate fusion of new and old nobility indicate that the traditional division of French society into the three legal orders was becoming superfluous.[34] The crucial link between social groups was determined by money, and the significant distinction was between those who were wealthy and those who were not; [35] educa-

[34] Bluche and Durye (*L'anoblissement par charges avant 1789,* I, 6) indeed state that the distinction and implicit rivalry between the aristocracy and the *bourgeoisie* have been exaggerated: "More than all economic developments, the social policy of the Capetians [i.e., ennoblement] progressively killed the feudality and its many survivals. At the end of the *ancien régime* the legally recognized structure of 'elites' announced, in many regards, the Napoleonic aristocratic system. Tocqueville perceived this truth without expressing it. In any case, the antinomy 'noblesse-roture' may become a false problem. *A social revolution thus loses its urgency.*" (Italics mine.)

[35] Cf. McManners, "France," *passim,* and Cobban, *Social Interpretation,* chs. 12–14. See also Egret, "The Origins of the Revolution in Brittany (1788–1789)," 143, and "The Pre-Revolution in Provence (1787–1789)," 167, in *New Perspectives on the French Revolution,* ed. Kaplow.

The relations and attitudes in turn of the poor or lower classes to those wealthier and higher in status are complex as well; because of traditional social attitudes or immediate economic grievances, the rural and urban poor did not uniformly or automatically ally with the *bourgeoisie* against the nobility. Economic and social difficulties involving all groups in France at the end of the eighteenth century comprehend many problems, conflicting interests, and attitudes, which cannot simply be explained in terms of the battle between the *bourgeoisie* and the aristocracy. Moreover, not all of these problems were causes of the Revolution, for they entered into play at different times, some at its origin and others during its course. Events must also be seen within their proper time sequence, for social and political conflicts during the Revolution were often produced by the unfolding of events and promoted by a newly gained consciousness of aims among the mass of Frenchmen, who, before 1789, were generally dormant and traditional in their political and social ideas. One must guard against projecting back into the period before 1789 (or late 1788) the social and political

tion, culture, and manners—*esprit*—assisted in this reordering of social relations. The *pays réal* in sum differed fundamentally from the *pays légal*.[36]

---

ideas and aims that emerged from the Revolution in response to new problems or because of decisions and actions taken or not taken by crucial individuals and groups.

[36] As early as 1766, in a letter to a friend, the royal minister Malesherbes (Chrétien Guillaume de Lamoignon de Malesherbes) reflected on changes being introduced into French society by the spread of wealth and luxury.

"Wealth is also in all countries a source of real inequality. . . . It places certainly a very real distinction between men, and this inequality is even the most far-reaching of all, felt as well by men in the highest and lowest ranks of society.

"It is not at all the philosophy of our modern Quakers which diminishes the homage rendered to the nobility. It is 'les grands' [those who have power and wealth], . . . whom I always distinguish from the nobles, who set the example of ignoring the power of the nobility because . . . they give more regard to wealth than to gentility. And they do this not only because of their need for wealthy men, but also because this rich man raised as they are, with the same manners as they have, is more agreeable company for them. I know that they make bitter remarks against the parvenus, but with all that M. de Villette who has assumed in Paris the manners of good society will be better entertained and receive some consideration at the home of a prince of the blood who has a high position in the army than would be the heir of the name of Coucy who is raised in a village. The latter will obtain the favors due to etiquette and after this duty is fulfilled he will be forgotten and the man of nothing who has been raised well will be admitted into familiarity if he will not be maladroit and cause himself to be chased away by excessive impertinence.

" 'Les grands' . . . who give the tone to public opinion must therefore reproach themselves more than others for having destroyed the consideration due to birth, because pleasure and agreeableness prevail with them over everything else. It is then effeminate manners, elegance, luxury, which have degraded the nobility at the same time that they have influenced it. . . .

". . . The attitude of 'les grands' is that contempt is the lot of poverty, and that the crime of being poor cannot be overcome either by birth or even by merit except in . . . very rare cases, . . . when it is altogether exceptionable birth or very brilliant merit.

In this context, in 1787 political discord broke out in France. From that year to the next, the Paris Parlement, the Assembly of Notables, and the Crown were locked in battle. Older nobles and the most recent ennobled bourgeois supported the magistrates and other leaders of the Second Estate against the government.[37] As the new nobles assumed the status and assimilated the mores of the older ones, so too they adopted their ambition: to make the nobility the dominant power in the state. Looking ahead to the following years, Lefebvre has termed this campaign the "aristocratic revolution"—the first stage of the Great Revolution. Yet this was also the "aristocratic reaction." In its origin and at its core this was a political movement whose roots run back into the eighteenth century, and even farther back into the history of France. The term has taken on many other meanings as historians use it to describe the sum of economic and social changes in the eighteenth century. True, there were such

---

"Wealth equalizes, and even without being equal the man in a fairly comfortable position to live in the world is treated very differently by 'les grands' than the man with nothing. A nobleman who is poor is not as well treated by them as the rich man who is a commoner. . . . It is not at all the ideas of philosophy [ideas of equality] which have diminished the respect due to birth. . . . The true cause of this change introduced into our mores . . . is luxury. . . . Everyone seeks only to have money because the respect accorded to wealth is so real that everything else is nothing in comparison. No longer is there honor in the military, nor in the magistracy, nor even in the offices of the Court because the superiority of wealth spoils everyone and eclipses all other distinctions." (See *Malesherbes et son temps*, ed. Pierre Grosclaude [Paris, 1965], 43–51.)

[37] Commoners generally remained quiescent at this time, though some, stirred up by their professional and social superiors in the Second Estate, did riot to support the nobility while in one province, Provence, some bourgeois and nobles began to oppose the program of the nobility. For a description and analysis of the conflict against the Crown during these two years see Egret, *La pré-Révolution française*, especially chs. IV and V, "The Pre-Revolution in Provence (1787–1789)," and "The Origins of the Revolution in Brittany (1788–1789)."

changes, but it remains questionable that these constituted an "aristocratic reaction" in the society and economy of the *ancien régime;* in a subtle and more limited sense did this "aristocratic reaction" have social implications and goals.

In August of 1788 the Crown announced that the Estates-General would meet in the spring of 1789. The following month, on September 25, 1788, the Paris Parlement declared that the three estates should convene as they had in 1614—sitting and voting in three separate orders. This was calculated to ensure the political predominance of the aristocracy, allied presumably with the clergy. It was also designed to preserve the existing, traditional social order, to guarantee the nobility their time-honored status. In short, at this late date the nobility attempted to reimpose the sharp lines of a legal hierarchy, of distinct and separate estates, upon a society that no longer conformed to its prescription. Social reality had diverged from legal fact, and so long as these differences had remained muted French society accepted them. Until this pronouncement the *bourgeoisie* had neither questioned, criticized, nor sought to change the traditional hierarchical order since it was not an insuperable barrier or hindrance to their activities. For a number of years bourgeois had mingled with noble, and some bourgeois had even become noble. Now, unexpectedly, the Second Estate turned about, and overnight the Third Estate turned against its long-time social superiors and recent political allies.

Historians recognize that this was a sudden and radical transformation in the *bourgeoisie's* attitude.[38] But it is not

[38] See, for example, Palmer, I, 89 and 457. The most thorough examinations of the response of the Third Estate and of the participation of nobles in the campaign for "doubling the Third" may be found in Egret, *La pré-Révolution française,* ch. 4, Pts. I, IV, ch. 6, Pts. III, V, and ch. 7, Pt. V (this last aptly entitled "Le réveil du Tiers Etat"), and also in his two articles, "The Origins of the Revolution in Brittany (1788–1789)," 142–44, and "The Pre-Revolution in Provence (1787–1789)," 158–66. Elizabeth Eisenstein ("Who Intervened in 1788?," 77–103) argues forcefully that the campaign for "doubling" was

unaccountable. Now for the first time in a long while, bourgeois could not easily feel that they could move outside their rank or even move into the higher order. Society might indeed become crystallized. Perhaps even more, an issue now opened up which was central, as crucial to the Third Estate as it was to the Second Estate: where would political power lie, who among the French people would exercise political power in the newly regenerated French state? So a new political question and an old social framework converged, an anomalous situation at a critical moment.[39] Is it necessary to

---

not simply a bourgeois movement but was initiated and led by a group that included prominent aristocrats. The campaign for "doubling of the Third" originated in some instances, as Egret indicates in the above works, before September 1788: the Patriot Party in Paris began to disseminate its ideas in July 1788 after the Crown announced its intention to convene the Estates-General; and even earlier in 1787, in Dauphiné and in Provence, "doubling" was demanded for representation in those two provincial estates.

[39] Some members of the royal government were aware that the changing character of society required new political forms regardless of legal hierarchy. In the 1760's Controller-General Laverdy proposed reforms for municipal government that would eliminate strict division into the three legal orders, but the Parlements blocked their implementation. (See Maurice Bordes, "La réforme municipale du contrôleur-général Laverdy et son application dans certaines provinces," *Revue d'Histoire Moderne et Contemporaine*, XII [Oct.–Dec. 1965], 241–70.) Voting not by order but by head was the procedure in the two provincial assemblies that Necker established in 1778. Calonne proposed to the first Assembly of Notables in 1787 a system of provincial assemblies without distinction of orders and with suffrage determined by landholding, but the Notables voted down the measure. (See Egret, *La pré-Révolution française*, 21–23, and Albert Goodwin, *The French Revolution* [New York, 1962], 30–32.) In mid-1788 the ministers debated the organization and voting procedures for the Estates-General which was to be summoned; Malesherbes, then minister of state, presented a challenging memorandum to the king, bold in its tone and design, which anticipated the events of the coming years:

"'What is this Estates-General which you propose? . . . It is an old debris of ancient barbarism; it is a field of battle where three factions of a single people come to fight together; it is the clash of all false interests

233

project back into the eighteenth century the change that occurred in September of 1788? [40] The events and developments of the French Revolution, which now unfolded, lose none of their force and significance; indeed the year 1789 assumes more of the character of a revolution since it wit-

against the general interest; it is inertia or obstinacy in the spirit of the body politic; it is a means of subversion; it cannot be at all a means of renovation. Take this old edifice for what it is, for a ruin. One can be attached to it only as a memory; gain the hold over national feelings by an institution which will astonish them and please them, which the Nation avows and where it can better predominate . . . ; let not a king at the end of the eighteenth century convoke the three orders of the fourteenth century; let him call the proprietors of a great Nation renewed by its civilization. A king who proposes a constitution gains the most beautiful glory there is among men and all that is most vital and constant in their gratitude. A constitution must be appropriate to the wisest ideas which discussion has prepared and fixed. Conceive the constitution of your century; take your place and do not fear to establish it on the rights of the people. Your nation, seeing you abreast of its wishes, will but perfect your work before sanctioning it. It is in this way that you can master a great event in accomplishing it yourself. . . .' " (See Egret, 322.)

Malesherbes' advice was ignored in the summer of 1788 and in the year that followed. Egret (361–67) gives some indications of the conflicting ideas of the ministers and members of the royal family who fought to win over the king to their views in 1788 and 1789; more work should be done on this problem, for the Crown's decision was crucial in determining the course of the Revolution. I hope to examine the social and political ideas of the eighteenth-century intendants, particularly those who were still in government between 1787 and 1789.

[40] One may further attempt to explain and understand the sudden opposition of the Third to the historic legal hierarchy by analogy with the response of nobles suddenly deprived of their rights to vote for or become deputies of the Second Estate who then, like Mirabeau and Merlin de Douai, supported the movement for "doubling" and became leaders of the Revolution. See Egret, *La pré-Révolution française,* 352–53, "The Origins of the Revolution in Brittany (1788–1789)," 142–44, and "The Pre-Revolution in Provence (1787–1789)," 158–66; and also Lefebvre, *Etudes Orléanaises,* I, 194–95. The ideas and motives of the various "Patriot" leaders in 1788 and 1789, nobles and bourgeois, should be further studied.

nessed also a profound change in basic ideas and historic beliefs.[41]

The Revolution began in 1789, but this should not cause us to look back upon French government and society in the eighteenth century and force the facts to fit the dénouement or to conform to theories which are generalizations drawn from later revolutions. There was a revolution in 1789; there were fundamental economic and social changes in the course of the century; but these changes did not necessarily or in all ways produce the Revolution. Between romantic adulation of the *ancien régime* and total commitment to the Revolution there remains a third way which combines an understanding and appreciation of pre-Revolution France with an acceptance of the Revolution and its achievements. The problems that brought on the Revolution and the course it took must be thought anew.

[41] Cf. Franklin L. Ford, "The Revolutionary and Napoleonic Era: How Much of a Watershed?" *American Historical Review,* LXIX (1963), 24–28. Still in late 1788 and early 1789 few of the Patriots and few even in the Third Estate conceived of totally overthrowing the social hierarchy; they wanted to eliminate the nobility's legal and fiscal privileges (the latter was acceptable to many nobles) and their disproportionate political power, but were willing to preserve their honorific privileges and to recognize their social pre-eminence. See Egret, *La pré-Révolution française,* 334–36, and Lefebvre, I, 203–204 and 209–10.

Comparative Incomes of Magistrates of the Paris Parlement and Members of the Royal Council

Did the prospect of greater income also serve to draw magistrates into service on the Royal Council? This question can only be answered by comparing the incomes of sovereign-court judges and of members of the Royal Council on related levels of the judicial and administrative hierarchies. The following figures are minimum approximations drawn from various sources and are given in livres, the unit of money in the *ancien régime.*

The figures shown for the parlementarians represent the income from the *gages* (interest from the capital invested in the office) and from the *casuels* (payments for work done as a member of a court). The *appointements* and *traitement,* which made up part of the income of royal functionaries, represent fixed salaries for certain official posts or for functions performed by specific members of the Royal Council. The *pension* were in effect bonuses given by the Crown to its agents in order to supplement regular income or to reward individuals for able work.

Paris Parlement:

Conseiller aux Enquêtes
  1,200–3,000

Conseiller au Grand'chambre
  7,000–8,000

Président à Mortier (1743)
  10,000 (not including *pension* and gifts)
  20,000 maximum

Appendix I

Procureur-général (1739)
34,000 (not including *pension* and gifts)
44,000 maximum

Premier président (1763)
41,950 (*gages*)
20,000 (*pension*)
10,000 (free residence)
10,000 (*casuels*)

Total: 81,950

Royal Council:

Maîtres des requêtes:
1,600 (*gages*)
1,000 (supplement for service on each bureau)
1,500 (*appointements* for the *doyen* of each *quartier*)
3,300 (*appointements* for the *doyen* of the entire corps)
3,000 (*appointements* as member or president of the Grand Conseil)

Total: 2,600–4,900

Intendant:
6,000–12,000   (*traitement*)
varying amounts (supplements)
2,000–6,000   (*pension* from the Crown)
varying amounts (*gratifications* from the Crown and the provinces)

Total: 15,000–70,000

(According to the budget of 1786, the total royal expenses for the provincial intendants were 1,150,000 livres. There was no uniform pay scale for all the intendants; nevertheless, if we divide this total by the number of *généralités* in that year—thirty-four—we arrive at the average payment to each intendant: 33,823 livres.)

Conseiller d'état:
3,000– 3,300 *semestre* (*appointements*)
5,100– 5,500 *ordinaire* (*appointements*)
10,000   conseiller au Conseil Royal des finances (*traitement*)
16,000   *doyen* (*appointements*)
6,000   (*pension*)
2,000– 3,000 (*appointements* as member of a bureau)
3,000–12,000 (*appointements* as President of the Grand Conseil)

Total: 9,000–19,000   *semestre*
          11,100–21,000   *ordinaire*
          24,000 minimum *doyen*

Secretaries of state (1775):
300,000 (includes: *appointements, pension, émoluments, dons, présents*)

Minister of state (under Louis XV):
20,000 (*traitement*)

Secretary and minister of state:
320,000

The disparity between the incomes of an intendant and a councilor of state does not affect the ranking of these two posts: the latter was definitely more important and prestigious, and obtaining it signified a promotion for a provincial intendant. Moreover, the figures for the intendant's income give only a partial indication of his actual earnings; from the total sum he received, he had to draw money to pay for administrative expenses in the *généralité*—e.g., the expenses of his office and the salaries of his subordinates—which exceeded the sums provided by the Crown and the provinces. Cf. Fréville, *L'intendance de Bretagne*, II, 324–25 and 353–54, and III, 31, 143 and note 29.

The above figures clearly indicate that, excepting the highest positions on both the Royal Council and the Paris Parlement, the other incomes were broadly equivalent. The great difference arises only for the incomes of the four to six secretaries of state. Thus, one may conclude that money did not constitute a strong lure for most of the young men who entered the Royal Council, since only a very small number of them could attain the posts of secretary of state.

Sources for the figures are: Bluche, *Les magistrats du Parlement de Paris*, 169 f., for the incomes of Paris parlementarians; PO 582, "Camus," f. 101, PO 2897, "Turgot," f. 72, and Aucoc, *Le conseil d'état*, 74–75, for the incomes of *maîtres des requêtes;* Chérin 24, "Bertin," f. 65 for the income of members of the Grand Conseil (Kerviler, "Etudes sur les Bignon," *Bibliophile le français*, [Sept.–Nov. 1872], 337, gives the sum of 12,000 livres as the *appointements* for the President of the Grand Conseil, but the document in Chérin attributing only 3,000 livres to Bertin evidently refutes the former) ; Aucoc, *ibid.,* 66, for the incomes of councilors of state and ministers of state; and Viollet, *Le roi et ses ministres*, 265 and note 3, and 270 for the incomes of secretaries of state. The figures for the incomes of provincial intendants are based on the following: Chérin 24, "Bertin," f. 72; Beaucorps, "Une province sous Louis XIV," *Mémoires de la Société archéologique et historique de l'Orléanais*, XXXIII (1911), 68; Boyé, "Le chancelier Chaumont de la Galaizière et sa famille," *Le Pays Lorrain*, XXX (1938), 458, note 3; Boyer de Sainte-Suzanne, *Les intendants de la généralité d'Amiens*, 33 and 588–89, "pièce justificative" no. vii; Charles Alexandre de Calonne, "Compte rendu au commencement de 1787 . . . ," *Pièces essentielle et indispensables; tableaux de régie, appendix, qui font suite au Mémoire de M. de Calonne* (Fevrier, 1788), 43; Fréville, *L'intendance de Bretagne*, I, 346, II, 361–62, III, 32 and 114; Jolly, *Calonne, 1734–1812*, 56; Louis Legrand, *Sénac de Meilhan et l'intendance de Hainaut et du Cambrésis sous Louis XVI* (Paris, 1868), 42 and 128; Néraud, *Les intendants de la généralité de Berry*, 167; Louis Vialatte, *Rossignol, intendant de la généralité de Riom et province d'Auvergne (1734–1750)* (Poitiers, 1924), 6; and H. Carré in *Histoire de France,* ed. Ernest Lavisse, t. 9¹, 208–209.

For a breakdown of the earnings of a councilor of state over a period of one year and nine months see Appendix II.

APPENDIX II

Breakdown of the Income of a Councilor of State during a Period of Twenty-one Months, 1754-1755

Etat des arrérages dus à M. Bernard Chauvelin, conseiller d'Etat ordinaire, au 16 octobre 1755 des appointements et pension qui luy avoient été accordé par Sa Majesté.

I: Appointements, Conseiller d'Etat
1754	5,100 l
1755	4,476 l, 13 s, 4 d
	9,576 l, 13 s, 4 d

II: Appointements, Bureau des Domaines
1754	3,000 l
1755	2,633 l, 6 s, 8 d
	5,633 l, 6 s, 8 d

III: Appointements, Bureau des Fermes
1754	2,000 l
1755	1,755 l, 11 s, 1 d
	3,755 l, 11 s, 1 d

IV: Appointements, Bureau des Comptes en Banque
1754	2,000 l
1755	1,755 l, 11 s, 1 d
	3,755 l, 11 s, 1 d

V: Appointements, Bureau des Péages
1754	2,000 l
1755	1,755 l, 11 s, 1 d
	3,755 l, 11 s, 1 d

VI: Pour un an 16 jours de la pension de
6,000 l que le Roy luy avoit accordé
échu depuis 1 septembre 1754 jusque
et compris 16 octobre 1755:   6,766 l, 13 s, 4 d

Total: 33,243 l, 6 s, 7 d

Sur quoy il sera retenu le dixième: 3,324 l, 6 s, 7 d
Et pour sa capitation personnelle pendant
1755:   960 l

Reste net...................... 28,959 livres

(Archives Nationales, Minutier Central, LXXXVII:1035, 8 mars 1756,
notaire Duval.

Proportions and Nature of the French Nobility in the Eighteenth Century

I. Noble origins of ninety intendants included in this study:

Office   72 out of 90 (80%)
  sovereign courts   19 out of 90 (21%)
          (37% ennobled during the eighteenth century)
  royal council   11 out of 90 (12%)
  secrétaire du roi 35 out of 90 (38.8%)
  financial magistracy 5 out of 90 (5.5%)
  commensal office 1 out of 90 (1%)
  municipal office 1 out of 90 (1%)
Feudal   3 out of 90 (3.3%)
Prescription   6 out of 90 (6.6%)
Letters patent 7 out of 90 (7.7%)
Official favor   1 out of 90 (1%)
Ducal service   1 out of 90 (1%)

II. Noble origins of royal ministers in the eighteenth century: [1]

A—Type of nobility

Feudal or ancient	15%
Letters patent	22%
Sovereign courts	30%
Secrétaire du roi	22%

[1] François Bluche, "L'origine sociale du personnel ministériel français au XVIIIᵉ siècle," *Bulletin de la Société d'Histoire Moderne*, 12ᵉ série, no. 1 (Jan.–Feb. 1957), 10–11.

Prescription

    (or unproved ancient nobility)   7%

    Financial and judicial magistracy   3%

B—Age of nobility

2 generations	15.5%
3 generations	12.7%
4 generations	9.9%
5 generations	12.7%
6 generations	11.6%
7, 8, and 9 generations	12.7%
10 generations and more	25.5%

III. Nobility in provincial towns: [2]

  A—Lyon, Saint-Malo, Nantes, Toulouse, La Rochelle, Bordeaux, and Bayonne

    5,000–6,000—total of nobles

    1,000—total of new nobles in 1789 created in less than one century

    16–20%: total of new nobles within the nobility

  B—Orléans in 1791 [3]

    Nobility 1,000

              2.5% of total population of 40,000.

    Samples 120 "d'épée et de date plus ou moins ancienne"

              137 "d'office et relativement récents."

  C—Lamballe in 1789 [4]

    Nobility 650

              18.6% of total population of 3,485

  D—Poitiers in 1789

    Nobles were in proportion of 1 out of 50 (2%)

---

[2] Guy Richard, "A propos de la noblesse commerçante de Lyon au XVIIIe siècle," *L'Information Historique,* no. 4 (Sept.–Oct. 1959), 156–61.

[3] George Lefebvre, *Etudes Orléanaises: I Contribution à l'étude des structures sociales à la fin du XVIIIe siècle* (Paris, 1962), 178–79.

[4] Figures for Lamballe and Poitiers are from Henri Carré, *La noblesse de France et l'opinion publique au XVIIIe siècle* (Paris, 1920), 15 and 16–17.

E—Beauvais in 1789 [5]
 58—Total *"gentilshommes"*
  10 (17%) —*"gentilshommes"* from the time of Henry IV
  27 (46%) —merchants at the time of Louis XIV
   (16[27.5%] were of families ennobled before 1740)
  21 (36%) —"des étrangers, robins et nobles de fraîche
   date venus de la capitale ou des provinces
   voisines."

IV. Proportion of older and newer nobility: [6]

 A—Second half of the eighteenth century
  4,000 noble families (or 20,000 nobles) were of *ancienne ex-
  traction*, i.e., 5 percent of 400,000.
 B—1789—Elections to the Second Estate
  130,000 nobles participated in the elections, i.e., 32.5 percent
  of 400,000.

[5] Pierre Goubert, *Beauvais et le Beauvaisis de 1600 à 1730: contribution à l'histoire sociale de la France du XVII*e* siècle* (Paris, 1960), 221.
The author comments: "La noblesse de bailliage [of Beauvais], tout
injectée de marchands anoblis, s'était presque entièrement renouvellée."
 [6] These figures are from Carré, *La noblesse de France*, 17–18. According to the royal declaration of January 24, 1789 (as explained by
Carré), nobles eligible to vote in the Second Estate were limited to
those who were *"possedants-fiefs"* and those who enjoyed *"noblesse
acquisse et transmissible";* nobility that was fully acquired and hereditary
would mean three or more generations of nobility. Those nobles not
eligible to vote in the assemblies of the Second Estate were those who
were *"anoblis"*, who held *"noblesse personnelle"*, who were *"titulaire[s]
d'office dont la noblesse ne sera transmise qu'à la troisième génération"*,
and who were *"anobli[s] de noblesse militaire"* (*ibid.*, 17).

The Intendants Studied and Their Intendancies

François Marie Bruno d'Agay de Mutigney
   Rennes (Brittany), 1767–1771; Amiens (Picardy), 1771–1789
Marie Jean Baptiste Nicolas d'Aine
   Pau (Navarre and Béarn), 1767–1774; Limoges (Limousin),
   1774–1783; Tour (Touraine Anjou, and Maine), 1783–1790
Etienne Jean François Marie d'Aligre de Boislandry
   Pau and Auch (Navarre, Béarn, and Gascony), 1749–1751;
   Amiens (Picardy) and Artois, 1751–1754
Antoine Jean Amelot de Chaillou
   Dijon (Burgundy), 1764–1776
Louis Urbain Aubert de Tourny
   Limoges (Limousin), 1730–1743; Bordeaux (Guyenne),
   1743–1757
Antoine Jean Baptiste Robert Auget de Montyon
   Riom (Auvergne), 1767–1771; Aix (Provence), 1771–1773; La
   Rochelle (Aunis and Saintonge), 1773–1775
Dominique Claude de Barberie de Saint-Contest
   Metz (Three Bishoprics), 1700–1712?
Henri Louis de Barberie de Saint-Contest de la Chataîgneraye
   Limoges (Limousin and Angoumois), 1743–1750; Châlons
   (Champagne), 1750–?
Charles Amable Honoré de Barentin
   La Rochelle (Aunis and Saintonge), 1736–1747; Orléans (Or-
   léanais), 1747–1760?
Antoine Barrillon d'Armoncourt
   Perpignan (Foix and Roussillon), 1708?–1710; Pau (Navarre
   and Béarn), 1711–1712 or 1713

Nicolas Prosper Bauyn d'Angervilliers
Alençon (Normandy), 1702–1705; Grenoble (Dauphiné), 1705–1715; Strasbourg (Alsace), 1715–1724
François de Beauharnois
Canada, 1702–1704; intendant of the navy, 1704–1715; La Rochelle (Aunis and Saintonge), 1710–1715
Louis de Bernage
Limoges (Limousin and Angoumois), 1694–1702; Besançon (Franche-Comté), 1702–1708; Amiens (Picardy), 1708–1718; Toulouse and Montpellier (Languedoc), 1718–1724
Jean Louis de Bernage de Vaux
Moulins (Marche, Bourbonnais, and Nivernais), 1744–1756; Metz (Three Bishoprics), 1756–1767?
Louis Bénigne François Bertier de Sauvigny
Paris (Ile-de-France—*adjoint*, 1768–1776), 1776–1789
Louis Jean Bertier de Sauvigny
Moulins (Marche, Bourbonnais, and Nivernais), 1737–1740; Grenoble (Dauphiné), 1740–1744; Paris (Ile-de-France), 1744–1776
Henri Léonard Jean Baptiste Bertin de Bellisle
Perpignan (Foix and Roussillon), 1750–1753; Lyon (Lyonnais), 1754–1757
Claude François Bertrand de Boucheporn
Corsica, 1775–1785; Pau (Navarre and Béarn), 1785–1787; Auch (Gascony), 1787–1790
Roland Armand Bignon de Blanzy
Paris, 1709–1724
Louis Guillaume de Blair de Boismont
La Rochelle (Aunis and Saintonge), 1749–1754; Valenciennes (Hainaut), 1754–1764; Strasbourg (Alsace), 1764–1777
Charles Boucher d'Orsay
Limoges (Limousin and Angoumois), 1710–1719; Grenoble (Dauphiné), 1720–1724?; Limoges (Limousin and Angoumois), 1724–1730
Jean Benoît Cachet de Garnerans
Trévoux (Dombes), 1762–1782
Charles Alexandre de Calonne
Metz (Three Bishoprics), 1768–1778; Lille (Flanders and Artois), 1778–1783

247

Jean Baptiste Elie Camus de Pontcarré de Viarme
  Rennes (Brittany), 1734–1753
Gaspard Henri de Caze de la Bove
  Pau and Auch (Navarre, Béarn, and Gascony), 1744–1749;
  Châlons (Champagne), 1749–1750
Gaspard Louis de Caze de la Bove
  Rennes (Brittany), 1775–1785; Grenoble (Dauphiné),
  1784–1790
Antoine Chaumont de la Galaizière
  Montauban (Guyenne), 1756–1758; Nancy (Lorraine and Bar-
  rois—*adjoint,* 1758–1766), 1766–1777; Strasbourg (Alsace),
  1777–1790
Antoine Martin Chaumont de la Galaizière
  Soissons (Ile-de-France and Picardy), 1731–1737; Nancy (Lor-
  raine and Barrois), 1737–1766
Jacques Louis Chaumont de la Millière
  Limoges (Limousin and Angoumois), 1750–1756
Bernard Chauvelin de Beauséjour
  Tours (Touraine, Anjou, and Maine), 1709–1718?; Alençon
  Normandy),?; Bordeaux (Guyenne), 1717?; Amiens (Pic-
  ardy) and Artois, 1718?
Jacques Bernard Chauvelin de Beauséjour
  Amiens (Picardy) and Artois, 1731–1751
Charles Antoine Claude de Chazerat
  Riom (Auvergne), 1771–1790
Jean Etienne Bernard de Clugny de Nuis
  Santo Domingo (French Caribbean islands), 1760–1764?; Per-
  pignan (Foix and Roussillon), 1773–1775; Bordeaux (Guy-
  enne) and Bayonne, 1775–1776
François Pierre du Cluzel
  Tours (Touraine, Anjou, and Maine), 1766–1783
Jean François de Creil de Bournezeau
  La Rochelle (Aunis and Saintonge), 1719 or 1721–?; Metz
  (Three Bishoprics), 1721-beyond 1751
Denis Dodart
  Bourges (Berry), 1728–1767
Jean Charles Doujat
  Poitiers (Poitou), 1705–1708; Maubeuge (Hainaut),
  1708–1720; Moulins (Marche, Bourbonnais, Nivernais), ?

Guillaume Joseph Dupleix de Bacquencourt
  Pau (Navarre and Béarn)?, 1765?; La Rochelle (Aunis and
  Saintonge), 1765–1766; Amiens (Picardy), 1766–1771; Rennes
  (Brittany), 1771–1774; Dijon (Burgundy), 1774 or 1775–1780
Nicolas Dupré de Saint-Maur
  Bourges (Berry—*adjoint,* 1764–1767), 1767–1776; Bordeaux
  (Guyenne) and Bayonne, 1776–1785
Charles François Hyacinthe Esmangart
  Bordeaux (Guyenne), 1770–1775; Caen (Normandy),
  1775–1783; Lille (Flanders and Artois), 1783–1790
Antoine François Ferrand de Villemilan
  Dijon (Burgundy), 1694–1705; Rennes (Brittany), 1705–1716
Jacques de Flesselles
  Moulins (Marche, Bourbonnais, Nivernais), 1762–1765;
  Rennes (Brittany), 1765; Lyon (Lyonnais), 1765–1784
Etienne Hyacinthe Antoine Foullé de Martargis
  Bourges (Berry), 1708–1715; Alençon (Normandy),
  1715–1720
Charles Jean Baptiste des Gallois de la Tour
  Aix (Provence), 1744–1771 and 1775–1790
Jean Emmanuel de Guignard de Saint-Priest
  Montpellier and Toulouse (Languedoc), 1751–1785
Jean François Joly de Fleury de la Valette
  Dijon (Burgundy), 1749–1760 or 1767
Etienne Louis Journet
  Auch and Bayonne (Gascony), 1767–1776
Louis Guillaume Jubert de Bouville
  Alençon (Normandy), 1708–1713; Orléans (Orléanais),
  1713–1731
Antoine Jean Baptiste Jullien
  Alençon (Normandy), 1766–1790
Louis François de La Bourdonnaye
  Rouen (Normandy), 1732–1755
Yves Marie de La Bourdonnaye
  Poitiers (Poitou), 1690–1695; Rouen (Normandy),
  1695–1700; Bordeaux (Guyenne), 1700–1709; Orléans (Or-
  léanais), 1709–1713
Paul Esprit Marie de La Bourdonnaye de Blossac
  Poitiers (Poitou), 1751–1784; Soissons (Ile-de-France and Pi-
  cardy), 1784–1790

Pierre Arnaud de La Briffe
    Caen (Normandy), 1709–1711; Dijon (Burgundy), 1711–1740
Louis Arnaud de La Briffe des Ferrières
    Caen (Normandy), 1740–1751
Charles André de La Coré
    Montauban (Guyenne), 1758–1761; Besançon (Franche-Comté), 1761–1784
Louis François Lallemant de Lévignen
    Alençon (Normandy), 1726–1766
Nicolas de Lamoignon de Basville
    Poitiers (Poitou), 1682–1685; Montpellier and Toulouse (Languedoc), 1685–1718
Urbain Guillaume de Lamoignon de Courson
    Rouen (Normandy), 1704–1709; Bordeaux (Guyenne), 1709–1715 or 1720
Jean Baptiste François de La Porte de Meslay
    Perpignan (Foix and Roussillon), 1775–1778; Nancy (Lorraine and Barrois), 1778–1790
Pierre Jean François de La Porte de Meslay
    Moulins (Marche, Bourbonnais, Nivernais), 1740–1744; Grenoble (Dauphiné), 1744–1761
Louis Claude Le Blanc
    Riom (Auvergne), 1704–1708; Dunkerque and Ypres (maritime Flanders), 1708–1716
Cardin Le Bret
    Pau (Navarre and Béarn), 1701–1704; Aix (Provence), 1704–1734
Antoine Louis François Le Fèvre de Caumartin
    Metz (Three Bishoprics), 1754–1756; Lille (Flanders and Artois), 1756–1778
Antoine François de Paule Le Fèvre d'Ormesson de Chéray
    Rouen (Normandy), 1694–1695; Riom (Auvergne), 1695–1704; Soissons (Ile-de-France and Picardy), 1705–1712
Gaspard François Le Gendre de Saint-Aubin
    Montauban (Guyenne), 1700–1713; Auch (Gascony), 1713?–1717?; Tours (Touraine, Anjou, and Maine), 1717–1721
Pierre Hector Le Guerchois
    Alençon (Normandy), 1705–1708; Besançon (Franche-Comté), 1708–1717

Louis Le Peletier de Morfontaine
  Soissons (Ile-de-France and Picardy), 1765–1784
Félix Le Pelletier de la Houssaye
  Soissons (Ile-de-France and Picardy), 1694–1698; Montauban
  (Guyenne), 1698–1699; Strasbourg (Alsace), 1699–1715
César Charles de L'Escalopier
  Châlons (Champagne), 1711–1730
Gaspard César Charles de L'Escalopier
  Montauban (Guyenne), 1740–1756; Tours (Touraine, Anjou,
  and Maine), 1756–1766
Charles Etienne Maignard de Bernières
  Maubeuge (Hainaut), 1698–1705; Dunkerque (maritime
  Flanders), 1705–1708; Lille (Flanders and Artois), 1708–
  1715
Jean Nicolas Mégret de Sérilly
  Pau and Auch (Navarre, Béarn, and Gascony), 1740–1744;
  Besançon (Franche-Comté), 1744–1750; Strasbourg (Alsace),
  1750–1752
Antoine François Méliand
  Pau (Navarre and Béarn), 1704–1710; Lyon (Lyonnais),
  1710–1717
Charles Blaise Méliand
  Soissons (Ile-de-France and Picardy), 1743–1751?
Jean Louis Moreau de Beaumont
  Poitiers (Poitou), 1747–1750; Besançon (Franche-Comté),
  1750–1754; Lille (Flanders and Artois), 1754–1756
Jean Moreau de Séchelles
  Maubeuge (Hainaut), 1727–1743?; Lille (Flanders and Ar-
  tois), 1743–1754?
Jean François d'Orceau de Fontette
  Caen (Normandy), 1752–1775
Christophe Pajot de Marcheval
  Limoges (Limousin and Angoumois), 1756–1761; Grenoble
  (Dauphiné), 1761–1784
François Marie Peirenc de Moras
  Riom (Auvergne), 1750–1752; Maubeuge (Hainaut),
  1752–1755
Jean François Claude Perrin de Cypierre
  Orléans (Orléanais), 1760–1785

Jacques Pineau de Lucé
  Tours (Touraine, Anjou, and Maine), 1743–1745; Maubeuge (Hainaut), 1745–1752; Strasbourg (Alsace), 1752–1761
Jean Samuel de Pont de Monderoux
  Moulins (Marche, Bourbonnais, Nivernais), 1765–1778; Metz (Three Bishoprics), 1778–1790
Charles Bonaventure Quentin de Richebourg
  Rouen (Normandy), 1709–1712; Poitiers (Poitou), 1712–1715
Bonaventure Robert Rossignol
  Riom (Auvergne), 1734–1750; Lyon (Lyonnais), 1750–1754
Gaspard Louis Rouillé d'Orfeuil
  Châlons (Champagne), 1764–1790
Nicolas Etienne Roujault
  Bourges (Berry), 1699–1705; Maubeuge (Hainaut), 1705–1708; Poitiers (Poitou), 1708–1712; Rouen (Normandy), 1712–1715
Charles Pierre de Savelette de Magnanville
  Tours (Touraine, Anjou, and Maine), 1745–1756
Gabriel Sénac de Meilhan
  La Rochelle (Aunis and Saintonge), 1766–1773; Aix (Provence), 1773–1775; Valenciennes (Hainaut), 1775–1790
Louis Gabriel Taboureau des Réaux
  Valenciennes (Hainaut), 1764–1775
Antoine Jean Terray
  Montauban (Guyenne), 1773–1781; Moulins (Marche, Bourbonnais, and Nivernais), 1781–1784; Lyon (Lyonnais), 1784–1790
Louis Thiroux de Crosne
  Rouen (Normandy—*adjoint,* 1767–1768), 1768–1785
Charles Trudaine
  Lyon (Lyonnais), 1704–1710; Dijon (Burgundy), 1710–1711
Marc-Antoine Turgot de Saint-Clair
  Riom (Auvergne), 1708–1713; Moulins (Marche, Bourbonnais, Nivernais), 1714–1720, Soissons (Ile-de-France and Picardy), 1720–1722
Jacques Etienne Turgot de Soumons
  Metz (Three Bishoprics), 1696–1699; Tours (Touraine, Anjou, Maine), 1701–1709; Moulins (Marche, Bourbonnais, Nivernais), 1709–1713

Bibliography

The first task in undertaking this research was to determine who the intendants were during the three periods covered in this book: 1710–1712, 1749–1751, and 1774–1776. This information was obtained in the *Almanach Royal,* which lists all the offices and officials in all the branches, civil and military, of the royal government. Printed genealogies, particularly in the *nobiliaires* and *armorials* dating from the *ancien régime* or based upon genealogies published in that period, are too frequently exaggerated and fictitious since their purpose was to make the families' origins more ancient and more exalted than was true. Hence the only published genealogical guide that I depended upon and whose trustworthiness is assured is François Bluche's *L'origine des magistrats du Parlement de Paris au XVIII° siècle (1715–1771): Dictionnaire généalogique.* Occasionally, to supplement information about an intendant or his immediate antecedents where regular genealogies were sketchy, I referred to M. Michaud's *Biographie universelle ancienne et moderne.* The major part of the information in this book regarding the individual lives and careers of the intendants and the histories of their families I obtained from the genealogical collection, the Cabinet des Titres, in the Salle des Manuscrits of the Bibliothèque Nationale in Paris. In order of importance and historical veracity these consist of:

Bibliography

Pièces originales and *Dossiers bleus:* collections of various source materials in whole or in part relating to individual families, ranging from marriage contracts and baptismal records to receipts for *rentes,* together with occasional genealogical charts. Paternal lineage is first determined from the documentary evidence, which may then confirm or disprove the genealogical charts in these volumes and elsewhere; in turn, these genealogical charts may add information about various ancestors, thereby supplementing the documentary evidence.

Carrés d'Hozier: collections that often include complete copies of source materials, such as marriage contracts, which provide invaluable information to determine an intendant's lineage and to fill out details of the careers and status of his ancestors. Some of the genealogical charts also included in this series are not always valid and must be corroborated by the documentary materials.

Chérin: genealogical lists compiled by the royal genealogist serving Louis XVI. During the latter's reign, requirements respecting the age of a family's nobility were made more rigorous for entrance into military academies and schools for young ladies and for receiving the *honneurs de la cour;* Chérin's task was to investigate and determine a family's true genealogy regardless of verbal pretensions and falsified documents. Hence the genealogical lists included in this series are scrupulously exact, based on lineage attested to by documents which Chérin analyzed; the genealogies are also confirmed by the lineage determined on the basis of the source materials in the *Pièces originales* and the *Dossiers bleus.*

Cabinet d'Hozier and *Nouveau d'Hozier:* these should be perused only to supplement information about individual ancestors. A number of the genealogies included in these series were presented to gain entrance into the honored religious and military orders, such as the Order of Malta, which technically required four quarters of nobility; families frequently exalted their ancestry in order to gain admission for their sons, and their claims were accepted without question. On occasion valuable copies of original documents may be found in these two series.

The Bibliothèque Nationale also has additional genealogical and biographical information about the intendants and their ancestors—those who were *maîtres des requêtes*—in two manuscript collections: François Blanchard, *Les généalogies des maistres des requestes ordinaires de l'Hostel du Roi* (Paris, 1670), ms. fr. 32137 and 32514; and the *Biographie des maistres des requestes,* ms. fr. 14018, which is a continuation of Blanchard's work covering the first half of the eighteenth century. Generally, the information obtained from these two sources repeats and corroborates information from the genealogical sources in the Cabinet des Titres.

Notarial records, consisting of marriage contracts, testaments, and division of legacies, are an invaluable source of information regarding the intendants' ancestry, their circle of relations and acquaintances in the past or during their own times, and the status and wealth of their immediate families. These documents may sometimes be found, in part or complete, among the source material in the genealogical collection of the Bibliothèque Nationale. Otherwise these records are hidden away in the storehouse of material located in the Minutier Central of the Archives Nationales; this consists of the total collection of documents of all the Parisian notaries, and individual documents may be found only if the name of the notary and the date of the document are known. Historians of the *ancien régime* continue to hope that an easier system of classification may one day be devised.

PRIMARY SOURCES

ABBREVIATIONS

AN	Archives Nationales
BN	Bibliothèque Nationale

Bibliography

ABBREVIATIONS

DB   *Dossiers bleus*
MC   Minutier Central
ms. fr. manuscrits français
PO   *Pièces originales*

A. *Genealogy—unpublished* (listed by family name)

D'Agay de Mutigney
   PO 11; DB 4; Nouveau d'Hozier 3
D'Aine
   PO 18
D'Aligre de Boislandry
   PO 36–37; Nouveau d'Hozier 6; also BN ms. fr. 32138, fs. 471–474
Amelot de Chaillou
   PO 52; DB 16; Carrés d'Hozier 19; Nouveau d'Hozier 8
Aubert de Tourny
   PO 119 and 120; DB 36; Carrés d'Hozier 39; Nouveau d'Hozier 15; and BN ms. fr. 32138, f. 49
Auget de Montyon
   PO 137; DB 39; Nouveau d'Hozier 17
Barberie de Saint-Contest, and
Barberie de Saint-Contest de la Chataîgneraye
   PO 188; DB 56; Carrés d'Hozier 57
Barentin
   PO 195; DB 57; Carrés d'Hozier 59; Chérin 14; MC—LIV:402, 13 July 1692; XCVIII:355, 31 Oct. 1703
Barrillon d'Armoncourt
   PO 204; DB 61
Bauyn d'Angervilliers
   PO 231–232; DB 66; Carrés d'Hozier 70; Chérin 18
Beauharnois
   PO 242
Bernage, and
Bernage de Vaux
   PO 300; DB 87; Cabinet d'Hozier 41; MC—LXI:337, 11 Feb. 1714

Bertier de Sauvigny
PO 314; DB 90
Bertin de Bellisle
PO 315; DB 90; Chérin 24
Bignon de Blanzy
PO 341–344; DB 96; Carrés d'Hozier 93; MC—LXVI:388, 21
Aug. 1724; LXXV:473, 20 July 1706; CV:954, 2 Jan. 1697
Blair de Boismont
PO 359; DB 99; Chérin 27; Nouveau d'Hozier 45
Boucher d'Orsay
PO 432–433; DB 115; Carrés d'Hozier 118; MC—III:450, 18
Nov. 1619; III:479, 5 Feb. 1606; III:488, 26 Feb. 1610; III:489,
17 July 1610; III:497, 8 Oct. 1614; III:501, 16 May 1616;
III:507, 22 June, 20 Aug., and 18 Sept. 1618; III:509, 19 Jan.
and 3 May 1619; III:511, 7 Apr. 1620; XIV:110, 3 and 11 Mar.
1674; XIV:226, 8 May 1716; XIV:278, 24 Apr. 1730; XIV:306,
28 Feb. 1740; XIV:310, 8 Jan. 1741; XIV:345, 14 Aug. 1752;
XIV:363, 9 Feb. 1758; LXXXVII:505, 24 Jan. 1641; CXII:368A,
27 Feb. and 17 Mar. 1674
Cachet de Garnerans
PO 566; Cabinet d'Hozier 73
Calonne
PO 574; DB 149
Camus de Pontcarré de Viarme
PO 582; DB 150; Carrés d'Hozier 148; Cabinet d'Hozier 76;
and BN ms. fr. 14018
Caze de la Bove
PO 631; DB 161; Carrés d'Hozier 158; Chérin 47; Cabinet
d'Hozier 81; Nouveau d'Hozier 85
Chaumont de la Galaizière, and
Chaumont de la Millière
PO 716; DB 178; Carrés d'Hozier 179
Chauvelin de Beauséjour
PO 722; Carrés d'Hozier 180–181; Cabinet d'Hozier 91; Nouveau d'Hozier 95; MC—LXXXVII:1035, 6 Feb. and 8 Mar.
1756
Chazerat
PO 729; DB 181

Bibliography

Clugny de Nuis
  PO 791; DB 198
Cluzel
  PO 792; DB 198
Creil de Bournezeau
  PO 924; DB 222
Dodart
  PO 1007; DB 237
Doujat
  PO 1021; DB 241; Cabinet d'Hozier 122; MC—XLIII:57, 26
  May 1649
Dupleix de Bacquencourt
  PO 2299, "Pleix"; Nouveau d'Hozier 121
Dupré de Saint-Maur
  PO 2372 and 2373; DB 543; Carrés d'Hozier 513; Nouveau
  d'Hozier 274; MC—XXXIV:355, 25 July 1711; CXV:274, 3
  June 1691
Esmangart
  PO 1063; Chérin 73, "Esmangard"; Nouveau d'Hozier 125,
  "Esmangard"
Ferrand de Villemilan
  PO 1127; DB 265; Carrés d'Hozier 254; Chérin 79; Cabinet
  d'Hozier 138; Nouveau d'Hozier 132; MC—XXII:438, 28 Oct.
  1719
Flesselles
  PO 1163; Carrés d'Hozier 258; Chérin 81; Nouveau d'Hozier
  135 and 136
Foullé de Martargis
  PO 1215; DB 278; Carrés d'Hozier 269; Cabinet d'Hozier 147;
  Nouveau d'Hozier 141; MC—XXVII:60, 23 Nov. 1709
Gallois de la Tour
  PO 995, 1271, and 2860; DB 300
Guignard de Saint-Priest
  PO 1440; DB 339; Nouveau d'Hozier 169
Joly de Fleury de la Valette
  PO 1585; DB 369
Journet
  PO 1591

Jubert de Bouville
PO 1596; Carrés d'Hozier 358; Chérin 112
La Bourdonnaye, and
La Bourdonnaye de Blossac
PO 465; DB 123; Carrés d'Hozier 122; Chérin 34; Nouveau
d'Hozier 61; also Nouveau d'Hozier, "le Fèvre d'Ormesson,"
f. 62; MC—LIV:391, 12 Jan. 1687; CXVII:676, 3 Nov. 1705
La Briffe, and
La Briffe des Ferrières
PO 518 and 1614; DB 135; Carrés d'Hozier 134; Chérin 37;
Nouveau d'Hozier 69
La Coré
PO 855 and 1615; DB 375
Lallemant de Lévignen
PO 1624; DB 377; Carrés d'Hozier 365; Nouveau d'Hozier 200;
MC—LXXXIV:476, 29 Apr. 1761
Lamoignon de Basville, and
Lamoignon de Courson
PO 1631; DB 379; Chérin 115; Nouveau d'Hozier 201; MC—
XVI:15, 9 June 1597; CXII:434, 22 May 1706
La Porte de Meslay
PO 2345 and 2346; DB 537
Le Blanc
DB 99
Le Bret
PO 502 and 1677; DB 132; Cabinet d'Hozier 64
Le Fèvre de Caumartin
PO 1140 and 1680; DB 268; Nouveau d'Hozier 134
Le Fèvre d'Ormesson de Chéray
PO 1138, 1139, 1145, and 1680; DB 267; Cabinet d'Hozier 139;
Nouveau d'Hozier 134; MC—XIX:420, 22 July 1640; XXVI:
234, 22 Apr. 1708; LXXV:215, 20 Dec. 1682; C:327, 13 Jan.
1676
Le Guerchois
PO 1427; DB 177
Le Peletier de Morfontaine
PO 2223; DB 515; Carrés d'Hozier 487; Cabinet d'Hozier 264;
Nouveau d'Hozier 261; MC—XXXV:406, 16 Oct. 1656

Bibliography

Le Pelletier de la Houssaye
 PO 2225 and 2226; DB 515; Carrés d'Hozier 487; Chérin 154;
 Cabinet d'Hozier 264; MC—LX:111, 13 Jan. 1687; CIX:202,
 25 Apr. 1657
L'Escalopier
 PO 1690; DB 390; Chérin 120; Nouveau d'Hozier 124
Maignard de Bernières
 PO 1794; DB 415; Chérin 127; Nouveau d'Hozier 218; MC—
 LXXXVIII:458, 18 Mar. 1719
Mégret de Sérilly
 PO 1912; DB 440
Méliand
 PO 1914; DB 440; Carrés d'Hozier 426; Cabinet d'Hozier 233;
 MC—XLI:242, 1 Sept. 1671
Moreau de Beaumont, and
Moreau de Séchelles
 PO 2046; DB 471; Carrés d'Hozier 453; Nouveau d'Hozier 246;
 MC—XLI:276, 12 July 1682; LXI:337, 11 Feb. 1714; LXVI:380,
 7 Apr. 1721
Orceau de Fontette
 PO 2147; DB 501; Carrés d'Hozier 473; Nouveau d'Hozier 255
Pajot de Marcheval
 PO 2184; DB 507; Carrés d'Hozier 479; Chérin 151; Nouveau
 d'Hozier 258
Peirenc de Moras
 PO 2255, "Peyrenc"
Pineau de Lucé
 PO 2283; DB 524; Carrés d'Hozier 497; Nouveau d'Hozier 266
Quentin de Richebourg
 PO 2407, "Quantin," and 2411; DB 551 and 565; Carrés d'Ho-
 zier 520; Cabinet d'Hozier 282; MC—LXXXV:297, 24 Mar.
 1704; XCVI:169bis, 29 Sept. 1697
Rossignol
 PO 2550; DB 583; Nouveau d'Hozier 291
Rouillé d'Orfeuil
 PO 2560; DB 585; Chérin 179; Carrés d'Hozier 158, "Caze,"
 f. 240; MC—CV:967, 2 Dec. 1699
Roujault
 PO 2561; DB 585

Savalette de Magnanville
  PO 2648, "Savalete"; DB 601
Sénac de Meilhan
  DB 610
Taboureau des Réaux
  PO 1784; DB 623; Nouveau d'Hozier 309
Terray
  PO 1809; DB 629
Thiroux de Crosne
  PO 2830; DB 632; Carrés d'Hozier 600; Nouveau d'Hozier 314;
  MC—LII:315, 26 Jan. 1744; LII:394, 24 Nov. 1757; LII:409,
  17 Mar. 1760; LXIX:321; 28 Feb. 1735
Trudaine
  PO 1892; DB 648; Carrés d'Hozier 613; Chérin 200; MC—LI:
  562, 9 Apr. 1666
Turgot de Saint-Clair, and
Turgot de Soumons
  PO 2897; DB 650; Carrés d'Hozier 614; Chérin 200; MC—
  XVI:37, 13 Mar. 1619; LXXXVIII:441, 15 June 1716

B. *Administration*

1. UNPUBLISHED

Mémoire pour M^{rs} les Ms. des req. Pretendants quils sont seuls en Droict et en possession destre envoyés dans les provinces en qualité dintendants. . . . Janvier 1717. Bibliothèque Nationale ms. fr. 7-013, f°558r°–566v°.

2. PUBLISHED

Almanach Royal, Paris, 1710–1713, 1749–1752, and 1774–1777.
Boislisle, A. M. de, ed. *Correspondance des contrôleurs généraux des finances avec les intendants des provinces (1683–1715).* 3 vols. Paris, 1874–1897.
——. *Mémoires des intendants sur l'état des généralités dressés pour l'instruction du duc de Bourgogne.* Vol. I. Paris, 1881.
Depping, Georges Bernard, ed. *Correspondance administrative sous le règne de Louis XIV.* 4 vols. Paris, 1850–1855.
Doisy, M., directeur de Bureau des Comptes des Parties Casuelles

Bibliography

du Roi. *Le royaume de France et les états de Lorraine.* Paris, 1753.

C. *Writings by the intendants*

D'Agay de Mutigney, François Marie Bruno. *Discours prononcé à la séance publique de l'Académie des Sciences, Belles-Lettres et Arts d'Amiens . . . sur les Avantages de la Navigation intérieure. . . .* 25 Aug. 1782. Amiens, J. B. Caron.

——. *Discours prononcé à la séance publique de l'Académie des Sciences, Belles-Lettres et Arts d'Amiens . . . sur l'utilité des Sciences et des Arts.* 25 Aug. 1774.

Auget de Montyon, Antoine Jean Baptiste Robert. *Eloge de Michel de l'Hôpital, chancelier de France.* Discours qui a obtenu le second accessit du Prix de l'Académie Françoise, en 1777. Paris, 1777.

——. *Examen de la Constitution de France de 1799 et comparaison avec la Constitution monarchique de cet état.* London, 1800.

——. *Mémoire des Princes presenté au Roi.* 1788. This declaration presented in the name of the Royal Princes, expressing their political views on the eve of the Estates-General, was written by Auget de Montyon, who was a political adviser to the Comte d'Artois.

——. *Particularités et observations sur les ministres des finances de France les plus célèbres, depuis 1600 jusqu'en 1791.* Paris, 1812.

——. *Quelle influence ont les diverses espèces d'impôt sur la moralité, l'activité, et l'industrie des peuples?* (1808). Included in *Mélanges d'Economie Politique,* Gustave de Molinari, ed., II (Paris, 1848) 365–493.

——. *Rapport fait à S. M. Louis XVIII sur le principe de la monarchie française contre le Tableau de l'Europe de M. de Calonne.* Constance, 1796.

——. *Recherches et considérations sur la population de la France.* Paris, 1778. (Sometimes attributed to M. Moheau, the secretary to Auget de Montyon.)

Bauyn d'Angervilliers, Nicolas Prosper. "Lettres écrites à la cour." Drawn from *Bulletin de la Société pour la conservation des monuments historiques d'Alsace,* Strasbourg, 1878.

Calonne, Charles Alexandre de. *De l'état de la France, présent et à venir.* London, Oct. 1790.

——. *De l'état de la France, tel qu'il peut et qu'il droit être.* London, Nov. 1790.

——. *2ᵉ Lettre au Roi.* London, 5 Apr. 1789.

——. *Discours prononcé de l'ordre du roi et en sa présence à l'Assemblée des notables, tenue à Versailles le 22 février 1787.* Versailles, 1787.

——. *Esquisse de l'état de la France.* Paris, Feb. 1791.

——. *Lettre adressé au roi, le 9 février 1789.* London, 1789.

——. *Lettre de M. de Calonne au citoyen auteur du prétendu Rapport fait à S.M. Louis XVIII.* London, 26 July 1796.

——. *Lettre de M. de Calonne, ministre d'Etat, à M. l'Evêque de Blois, sur le cahier de Madon.* 15 June 1789.

——. *Lettres surprises à M. de Calonne.* Paris, 1787. (This also includes Calonne's answers to these letters.)

——. *Mémoire concernant la navigation des rivières de la province des Trois-Evêchés et le commerce de la ville de Metz; lue dans l'Assemblée publique de la Société Royale des Sciences et des Arts de Metz, tenue le 18 novembre 1772.* Metz, 1773.

——. *Observations de M. de Calonne sur la déclaration de Leurs Majestés Imperiale et Prussienne signée à Pillnitz . . .* , Paris.

——. *Pièces essentielles et indispensables; tableaux de régie, appendix, qui font suite au Mémoire du M. de Calonne.* Feb. 1778.

——. *Réponse de M. de Calonne à l'écrit de M. Necker . . . contenant l'examen des comptes de la situation des finances rendus en 1774, 1776, 1781, 1783, et 1787, avec des observations sur les résultats de l'Assemblée des Notables.* London, 1788.

——. *Requête au roi.* Paris, 1787. This is Calonne's reply to accusations leveled against him and his defense of his actions as royal minister.

——. *Tableau de l'Europe, jusqu'au commencement de 1796 et pensées sur ce que peut procurer une paix solide.* London, Mar. 1796.

Chaumont de la Galaizière, Antoine. *Mémoire sur les corvées.* 1785.

Moreau de Beaumont, Jean Louis. *Mémoire concernant les impositions et droits en Europe.* Mᵉ Poullin de Vieville, éditeur. 5

vols. Nouvelle édition. Paris, 1787–1789. This is a thorough, extensive, and detailed examination of the complex system of taxes in France and in all the states of Europe. Moreau de Beaumont originally undertook this study for the royal government to serve as the basis for projected reforms in the French fiscal system. The first edition, published in 1768–1769, was studied by Adam Smith as a factual basis for his own work, *The Wealth of Nations.*

Sénac de Meilhan, Gabriel. *Le caractère des principaux personnages du règne de Louis XVI.* Hamburg, 1795.

——. *Considérations sur l'esprit et les moeurs.* London, 1787.

——. *Considérations sur les richesses et le luxe.* Amsterdam, 1787.

——. *Des principes et des causes de la Révolution en France.* London, 1790.

——. *Du gouvernement, des moeurs, et des conditions en France avant la Révolution.* Hamburg, 1795. The purpose of this essay was to show that the Revolution was not caused by an uprising of a people oppressed by a tyrannical government; this Sénac does by describing conditions in pre-Revolution France, thereby demonstrating that Frenchmen were not oppressed and the monarchy was not tyrannical. Although the essay is more vindictive in tone than his other writings, since Sénac wrote it in the midst of the Revolution, nevertheless he does not distort the political and social conditions in the *ancien régime.*

——. *L'émigré.* (Brunswick, 1797). Publié par Casimir Stryienski and Frantz Funck-Brentano. 4 vols. in 2. Paris, 1904. This is a rather sentimental novel about the hardships of émigré life, in the typical epistolary form of many eighteenth-century novels. It was written around 1793, when Sénac himself was an émigré.

——. *Lettre de Monsieur de M**, à M. l'abbé Sabatier de Castres sur la République Françoise.* Vienna, 1792.

——. *Portraits et caractères du XVIIIᵉ siècle* (1789). Paris, 1945.

D. *Writings relating to the intendants*

La Briffe des Ferrières, Louis Arnaud de. *Poésies dédiées à l'intendant de La Briffe par les rhétoriciens du Collège de Bourbon à Caen.* (Caen, 1740). Included in *Recueil des Poésies Scolaires composées dans les Collèges de Rouen et de Caen.* Publiés par plusieurs Bibliophiles Normands. Rouen, 1924.

SECONDARY SOURCES

A. *Manuals, dictionaries, encyclopedias,*
and treatises about
the ancien régime

1. GENEALOGICAL AND BIOGRAPHICAL

Bluche, François. *L'origine des magistrats du Parlement de Paris au XVIIIe siècle (1715–1771) : Dictionnaire généalogique.* Thèse complémentaire pour le doctorat ès lettres présentée à la Faculté des Lettres de l'Université de Paris. Paris, 1956.

Bouillet, J.-B. *Nobiliaire d'Auvergne.* T. II. Clermont-Ferrand, 1847.

Dictionnaire biographiques des origines à 1800, les Bouches-Rhône. "La Tour de Glené," t. IV², p. 291.

Histoire héroique et universelle de la noblesse de Provence. "Gallois," t. I, pp. 446–447. Avignon, 1776.

La Chesnaye-Desbois, François Alexandre Aubert de. *Dictionnaire de la noblesse.* 19 vols. Paris, 1863–1876.

Laîné, P. Louis. *Dictionnaire véridique des origines des maisons nobles ou anoblies du royaume de France.* 2 vols. Paris, 1818–1819. Both Laîné and La Chesnaye-Desbois should be used only to obtain biographical information about the intendants themselves or their immediate forebears, since the genealogies relating to earlier periods of their family histories may not be accurate.

Meurgey de Tupigny, Jacques. *Guide des recherches généalogiques aux Archives Nationales.* Paris, 1956.

Michaud, M. *Biographie universelle ancienne et moderne.* Rev. ed., 45 vols. Paris, 1843.

2. POLITICAL AND SOCIAL

Antoine, Michel. *Le Fonds du Conseil d'Etat du Roi aux Archives Nationales.* Paris, 1955. The introduction is an excellent survey of the evolution of the Royal Council and its many organs during the eighteenth century.

Bluche, François, and Pierre Durye. *L'anoblissement par charges avant 1789.* 2 vols. La Roche-sur-Yon, 1962.

Chérin, Louis Nicolas Henri. *Abrégé chronologique d'édits déclarations, règlements, arrêts et lettres patentes des rois de France concernant le fait de noblesse.* In Charles Grandmaison, *Dictionnaire héraldique* (Paris, 1852).

Chéruel, A. *Dictionnaire historique des institutions, moeurs et coutumes de la France.* 7th ed., 2 vols. Paris, 1899.

Encyclopédie méthodique. Volumes: "Economie Politique," "Finances," and "Jurisprudence." Paris, 1784–1788.

Fréminville, Edme La Poix de. *Les vrais principes des fiefs.* Vols. I, II. Paris, 1769.

Furetière, Antoine. *Dictionnaire universel de Furetière.* Rev. ed., 5 vols. Paris, 1732.

Gasquet, Amédée. *Précis des institutions politiques et sociales de l'ancienne France.* 2 vols. Paris, 1885.

La Grande encyclopédie. Ed. by Berthelot *et al.* 31 vols. Paris, 1886–1902.

Guyot, Pierre. *Traité des droits, fonctions, franchises, exceptions, prérogatives et privilèges annexés en France à chaque dignité, à chaque office et à chaque état.* Vols. II, III, IV. Paris, 1786–1788.

La Roque, Gilles André de. *Traité de la noblesse et de toutes ses différentes espèces.* Rev. ed. Rouen, 1734.

Loyseau, Charles. *Traité des seigneuries: Oeuvres.* 7th ed. Paris, 1666.

Marion, Marcel *Dictionnaire des institutions de la France aux XVIIᵉ et XVIIIᵉ siècles.* Paris, 1923.

Necker, Jacques. *De l'administration des finances de la France.* 3 vols. [1785].

Puy de Clinchamps, Philippe de. *La noblesse.* Paris, 1959.

B. *Works relating to the intendants and the intendancies*

Angot des Rotours. "Le dernier intendant de la généralité d'Alençon," *Bulletin de la Société Historique et Archéologique de l'Orne,* XII (1893), 503–14.

D'Arbois de Jubainville, Henri. *L'administration des intendants d'après les archives de l'Aube.* Paris, 1880.

Ardascheff, Paul. *Les intendants de province sous Louis XVI.* Trans. by Louis Jousserandot. (Vol. II of the original work in

Russian, *L'administration provinciale en France dans les derniers temps de l'ancien régime, 1774–1789.*) Paris, 1909.

Astre, F. "Les intendants de Languedoc," *Mémoires de l'Académie des Sciences et Belles-Lettres de Toulouse.* 5ᵉ série (1859–1861), III, 7–36; IV, 421–43; V, 102–24.

Beaucorps, Charles de. "Une province sous Louis XIV: l'administration des intendants d'Orléans, de Creil, Jubert de Bouville, de la Bourdonnaye, 1686–1713," *Mémoires de la Société Archéologique et Historique de l'Orléanais,* XXXIII (1911), 37–500.

Bertier, Christian de. *Réponse à une note généalogique sur les origines et les armoiries de la maison de Bertier de Sauvigny.* Paris, 1939.

Bertier de Sauvigny, Charles de. *Quelques notes généalogiques sur la famille de Bertier.* Lille, 1887.

Bertier de Sauvigny, Guillaume de. *Le comte Ferdinand de Bertier (1782–1864) et l'énigme de la congrégation.* Paris, 1948.

Bonnefoy, Georges. *Histoire de l'administration civile dans la province d'Auvergne.* Vol. I. Paris, 1895.

Bordes, Maurice. "Les intendants de Louis XV," *Revue Historique,* CCXXIII (Jan.–Mar. 1960), 45–62.

——. "Les intendants éclairés de la fin de l'ancien régime," *Revue d'Histoire Economique et Sociale,* XXXIX (1961), 57–83.

——. "Une grande circonscription administrative sous l'ancien régime: l'intendance d'Auch au XVIIIᵉ siècle," *Académie de Toulouse; Bulletin régional d'informations universitaires,* No. 4 (Feb. 1951), 6–9.

Boy, C. "Les Peirenc de Moras," *Bulletin de la Diana,* XXIV (1931–1934), 154–61.

Boyé, Pierre. "Le chancelier Chaumont de la Galaizière et sa famille," *Le Pays Lorrain,* XXVIII (1935), 113–32, 441–60, 537–52; XXIX (1937), 129–57; XXX (1938), 481–507.

——. "Les travaux publics et le régime des corvées," *Annales de l'Est* (1899), 533ff. (About Antoine Martin Chaumont de la Galaizière.)

Boyer de Sainte-Suzanne, Charles Victor Emile, Baron de. "Les administrateurs sous l'ancien régime," in *Notes d'un curieux* (Monaco, 1878), pp. 115–237.

——. *Les intendants de la généralité d'Amiens.* Paris, 1865.

Bussière, G. "Henri Bertin et sa famille," *Bulletin de la Société Historique et Archéologique du Périgord,* XXXII (1905), 216–44, 381–418; XXX (1906), 72–113, 211–43, 311–31; XXXIV (1907), 53–83, 272–314, 373–88, 451–66; XXXV (1908), 274–313, 437–64; XXXVI (1909), 133–62, 210–81.

Chazet, René Alissan de. *Vie de M. de Montyon.* Paris, 1829.

Choullier, Ernest. *Les Trudaine.* Extract from *La revue de Champagne et de Brie.* Arcis-sur-Aube, 1884.

Coulaudon, Aimé. *Chazerat, dernier intendant de la généralité de Riom et province d'Auvergne (1774–1789).* Thèse pour le doctorat, la Faculté de droit de l'université de Poitiers. Paris, 1932.

Creutzer. "Les intendants de Lorraine," *Journal Officiel* (3 Apr. 1880), 3847.

Dartique-Peyron, Charles. *Dupré de Saint-Maur et le problème des corvées; le conflit entre l'intendant de Guyenne et le parlement de Bordeaux, 1776–1785.* Mont-de-Marsan, 1936.

Dubuc, Pierre. *L'intendance de Soissons sous Louis XIV.* Paris, 1902.

Dumas, François. *La généralité de Tours au XVIIIᵉ siècle; administration de l'intendant du Cluzel (1766–1783).* Paris, 1894.

Dumont, (F.?). "L'intendant de Dijon et le Mâconnais," *Société d'Histoire du Droit des Pays Bourguignons* (1939).

Durival, Nicolas Luton. *Description de la Lorraine et du Barrois.* Nancy, 1778–1783. (Information about Chaumont de la Galaizière.)

Durouvray, Edmond. "Comment Joly de Fleury devint ministre des finances," *Feuilles d'histoire,* VI (1911), 392–96.

Dutertre, A. P. "Notice sur la famille Taboureau," *Nouvelle Revue Historique,* (June–July 1935), 65–67.

Duval, Louis. *Etat de la généralité d'Alençon sous Louis XIV.* 1890.

Esmonin, Edmond. "Le Fèvre de Caumartin, intendant de Picardie pendant trente-deux ans," *Revue d'Histoire Moderne,* nouvelle série, no. 3 (May–June 1932), 272–83.

——. "Les intendants du Dauphiné des origines à la Révolution," *Annales de l'Université de Grenoble,* XXXIV (1923), 37–90.

Feugère, Léon. *Eloge de M. de Montyon*. Paris, 1834.

Fréville, Henri. *L'intendance de Bretagne, 1689–1790*. 3 vols. Rennes, 1953.

Godard, Charles. *Les pouvoirs des intendants sous Louis XIV*. Paris, 1901.

Gourbeyre, Alexis. *La petite propriété rurale dans la Puy-de-Dôme*. Paris, 1900. (Information about Chazerat.)

Grosriez, Fernand Le Fèvre du. "L'origine de la famille Le Fèvre de Caumartin," *Cabinet Historique de l'Artois et de la Picardie*, Nov. 1886.

Guérin, Louis. *L'intendant de Cypierre et la vie économique de l'Orléanais, 1760–1785*. Orléans, 1938.

Guérin, Paul. "L'exil d'un janséniste à Issoudun, le conseiller d'état Charles Maignard de Bernières," *Revue du Berry et du Centre*, XXII, 105–36; XXIII, 17–51.

Guimbaud, Louis. *Un grand bourgeois au XVIIIᵉ siècle: Auget de Montyon (1733–1820) d'après des documents inédits*. Paris, 1909.

Herlaut, Colonel. "Claude Le Blanc, intendant de la Flandre maritime (1708–1715)," *Bulletin Union Faulconnier*, XXV (1928).

Jolly, Pierre. *Calonne, 1734–1802*. Paris, 1949.

Kerviler, René. "Etudes sur les Bignon," *Bibliophile le francais*, Sept.–Nov. 1872, 275–83, 300–12, 322–42.

———. *Un évêque de Vannes à l'Académie française: Jean François Paul Lefebvre de Caumartin. Etude historique et biographique sur sa carrière administrative, et sur sa famille d'après des documents inédits*. Vannes, 1876.

Labour, Fernand Louis Edmond. *M. de Montyon*. Paris, 1880.

Lacour-Gayet, Robert. *Calonne: Financier, réformateur, contre-révolutionnaire, 1734–1802*. Paris, 1963.

Langlois, Abbé Marcel. "Ancêtres des parlementaires parisiens," *Bulletin de la Société de l'Histoire de Paris et de l'Ile-de-France*, 1924, 125–26; 1926, 60–62.

Le Bret, le Comte Robert Cardin. *Maison Le Bret: Généalogie historique*. Le Mans, 1889.

Legrand, Louis. *Sénac de Meilhan et l'intendance de Hainaut et du Cambrésis sous Louis XVI*. Thèse pour le doctorat présentée à la Faculté des Lettres de l'Université de Paris. Paris, 1868.

Bibliography

Lhéritier, Michel. *L'intendant Tourny (1695–1760)*. 2 vols. Paris, 1920.

Livet, Georges. *L'intendance d'Alsace sous Louis XIV, 1648–1715*. Paris, 1956.

Lombardon-Montézan, Eudoxe de. *Notes et souvenirs d'ancienne principauté de Dombes et son Parlement. La famille Cachet de Montézan, des comtes de Garnerans*. Marseilles, 1885.

Lurion, Roger de. *M. de Lacoré, intendant de Franche-Comté (1761–1784)*. Extract from the *Bulletin de l'Académie des Sciences, Belles-Lettres et Arts de Besançon*, (1897). Besançon, 1898.

Marchand, J. *Un intendant sous Louis XIV; étude sur l'administration de Lebret en Provence (1687–1704)*. Paris, 1889.

Mentque, Robert de. "Notice sur la maison de Chaumont de la Galaizière," *Bulletin Archéologique de Tarn-et-Garonne*, XXX (1902), 165–71, 287.

Merle, Abbé. "Les Terray à Boen, notes généalogiques sur les ascendants de l'abbé Terray," *Bulletin de la Diana*, XXIV (1931–1934), 301–10.

Monin, Ernest. *Montyon; ou la vie d'un homme de bien*. Paris, 1867.

Mourlot, Félix. "Les quatre derniers intendants de la généralité de Caen: Fontette, Esmangard, Feydeau de Brou (1783–1787), Coudrès de Launay," *Congrès des Sociétés Savantes*, session of 6 Apr. 1904, in the *Journal Officiel*, Apr. 1904, 2183.

———. *Un intendant de Caen au XVIIIᵉ siècle: Intendant Fontette (1752–1775) notes biographiques*. Extract from the *Bulletin Historique et Philogique*, 1904. Paris, 1905.

Néraud, J. *Les intendants de la généralité de Berry*. Thèse pour le doctorat, la Faculté de droit de l'Université de Paris. Paris, 1922.

Pilotelle. "Notice sur P. E. M. de la Bourdonnaye de Blossac," *Mémoires de la Société des Antiquaires de l'Ouest*, XXII (1855), 287–366.

Prévost de Levaud, Etienne. *Les théories d'intendant Rouillé d'Orfeuil*. Thèse pour le doctorat, la Faculté de droit de l'Université de Poitiers. Rochechouart, 1909.

Rossignol. "Le livre de dépenses de Dupré de Saint-Maur, intendant de Guyenne," Congrès des Sociétés Savantes, session of 7 Apr. 1904, in the *Journal Officiel,* Apr. 1904, 2209.

Sauvage, R. N. "L'intendant Fontette et les concessions de terre," *Normannia,* Oct.–Dec. 1939, 487–502.

Schwartz, Camille. "L'intendant Mégret de Sérilly et son oeuvre en Alsace, 1750–1752," *Vie en Alsace,* 1927, 80–88.

Sée, Henri. "L'industrie et le commerce de la Bretagne dans la première moitié du XVIIIᵉ siècle, d'après le mémoire de l'intendant des Gallois de la Tour," *Annales de Bretagne,* XXXV (1922).

Swarte, Victor de. "Un intendant secrétaire d'Etat; Claude Le Blanc, sa vie, sa correspondance," *Bulletin Historique et Philologique,* Nos. 1 and 2, année 1900 (Paris, 1901), 319–44.

Uzureau, F. "Les 31 intendants de la Touraine, du Maine et de l'Anjou (1618–1790)," *Andegaviana,* 15ᵉ série (Paris, 1914), 343–49.

Vialatte, Louis. *Rossignol, intendant de la généralité de Riom et province d'Auvergne (1734–1750).* Thèse pour le doctorat, la Faculté de Droit de l'Université de Poitiers. Poitiers, 1924.

Vian, Louis. *Les Lamoignon, une vieille famille de robe.* Paris, [1896].

C. *Education and intellectual formation of magistrates in the* ancien régime

Delbeke, Baron François. *L'action politique et sociale des avocats au XVIIIᵉ siècle.* Louvain, 1927.

Gilmore, Myron P. *Argument from Roman Law in Political Thought, 1200–1600.* Cambridge, Mass., 1941.

Glasson, Ernest. "Les examens d'entrée dans l'ancienne magistrature," *La Grande Revue,* I (1897), 34–53.

Jourdain, Charles M. *Histoire de l'université de Paris au XVIIᵉ et XVIIIᵉ siècles.* 2 vols. Paris, 1862–66.

Péries, Abbé G. *La faculté de droit dans l'ancienne université de Paris (1160–1793).* Paris, 1890.

Sicard, Abbé Augustin. *L'éducation morale et civique avant et pendant la Révolution (1700–1808).* Paris, 1913.

D. *Institutional history*

Antoine, M. "Le conseil des dépêches sous Louis XV," *Bibliothèque Ecole des Chartes*, 1953.

——. "Le conseil du roi sous Louis XV," *Congrès Sciences Historique*, VII (Rome, 1955), 259–61.

——. "Les comités de ministres sous le règne de Louis XV," *Revue Historique de Droit Français et Etranger* (1951), 193–230.

——. "Les conseils des finances sous le règne de Louis XV," *Revue d'Histoire Moderne et Contemporaine*, V (1958), 161–86.

Aucoc, Léon. *Le conseil d'état avant et depuis 1789: Ses transformations, ses travaux, et son personnel*. Paris, 1876.

Bisson de Barthélémy, Paul. *L'activité d'un procureur-général au Parlement de Paris à la fin de l'ancien régime: Les Joly de Fleury*. Paris, 1964.

Bordes, Maurice. "La réforme municipale du contrôleur-général Laverdy et son application dans certaines provinces," *Revue d'Histoire Moderne et Contemporaine*, XII (Oct.–Dec. 1965), 241–70.

Bosher, J. F. "French Administration and Public Finance in Their European Setting," in *The New Cambridge Modern History*, VIII (*The American and French Revolutions, 1763–93*), ed. A. Goodwin (Cambridge, Eng., 1965), 565–91.

Chéruel, A. *Histoire de l'administration monarchique en France depuis l'avènement de Philippe-Auguste jusqu'à la mort de Louis XIV*. Paris, 1855.

Dakin, Douglas. "The Breakdown of the Old Régime in France," in *The New Cambridge Modern History*, VIII (*The American and French Revolutions, 1763–93*), ed. A. Goodwin (Cambridge, Eng., 1965), 592–617.

——. *Turgot and the Ancien Régime in France*. London, 1939.

Esmonin, Edmond. "Observations critiques sur le livre de M. Hanotaux," *Bulletin de la Société d'Histoire Moderne*, 7ᵉ série, No. 40 (Dec. 1932—Jan. 1933), 6–9.

——. "L'origine des intendants jusqu'en 1665," *Bulletin de la Société d'Histoire Moderne*, No. 22 (6 Apr. 1910), 122–24.

Hanotaux, Gabriel. *Origines de l'institution des intendants des provinces: Les premiers intendants des provinces* (1550–1631). Paris, 1884.

Major, J. Russell. "Henry IV and Guyenne: A Study Concerning the Origins of Royal Absolutism," *French Historical Studies*, IV (Fall 1966), 363–83.

McCloy, Shelby T. *Government Assistance in Eighteenth-Century France*. Durham, N.C., 1946.

Monnet, Emile. *Histoire de l'administration en France*. Paris, 1885.

Mousnier, Roland. "Etat et commissaire: Recherches sur la création des intendants des Provinces (1634–1648)," in *Forschungen zu Staat und Verfassung, Festgabe für Fritz Hartung* (Berlin, 1958).

——. "La participation des gouvernés à l'activité des gouvernants dans la France du XVIIe et XVIIIe siècles," *Schwiezer Beiträge zur Allgemeinen Geschichte*, XX (1962–1963), 200–29.

——. "Recherches sur les Syndicats d'officiers pendant la Fronde: Trésoriers généraux de France et Elus pendant la Révolution," *Bulletin de la Société d'Etude du XVIIe Siècle*, Nos. 42–43 (Paris, 1959), 76–117.

——. *La vénalité des offices sous Henri IV et Louis XIII*. Rouen, [1945].

——, ed. *Lettres et mémoires adressés au Chancelier Séguier (1633–1649)*. 2 vols. Paris, 1965. The lengthy introductory essay examines the system of intendancies and the individual intendants in the period before the Fronde under the governments of Cardinals Richelieu and Mazarin.

——, and Fritz Hartung. "Quelques problèmes concernant la monarchie absolue," *Congrès Sciences Historiques*, IV (Rome, 1955), 4–12.

Pagès, Georges. "Essai sur l'évolution des institutions administratives en France du commencement du XVIe siècle à la fin du XVIIe," *Revue d'Histoire Moderne*, NS, VII (1932), 8–57, 113–37.

——. "La vénalité des offices dans l'ancienne France," *Revue Historique*, CLXIX (1932).

Temple, Nora. "The Control and Exploitation of French Towns during the Ancien Régime," *History*, LI (Feb. 1966), 16–34.

Viollet, Paul Marie. *Le roi et ses ministres pendant les trois derniers siècles de la monarchie.* Paris, 1912.

E. *Social history*

Ariès, Philippe. *Centuries of Childhood: A Social History of Family Life.* Trans. by Robert Baldick. New York, 1962.

Barber, Bernard. *Social Stratification: A Comparative Analysis of Structure and Process.* New York, 1957.

Barber, Elinor. *The Bourgeoisie in 18th Century France.* Princeton, N.J., 1955.

Barthélémy, Anatole de. "De la qualification de chevalier," *Revue Nobiliaire* (1868).

——. "Essai sur les lettres d'anoblissement," *Revue Historique Nobiliaire et Biographique* (1869).

Behrens, Betty. "Nobles, Privileges and Taxes in France at the End of the Ancien Régime," *Economic History Review,* 2nd ser., XV (Nov. 1963), 451–75.

——. " 'Straight History' and 'History in Depth': The Experience of Writers on Eighteenth-Century France," *The Historical Journal,* VIII (1965), 117–26.

Bertin, Ernest. *Les mariages dans l'ancienne société française.* Paris, 1879.

Bloch, Jean Richard. "L'anoblissement en France au temps de François 1er: Essai d'une définition de la condition juridique et sociale de la noblesse au début du XVIe siècle," *Bibliothèque de la Revue Historique* (Paris, 1934). (A review of this article by Marc Bloch may be found in *Revue de Synthèse,* 1935, 157.)

Bloch, Marc. "Sur le passé de la noblesse française: Quelques jalons de recherche," *Annales d'Histoire Economique et Sociale,* VIII (1936), 366–78.

Bluche, François. *Les magistrats du Parlement de Paris au XVIIIe siècle (1715–1771). (Annales littéraires de l'Université de Besançon,* XXXV.) Paris, 1960.

——. "L'origine sociale des secrétaires d'état de Louis XIV (1661–1715)," *Bulletin de la Société d'Etude du XVIIe Siècle,* Nos. 42–43 (Paris, 1959), 8–22.

——. "L'origine sociale du personnel ministériel française au XVIIIe siècle," *Bulletin de la Société d'Histoire Moderne,* 12e série, No. 1 (Jan.–Feb. 1957), 9–13.

274

Carré, Henri. *La noblesse de France et l'opinion publique au XVIIIᵉ siècle.* Paris, 1920.

——. "La noblesse de robe au temps de Louis XV," *Bulletin de la Faculté des Lettres de Poitiers* (1890), 344–55, 385–94.

Clavel, Bernard. "La politique dans l'oeuvre de Beaumarchais," *Revue Politique et Parlementaire*, No. 754 (1965), 44–57.

Cobban, Alfred. *The Myth of the French Revolution.* An Inaugural Lecture delivered at University College, London, 6 May 1954. London, 1955.

Corvisier, André. *L'armée française de la fin du XVIIᵉ siècle au ministère de Choiseul: Le soldat.* 2 vols. Paris, 1964.

——. "Les généraux de Louis XIV et leur origine sociale," *Bulletin de la Société d'Etude du XVIIᵉ siècle*, Nos. 42–43 (Paris, 1959), 23–53.

Dainville, P. François de. "Effectifs des collèges et scolarité aux XVIIᵉ et XVIIIᵉ siècles dans le Nord-Est de la France," *Population*, No. 3 (1955), 455–88.

Daumard, A. and F. Furet. *Structures et relations sociales à Paris au milieu du XVIIIᵉ siècles.* Paris, 1961.

Dawson, John Philip, 3rd. "The Bourgeoisie de Robe in 1789," *French Historical Studies*, IV (Spring, 1965), 1–21.

——. "The Judges in the *Bailliages* and *Sénéchaussées*, 1763–1800: A Study of Middle-Class Officeholders before and during the French Revolution." Unpublished Ph.D. thesis, Harvard University, 1960.

Dupront, Alphonse, "Livre et culture dans la société française au XVIIIᵉ siècle: Réflexions sur une enquête," *Annales: Economies, Sociétés, Civilisations*, No. 5 (Sept.–Oct. 1965), 887–922.

Egret, Jean. "L'aristocratie parlementaire française à la fin de l'ancien régime." *Revue Historique*, CCVIII (July–Sept. 1952), 1–147.

——. "L'opposition aristocratique en France au XVIIIᵉ siècle," *L'Information Historique*, No. 5 (Nov.–Dec. 1949), 181–86.

——. "The Origins of the Revolution in Brittany (1788–1789)," in *New Perspectives on the French Revolution*, ed. Jeffry Kaplow (New York, 1965), pp. 136–52.

——. *La pré-Révolution française (1787–1788).* Paris, 1962.

——. "The Pre-Revolution in Provence (1787–1789)," in *New Perspectives on the French Revolution*, ed. Jeffry Kaplow (New York, 1965), pp. 153–69.

Eisenstein, Elizabeth. "Who Intervened in 1788? A Commentary on 'The Coming of the French Revolution'," *American Historical Review,* LXXI (Oct. 1965), 77–103.

Ford, Franklin L. "The Revolutionary and Napoleonic Era: How Much of a Watershed?" *American Historical Review,* LXIX (Oct. 1963), 18–29.

———. *Robe and Sword: The Regrouping of the French Aristocracy after Louis XIV.* Cambridge, Mass., 1953.

———. *Strasbourg in Transition, 1648–1789.* Cambridge, Mass., 1958.

Forster, Robert. *The Nobility of Toulouse in the Eighteenth Century.* Baltimore, 1960.

———. "The Provincial Noble: A Reappraisal," *American Historical Review,* LXVIII (April 1963), 681–91.

Goodwin, Albert. "The Social Origins and Privileged Status of the French Eighteenth-Century Nobility," *Bulletin John Rylands Library,* XLVII (Mar. 1965), 382–403.

——, ed. *The European Nobility in the Eighteenth Century: Studies of the Nobilities of the Major European States in the Pre-Reform Era.* London, 1953. The chapter by J. McManners is an intelligent and perceptive analysis of the French nobility.

Goubert, Pierre. *Beauvais et le Beauvaisis de 1600 à 1730: Contribution à l'histoire sociale de la France du XVIIe siècle.* Paris, 1960.

———. "Les officiers royaux des présidiaux, bailliages et élections dans la société française du XVIIe siècle," *Bulletin de la Société d'Etude du XVIIe Siècle,* Nos. 42–43 (Paris, 1959), 54–75.

Grosclaude, Pierre, ed. *Malesherbe et son temps.* Paris, 1964.

Hyslop, Beatrice. *French Nationalism in 1789 According to the General Cahiers.* New York, 1934.

Kaplow, Jeffry. *Elbeuf during the Revolutionary Period: History and Social Structure.* Baltimore, 1964.

Kolabinska, Marie. *La circulation des élites en France: Etude historique depuis la fin du XIe siècle jusqu'à la Grande Révolution.* Lausanne, 1912.

Lefebvre, Georges. *Etudes orléanaises: I. Contribution à l'étude des structures sociales à la fin du XVIIIe siècle.* Paris, 1962.

——. "The French Revolution and the Peasants," in *The Economic Origins of the French Revolution: Poverty or Prosperity?,* ed. Ralph W. Greenlaw (Boston, 1958), 73–83.

Le Guin, Charles A. *Roland de la Platière, A Public Servant in the Eighteenth Century. (Transactions of the American Philosophical Society,* NS, LVI, pt. 6.) Philadelphia, November, 1966.

Lemoine, Robert-J. "Classes sociales et attitudes révolutionnaires," *Annales,* VII (1935), 167.

Léon, Pierre. "La crise de l'économie française à la fin du règne de Louis XIV (1685–1715)," *L'Information Historique,* No. 4 (Sept.–Oct. 1956), 127–37.

———. "Recherches sur la bourgeoisie française de province au XVIII⁰ siècle," *L'Information Historique,* No. 3 (May–June 1958), 101–105.

Léonard, E. G. *L'armée et ses problèmes au XVIII⁰ siècle.* Paris, 1958.

Marsay, Jacques Marie Joseph, Vicomte de. *De l'âge des privilèges au temps des vanités: Essai sur l'origine et la valeur des prétentions nobiliaires.* Rev. ed. Paris, 1946.

Pilon, Edmond. *La vie de famille au XVIII⁰ siècle.* Paris, 1928.

Ravitch, Norman. "Robe and Sword in the Recruitment of French Bishops," *Catholic Historical Review,* L (Jan. 1965), 494–508.

———. *Sword and Mitre: Government and Episcopate in France and England in the Age of Aristocracy.* Paris, 1966.

Reinhard, Marcel. "Elite et noblesse dans la seconde moitié du XVIII⁰ siècle," *Revue d'Histoire Moderne et Contemporaine,* III (1956), 5–37.

Ribbe, Charles de. *Les familles et la société en France avant la Révolution, d'après des documents originaux.* Paris, 1874.

Richard, Guy. "A propos de la noblesse commerçante de Lyon au XVIII⁰ siècle," *L'Information Historique,* No. 4 (Sept.–Oct. 1959), 156–61.

———. "La noblesse commerçante à Bordeaux et à Nantes au XVIII⁰ siècle," *L'Information Historique,* No. 5 (Nov.–Dec. 1958), 185–90.

———. "Les corporations et la noblesse commerçante en France au XVIII⁰ siècle," *L'Information Historique,* No. 5 (1957), 185–89.

———. "Un essai d'adaptation sociale à une nouvelle structure économique: La noblesse de France et les sociétés par actions à la fin du XVIIIe siècle," *Revue d'Histoire Economique et Sociale,* XLI (1962), 484–523.

Roche, Daniel. "La diffusion des lumières. Un exemple: L'académie de Châlons-sur-Marne," *Annales: Economies, Sociétés, Civilisations,* Sept.–Oct. 1964, 887–922.

Sagnac, Philippe. "Les grands courants d'idées et de sentiments en France vers 1789," *Revue d'Histoire Politique et Constitutionnelle,* II (1938), 317–41.

Saint-Jacob, P. de. *Les paysans de la Bourgogne du Nord.* Paris, 1960.

Snyders, Georges. *La pédagogie en France aux XVIIe et XVIIIe siècles.* Paris, 1965.

Taylor, George V. "Noncapitalist Wealth and the Origins of the French Revolution," *American Historical Review,* LXXII (Jan. 1967), 469–96.

——. "Types of Capitalism in Eighteenth-Century France," *English Historical Review,* LXXIX (July 1964), 478–97.

Trénard, L. "The Social Crisis in Lyons on the Eve of the French Revolution," in *New Perspectives on the French Revolution,* ed. Jeffry Kaplow (New York, 1965), pp. 68–100.

Tuetey, Louis. *Les officiers sous l'ancien régime: Nobles et roturiers.* Paris, 1908.

Vovelle, M. and D. Roche. "Bourgeois, Rentiers, and Property Owners: Elements for Defining a Social Category at the End of the Eighteenth Century," in *New Perspectives on the French Revolution,* ed. Jeffry Kaplow (New York, 1965), pp. 25–46.

F. *General works of analysis and interpretation of the* ancien régime

Behrens, C. B. A. *The Ancien Régime.* New York, 1967.

Cobban, Alfred. *A History of Modern France,* Vol. I. London, 1957.

——. *The Social Interpretation of the French Revolution.* Cambridge, Eng., 1964.

Lefebvre, Georges. *The Coming of the French Revolution.* Trans. by R. R. Palmer. Princeton, N.J., 1947.

Méthivier, Hubert. *L'ancien régime.* Paris, 1961.

Mousnier, Roland, Ernest Labrousse, and Marc Bouloiseau. *Le XVIIIe Siècle: L'epoque des 'Lumières' (1715–1815). (Histoire*

Générale des Civilisations, V, ed. Maurice Crouzet.) Paris, 1959.

Palmer, R. R. *The Age of the Democratic Revolution: A Political History of Europe and America: 1760–1800.* Vol. I, *The Challenge.* Princeton, N.J., 1959.

Sagnac, Philippe. *La formation de la société française moderne, 1661–1789.* 2 vols. Paris, 1945–1946.

Soboul, Albert. *Précis d'histoire de la Révolution française.* Paris, 1962.

Tocqueville, Alexis de. *L'ancien régime et la Révolution.* 8th ed., 2 vols. Paris, Gallimard, 1953.

G. *Comparative works of institutional-social analysis*

Aronson, S. H. *Status and Kinship in the Higher Civil Service.* Cambridge, Mass., 1964.

Aylmer, G. E. *The King's Servants: The Civil Service of Charles I, 1625–1642.* New York, 1961.

Ho, Ping-ti. *The Ladder of Success in Imperial China.* New York, 1964.

Matthews, George T. *The Royal General Farms in Eighteenth-Century France.* New York, 1958.

Namier, Sir Lewis. *The Structure of Politics at the Accession of George III.* 2nd ed. London, 1961.

Pegues, Franklin J. *The Lawyers of the Last Capetians.* Princeton, N.J., 1962.

Richardson, Nicholas. *The French Prefectoral Corps, 1814–1830.* Cambridge, Eng., 1966.

Rosenberg, Hans. *Bureaucracy, Aristocracy and Autocracy: The Prussian Experience, 1680–1815.* Cambridge, Mass., 1958.

Index

Abbeville, 146; *see also* Picardy

Absolutism, 2-3, 8, 10-11, 59, 93n., 146, 212-214; *see also* Administration, royal; Centralization; Councils, royal; Crown; Intendants, role and functions, *and* historical origins of the office; King of France; *and* Sovereign and sovereignty

Academies, 213, 219, 225

Administration, royal: social character of recruitment, viii, ix, 206, 209, 211, 219, 220-222; structure and operations, 2-6, 51, 59, 71-89, 92-93n., 102, 109, 110-113, 161, 193-194, 208-209, 211, 214-215 and 215n.; selection for and recruitment into, 42-51, 45-46n., 60-61, 63-70, 81, 82, 87-89, 91, 101-103, 108, 193-194; promotion and advance within, 45 and n., 52-56, 59, 70, 81, 82, 87-89, 209, 211; prestige and privileges in, 56-58; lower civil service, 90n., 211, 227-228n.; intendants' families in the high administration, 117, 134, 143ff.; *see also* Absolutism; *Bureau des finances;* Bureaus, of the royal councils; Centralization; Chancellery; Commissions, of the royal councils; Commissions and commissioners, royal; *Conseillers d'état;* Councils, royal; Crown; Intendants, role and functions, *and* historical origins of the office; *Maîtres des requêtes,* numbers, role, and functions; Ministers, royal; *and* Secretaries of state

Affairistes, see Tax farmers

D'Agay de Mutigney, François Marie Bruno, 27n.

D'Aiguillon, Emmanuel-Armand, Duc, 84

D'Aine, Marie Jean Baptiste, 17n., 43n.

Aix-en-Provence, 38, 39, 40n., 45n., 54n., 64, 65, 90n., 117n.; *see also* Parlements, provincial, Aix

Alençon, 39n., 41n., 65, 88, 90n.; *see also* Normandy

D'Aligre de Boislandry, Etienne Jean François Marie, 143, 184n.

Alsace, 8, 54n., 79; *see also* Colmar

Amelot (de Chaillou), family, 111, 143

Amelot de Chaillou, Antoine Jean, 17n., 43n., 181n., 184n.

America, 214

Amiens, 27n., 65, 146; *see also* Picardy

Ancienne noblesse, see Nobles and nobility, categories of

Anobli, see Nobles and nobility

Appointements, 237-239

Ardascheff, Paul, vii, ix

D'Argenson, Voyer de Paulny, family and minister, 171, 204

"Aristocratic reaction," 181-207, 206n., 217-235; *see also* "Feudal reaction"

Arras, 178n.; *see also* Artois *and* Parlements, provincial, Arras

Artois, 146

Assemblies, provincial, 213, 233n.

Assembly of Notables, 231, 233n.

Aubert de Tourny, Louis Urbain, 61, 63 and n., 78, 84

Auch, 14n., 17n., 117n., 175n.; *see also* Bayonne; Gascony; *and* Navarre

Audience de France, 72

Auget de Montyon, Jean Baptiste Robert, 45-46 and n., 65, 110

Auvergne, 27n., 45n., 53 and n., 65, 98n., 144, 147, 148; *see also* Chazerat; Cour des Aides, of Clermont-Ferrand; *and* Riom
Avocat-général (of the Parlements), 38, 39, 46-47 and 47n., 74, 111, 151, 152
Avocats, 21-22, 24-29; *see also* Lawyers *and* Legal education

Bailliage, 156; *see also* Judges
Barberie de Saint-Contest, Dominique Claude de, 98n.
Barberie de Saint-Contest de la Chataîgneraye, Henri Louis de, 98n., 143
Barbézieux, Marquis de, *see* Le Tellier-Louvois
Barbier, Edmond Jean François, 64n.
Barentin, Charles Amable Honoré de, 143
Barrillon d'Armoncourt, Antoine 184n.
Barrois, 161; *see also* Lorraine *and* Nancy
Bauyn d'Angervilliers, Nicolas Prosper, 28n., 90n., 184n.
Bayonne, 14n., 17n., 53n., 117n., 175n., 244; *see also* Gascony *and* Navarre
Beauharnois, François de, 18n., 43n., 53n., 98n., 116n.
Beaune, 151; *see also* Burgundy
Beauvais, 245
Belle-Isle, Charles Fouquet de, Maréchal and Comte de, 87
Bernage, Louis Bazile de, 61n., 65, 66n.
Bernage, Louis de, 65, 98n., 171, 204
Bernage de Vaux, Jean Louis de, 40-41n., 65, 90n., 98n., 184n.
Bernard, Samuel, 159
Berry, 145, 147, 161; *see also* Bourges
Bertier de Sauvigny, Louis Bénigne François, 87 and n., 99n., 116n., 143, 185, 192n.
Bertier de Sauvigny, Louis Jean, 87 and n., 90n., 99n., 116n., 143, 185, 192n.
Bertin de Bellille, Henri Léonard Jean Baptiste, 32n., 42n., 64, 66 and n., 78, 84, 239

Bertrand de Boucheporn, Claude François Bertrand, 27n.
Bignon de Blanzy, Roland Armand, 30
Bishops, *see* Church
Blair, Melchior de, 128
Blair de Boismont, Louis Guillaume de, 128
Blois, Estates of and ordinance of, 119n., 129-130
Bluche, François, 220, 222n., 253
Bordeaux, 14n., 41n., 53n., 61, 162, 226-227n., 244
Boucher d'Orsay, family, 111, 127, 143, 184n.; Arnoul Boucher, 143
Boucher d'Orsay, Charles, 143, 184n.
Boulainvilliers, Henri de, 11, 107
Bourbon, Duchesse de, 165
Bourbonnais, 147; *see also* Moulins
Bourgeois and *bourgeoisie,* 12, 107-108, 113, 115, 116, 122, 129, 132, 135, 138, 144, 146, 212, 213, 220, 223, 225-230 and nn., 232-233; *see also* Nobles and nobility, ennoblement, offices and modes of, *and* noble way of life; Offices and office-holders, ennoblement through offices; *and* Roturiers
Bourges, 17n., 88n., 90n., 183n.; *see also* Berry
Brittany, 8, 19n., 28n., 38, 53n., 69n., 84, 107, 147, 148, 152, 184n.; *see also* Nantes *and* Parlements, provincial, Rennes
Brittany, Duke of, 153
Bureaucracy, viii; *see also* Administration, royal; Bureaus, of the royal councils; Centralization; Commissions, of the royal councils; Councils, royal; Crown; Intendants, role and functions; *and Maîtres des requêtes,* numbers, role, and functions
Bureau de Commerce, *see* Commissions, of the royal councils
Bureau des Domaines et Aides, *see* Commissions, of the royal councils
Bureau des finances, 5, 6-7n., 124n., 178n.; *see also Elus;* Magistrates, financial; *Receveurs; and Trésoriers*

Bureau des Gabelles, Cinq Grosses Fermes, Tailles et Autres Affaires de Finance, *see* Commissions, of the royal councils

Bureau des Parties Casuelles, 69

Bureau des Postes et Messageries, *see* Bureaus, of the royal councils

Bureaus, of the royal councils, 52, 75-79, 238, 241; *see also* Commissions, of the royal councils; Councils, royal; *and Maîtres des requêtes*, numbers, role, and functions

Burgundy, 31, 38, 82, 110, 127, 151, 160; estates of, 161; *see also* Dijon *and* Parlements, provincial, Dijon

Burgundy, Duke of, 128, 151

Businessmen, *see* Bourgeois and *bourgeoisie;* Merchants; *and Roturiers*

Cachet de Garnerans, Jean Benoît, 38 and n., 46n., 53n., 98n.

Caen, 40n., 145, 162; *see also* Normandy

Cahiers, 76

Cahiers de doléances (of 1789), 227-228n.

Calas affair, 85

Calonne, Charles Alexandre de, 19n., 62, 85, 156, 162, 168, 233n.

Camus de Pontcarré de Viarme, Jean Baptiste Elie, 19n., 184n.

Capitation, 242; *see also* Taxes

Capitoul (of Toulouse), 120

Carré, Henri, 180

Casuels, 237-238

Catholic League, 147

Caze de la Bove, Gaspard Henri de, 54n., 99n., 184n.

Caze de la Bove, Gaspard Louis de, 28n., 69n., 84, 99n., 184n.

Centralization, 3, 8-9, 11, 93n., 102, 146, 155, 161, 211, 212-214; *see also* Absolutism; Administration, royal; Councils, royal; Crown; Intendants, role and functions, *and* historical origins of the office; *and* Sovereign and sovereignty

Cévennes, 164

Chambre des Comptes, 178n.; Paris, 57n., 125, 127, 144, 154; *see also* Magistrates, judicial, sovereign courts; Parlements; *and* Sovereign courts

Chambre de vacations, royal, 84

Chambre Royale de Justice, 84

Chamillart, family: Guy Chamillart, 170; Michel Chamillart, 170

Champagne, 54n., 64, 146, 148, 153, 184n.; *see also* Rheims

Chancellery, 72, 93n.

Chancellor, 63, 72, 73, 74, 75, 78, 80 and n., 81, 88, 112, 122

Charge, 68-69; *see also Droit annuel;* Offices and officeholders; *Paulette; and* Venality

Charles VI, king of France, 144

Charles VIII, king of France, 122

Châtelet, 28n., 39n., 41n., 48, 63n., 178n.; *see also* Judges

Chaumont de la Galaizière, Antoine, 62n., 63, 64n., 84, 87-88, 90n., 99n., 108, 168n., 171n.

Chaumont de la Galaizière, Antoine Martin, 87, 98n., 99n., 108, 136, 168n., 170n., 171n.

Chaumont de la Millière, Jacques Louis, 98n., 99n., 108, 136, 168n., 170n.

Chauvelin, family, 99n., 108, 130; Louis Chauvelin, 169

Chauvelin de Beauséjour, Bernard, 29 and 29-30n., 99n., 108, 130, 169-170, 204, 241-242

Chauvelin de Beauséjour, Jacques Bernard, 130

Chazerat, Antoine Claude de, 27n., 44-46n., 53n., 98n., 116n.

Chevalier, 105, 106, 107; *see also* Nobles and nobility, categories of

Church, 222 and n., 224, 227n.

Clugny de Nuis, Jean Etienne Bernard de, 53n.

Cluzel, François Pierre du, 84, 116n.

Cobban, Alfred, 212, 220

Colbert, Jean Baptiste, vii, 8-9, 102

Collèges, 19 and n.; *see also* Education; Intendants, legal education; *and Maîtres des requêtes*, education in the law schools

Colmar, 178n.; *see also* Alsace

Commensal office, *see* Household, royal

Commission des Péages, *see* Commissions, of the royal councils

Commission des Vivres et Etapes, *see* Commissions, of the royal councils

Commissions, of the royal councils, 75-79, 81, 84, 241; *see also* Bureaus, of the royal councils; Councils, royal; *and Maîtres des requêtes,* numbers, role, and functions

Commissions and commissioners, royal, 6n., 46, 82, 85, 86, 104, 148; *par commission,* 68-70; *see also* Crown, control over officials

Committees, royal, 82-83; *see also* Bureaus, of the royal councils; Commissions, of the royal councils; and Councils, royal

Compiègne, 162, 163

Conseillers: Parlementary, 25-26, 28-30, 37ff., 46, 47, 90n., 111, 115, 237 (*see also* Magistrates, judicial, sovereign courts; Offices and officeholders; Parlements; *and* Venality) ; princely or ducal, 110

Conseillers d'état, 49, 52-53, 54-55 and 55n., 58 and n., 73-75, 78, 81, 82, 83, 87, 112, 114, 115, 120, 122; income, 238-239, 241-242; *see also* Bureaus, of the royal councils; Commissions, of the royal councils; *and* Councils, royal

—*honoraires,* 39 and n.; *see also Lettre de vétérance*

Conseil Provincial, *see* Parlements, provincial, Arras

Conseil Supérieur: in Auvergne, 45 and n.; of Lyon, 55

Controller-general, 32n., 55, 56n., 64, 70, 73, 75, 80 and n., 81, 85, 90, 93n., 133; *see also* Calonne; Colbert; Laverdy; Ministers, royal; *and* Necker

Corsica, 14n., 27n.

Councilors, *see Conseillers*

Councilors of state, *see Conseillers d'état*

Councils, royal (*conseils*), 2-3, 9, 49, 54, 56n., 57 and n., 59, 66, 72-86, 88, 90, 91, 92n., 93 and n. 110-114, 120, 124, 126, 134, 136ff., 146, 199, 204ff., 239, 243; Council of State

(*Conseil d'état*), 56n., 58, 72, 79-80 and 80n.; Conseil des Dépêches, 72, 73, 77, 79-83; Conseil Royal des Finances, 72, 74, 77, 78, 79-83, 238; Conseil Royal de Commerce, 72, 79, 80; "Conseil du Roi," 73, 74n.; Conseil d'Etat Privé Finances et Direction, 72-79, 81; Conseil Privé (Conseil des Parties), 73-79, 80; Conseil d'Etat et des Finances, 73-79, 80; "Conseil de Direction," 76; *see also* Absolutism; Administration, royal; Centralization; Crown; *Maîtres des requêtes,* numbers, role, and functions; *and* Sovereign and sovereignty

Cour des Aides, 53, 178n.; of Clermont-Ferrand, 27n., 39, 45 and n.; of Paris, 30, 38-39, 48-49, 57n., 152; *see also* Magistrates, judicial, sovereign courts; Parlements; *and* Sovereign courts

Cour des Monnaies, 178n.

Courts, judicial, *see* Judges; Magistrates; Offices and officeholders; Parlements; Sovereign courts; *and* Venality

Creil de Bournezeau, Jean François de, 65, 143

Crown, viii, 3-6, 93n., 110; relations with sovereign courts, 42-51 and 50n., 81, 82, 83-86, 93n., 208, 231; control over officials, 45 and n., 46-47 and 47n., 69-70, 87-88, 91, 93n., 126, 193-194, 208-209; relations with businessmen and financiers, 103, 111, 112; Great Offices of the Crown, 122 (*see also* Chancellor) ; *see also* Absolutism; Administration, royal; Centralization; Councils, royal; Ministers; Parlements, relations with the Crown, *and* Parlement, Paris, relations with the Crown; Secretaries of state; *and* Sovereign and sovereignty

Dauphiné, 99, 124, 233n.; *see also* Grenoble *and* Parlements, provincial, Grenoble

Dijon, 17n., 38, 40n., 43n.; *see also* Burgundy *and* Parlements, provincial, Dijon

Dispensation, letters of, 70; for law students, 19 and n.; for *avocats*, 24-25; for *conseillers*, 29, 30-31, 32 and n., 33n.; for *maîtres des requêtes*, 60 and 61n., 66
Dixième, 242; *see also* Taxes
Dodart, Denis, 17n., 90n., 172n.
Dombes, 14n., 38 and n., 46n., 98n., 110, 128; *see also* Cachet de Garnerans
Doujat, Jean Charles, 40, 184n.
Droit annuel, 66, 68; *see also Charge; Offices* and officeholders; *Paulette; and* Venality
Dubois, Guillaume, Abbé, 28
Dunkerque and Ypres, 40n., 64; *see also* Flanders
Dupleix, family, 159-160; René François Dupleix, 159; Joseph François Dupleix, 160
Dupleix de Bacquencourt, Guillaume Joseph, 82, 85, 108, 160, 162, 168
Dupré de Saint-Maur, Nicolas III, 88n., 183n.

Echevin (of Paris), 120
Ecuyer, 105, 106, 129; *see also* Nobles and nobility, categories of
Education, 173-174 and 174n.; *see also Collèges;* Intendants, legal education; *and Maîtres des requêtes,* education in the law schools
Egret, Jean, 221, 222n.
Elus, 4-5, 7, 212; *see also Bureau des finances;* Magistrates, financial; *Receveurs; and Trésoriers*
England and English government and aristocracy, 147, 176, 177n., 214
Ennoblement, *see* Nobles and nobility *and* Offices and officeholders
En survivance, see Survivance, à titre de
En titre, see Charge
Esmangart, family, 162-163
Esmangart, Charles François Hyacinthe, 41n., 162-163, 168, 169
Estates: provincial, 76, 148, 161, 208, 209n., 213; Estates-General, 212, 232, 233-234n.; Second Estate, 231-233, 234n., 245n. (*see also* Nobles and nobility) ; Third Estate, 232-

233, 234n., 235n.; "doubling of the Third," 233-234n.; *see also* Bourgeois and *bourgeoisie, and Rotu-riers*

Families of intendants: noble origins and antiquity, vii, 117-118, 175, 195-200, 202, 210, 243-244; influence of, 34, 40, 42, 61, 63-68, 87, 90, 98-99n., 99-100, 193-195, 209; origins of, 41, geographic, 97-103, 182-183, social, 103-116, 183-185; social evolution of, 41, 100-141, 175-176, 183-206, 210; succession in offices, 65-68, 87-89, 98-99n.; antiquity of, 103-105, 183-184; status and professions of first ancestors, 105-116, 183-185; length of service in magistracy, 133-134, 176, 201-202, 204-206; length of service in the high administration, 134, 136ff., 176, 184-190, 201-202, 204-206; status and professions of grandfathers, 134-135, 137-139, 186-190, 189-190n., 204-205; status and professions of fathers, 134, 136-139, 187-190, 189-190n., 204-205; wealth, 173-175, 204-206; professions of intendants' sons, 190-194, 192-193n.; *see also* Social mobility
Fargès, 164; Anne Marie Josephe Fargès, 164; *see also* Peirenc, family
Farmers-general, *see* Tax farmers
Favier du Boullay, Jacques, 145
Ferrand de Villemilan, Antoine François, 79
"Feudal reaction," 11-12, 212, 220; *see also* "Aristocratic reaction"
Fiefholder and fiefs, 107, 108, 126, 129, 130, 144, 152; *see also* Blois, Estates of and ordinance of; Nobles and nobility; *and* Normandy, Charter of 1470
Financiers, *see* Bourgeois and *bourgeoisie;* Merchants; *Roturiers; and* Tax farmers
Flanders, 8, 14n., 38, 40n., 146; *see also* Dunkerque and Ypres; Lille; *and* Parlements, provincial, Douai
Flesselles, Jacques de, 32n.
Fleury, André-Hercule, cardinal, **28**, **82**

Foullé de Martargis, Hiacinthe Guillaume, 6in., 184n.
Franc-fief, 129
Franche-Comté, 8, 38, 54n.; *see also* Parlements, provincial, Besançon
Francis I, king of France, 124
French Indies Company, 108, 113, 159-160, 164, 172
Fronde, 7, 102

Gabriel, Jacques *(père)*, 165
Gages, 68, 237-238
Gallican, *see* Church
Gallois, Jean Baptiste des, 117n., 143
Gallois de la Tour, Charles Jean Baptiste des, 40n., 107, 116n., 117n., 143
Garde des sceaux, 148, 171; *see also* Chancellery *and* Chancellor
Gascony, 99; *see also* Bayonne *and* Navarre
Genealogy and genealogists, vii, 17-18n., 97 and 97n.; mode of determining genealogies, 104-106, 253-255
Généralité, 5-6, 8, 13-14n., 87, 209, 238, 239; *see also* Intendants, role and functions, *and* numbers of
Gens du roi, see Avocat-général and Procureur-général
Gentilshommes, 218, 245; *see also* Nobles and nobility, categories of, *ancienne noblesse; and Seigneurs*
Germans, *see* Holy Roman Empire
Government, royal, *see* Absolutism; Administration, royal; Bureaus, of the royal councils; Centralization; Chancellery; Commissions, of the royal councils; Commissions and commissioners, royal; Committees, royal; *Conseillers d'état;* Councils, royal; Crown; Intendants; Magistrates; *Maîtres des requêtes;* Ministers, royal; Parlements; Secretaries of state; Sovereign and sovereignty; *and* Sovereign courts
Governor, royal, 84
Grand Conseil, 39, 40n., 48-51 and 50n., 55, 56n., 63, 66, 86, 125, 145, 147, 148, 151, 160, 163, 171, 178n., 199, 238, 239; *see also* Magistrates,

judicial, sovereign courts; *and* Parlements
Grenoble, 28n., 38, 41n., 90n., 124n.; *see also* Dauphiné *and* Parlements, provincial, Grenoble
Guignard de Saint-Priest, Jean Emmanuel de, 87 and n., 116n., 192n.
Guignard de Saint-Priest, Marie Joseph Emmanuel, 87 and n.
Guise, Duc de, 147
Guizot, François, 207

Hainaut (-Meubeuge), 31, 40n., 156; *see also* Valenciennes
Hapsburgs, *see* Holy Roman Empire *and* Spain
Henry IV, king of France, 102, 146, 147, 245
Hobereaux, 219; *see also* Fiefholder and fiefs; Nobles and nobility, categories of, *ancienne noblesse; and Seigneurs*
Holy Roman Empire, 4, 5
Honorary councilors, *see Conseillers d'état, honoraires; and Lettre de vétérance*
Hôtel-Dieu, 161
Household, royal, 56, 110, 113, 121, 132, 135, 136, 161, 243
Hungary, 176 and n.

India, 160
Intendants: role and functions, ii, iii, vii, ix, 3, 51, 55n., 74, 89, 92n., 208-209, 213-217, 215n., 239; social origins and status, vii-ix, 11-13, 94, 102-141, 175-176, 183-206, 208-211, 219, 221-222, geographical origins, 40-41 and 41n., 43, 97-103, 99n., 182-183, families' age, 103-105, 183-185, noble origins, 243-244; recruitment, training, and appointment, viii, ix, 10-11, 13, 42, 51, 52-54, 54n., 81, 82, 86, 87-89, 91-94, 93-94n., 98n., 209, 216-217, 221-222; historical origins of the office, 3-10 and nn.; numbers of, 13, 13-14n., 181n.; legal education, 17-24, 209; apprenticeship as lawyers, 24-29, 209; apprenticeship as judges, 35-37, 49-50, 90, 209; pattern of judicial careers, 37-40, 46-49; careers within

Intendants *(cont.)*
　the royal bureaucracy, 45n., 54,
　55n., 86-87, 92-93n.; honors, rights,
　and privileges, 56-57, 208-211, 239;
　age at appointment, 89-91, 89n.,
　90n.; income, 238-239; *see also*
　Families of the intendants
Intendants adjoints, 87-89, 193-194
Intendants of commerce, of finance,
　52, 54n., 55n., 73, 75, 86-87, 89, 92-
　93n., 148, 150
Intendants of the army, of the navy,
　55n., 79, 147
Invalides, 158

Jansenist, 222 and n.
Jesuit, 19 and n., 222
Joly, family, 151-152; Guillaume
　François Joly de Fleury, 47n., 152;
　Guillaume François Louis Joly de
　Fleury, 152; Jean Omer Joly de
　Fleury, 152
Joly de Fleury de la Valette, Jean
　François III, 31, 150-152
Journet, Etienne Louis, 17n., 117n.,
　175n.
Jubert de Bouville, André, 88n., 129
　and n.
Jubert de Bouville, Louis Guillaume,
　88 and n., 129 and n.
Judges, 8, 33, 74, 110; *see also Bailli-
　age;* Families of the intendants;
　Intendants, apprenticeship as
　judges; Magistrates, sovereign
　courts; *Maîtres des requêtes,* ap-
　prenticeship in the courts; Nobles
　and nobility, categories of, *noblesse
　de robe;* Offices and officeholders;
　Parlements; *Présidial;* Sovereign
　courts; *and* Venality
Jullien, Antoine Jean Baptiste, 39n.,
　41n., 62n., 65, 90n.

Keeper of the seals, *see Garde des
　sceaux*
King of France, 1-3, 57-58, 72-74, 79,
　80n., 81, 82, 83, 85, 93n., 100, 106n.,
　108; *see also* Absolutism; Charles
　VI *and* Charles VIII; Crown;
　Henry IV; Louis XI, Louis XIV,
　Louis XV, *and* Louis XVI; *and*
　Sovereign and sovereignty

La Bourdonnaye, family, 105, 107,
　116n., 152-153, 195n.; François de
　La Bourdonnaye, 153
La Bourdonnaye, Louis François de,
　98n., 153
La Bourdonnaye, Yves Marie de, 90n.,
　99n., 152-153
La Bourdonnaye de Blossac, Paul
　Esprit Marie de, 30, 32n., 42n., 98n.,
　99n., 192n.
Laboureur, 108, 136; *see also* Peasant
La Briffe (des Ferrières), family,
　98n., 111, 143
La Briffe des Ferrières, Louis Arnaud
　de, 40-41n., 98n., 111, 143
La Chalotais, Louis René de, 47n.,
　84-85
La Grande Direction des Finance,
　see Commissions, of the royal
　councils; *and* Councils, royal, "Con-
　seil de Direction"
Lamballe, 244
Lamoignon de Basville, Nicolas de,
　79, 98n., 112, 143, 183n., 184n.
Lamoignon de Courson, Urbain Guil-
　laume de, 61, 98n., 112, 143, 183n.,
　184n.
Lamoignon de Malesherbes, Chrétien
　Guillaume de, 230-231n., 233-234n.
Languedoc, 13n., 38, 87n., 99, 164;
　see also Parlements, provincial,
　Toulouse; *and* Toulouse
La Petite Direction des Finances, *see*
　Commissions, of the royal councils
La Porte de Meslay, family, 99n., 108
La Rochelle, 18n., 43n., 45n., 65, 128,
　244
Laverdy, Clément Charles François
　de, controller-general, 233n.
Law: canon, 19-20; French, 19-23;
　Roman, 19-21
Law, John, 159, 219; Law's "system,"
　61, 78, 103, 164, 205
Lawyers, 108, 113-114, 115, 135, 136,
　138, 227-228n.; *see also Avocats;*
　Intendants, legal education, *and*
　apprenticeship as lawyers; Legal
　education; *and Maîtres des re-
　quêtes,* education in the law schools
Learned societies, *see* Academies
Le Blanc, Louis Claude, 40-41n., 64,
　66, 70

Index

Le Bret, Cardin II, 40-41n., 64, 90n., 143, 184n.

Le Bret, Pierre Cardin, 64

Lefebvre, Georges, 212, 231

Le Fèvre de Caumartin, family, 128, 143, 146-148; Jean Le Fèvre, 146; Louis Le Fèvre de Caumartin, 147-148

Le Fèvre de Caumartin, Antoine Louis François, 90n., 146, 148, 181n.

Le Fèvre d'Ormesson, family, 111, 143

Legal education, 18-24, 34ff.

Le Peletier, family, 130; Claude, Jerome, Louis, and Michel Le Peletier, 170

Le Peletier de Morfontaine, family, 143

Le Pelletier (de la Houssaye) , family, 111

Le Pelletier de la Houssaye, Félix, 184n.

L'Escalopier, family, 153-155; Jean Lescalopier, 154

L'Escalopier, César Charles de, 64, 153-154

L'Escalopier, Gaspard César Charles de, 65

Le Tellier-Louvois, family, 130; Michel Le Tellier, Marquis de Louvois, vii, 149, 169; Louis Le Tellier, Marquis de Barbézieux, 169

Lettre de provision, 68; *see also Charge;* Offices and officeholders; *and* Venality

Lettre de vétérance, 122; *see also Conseillers d'état, honoraires*

Licence, 20-22, 24-26, 28; *see also* Intendants, legal education, *and* apprenticeship as lawyers; Legal education; *and Maîtres des requêtes,* education in the law schools

Lieutenant-general (of the police) , 55, 56n.

Lille, 40n., 70, 90n., 158; *see also* Artois *and* Flanders

Limoges, 17n., 43n., 143

Lits de justice, 83; *see also* Crown, relations with sovereign courts; *and* Parlements, relations with the Crown, *and* Parlement, Paris, relations with the Crown

Lorraine, 14n., 62n., 63, 87, 88, 90n., 157, 161; *see also* Nancy

Louis XI, king of France, 129, 144

Louis XIII, king of France, 4, 111, 145-146, 148

Louis XIV, king of France, vii, 1, 4, 9n., 10, 13, 19, 21, 27, 60, 73, 80n., 82, 91, 100, 102, 125, 127, 129, 140, 144-145, 157, 158, 169, 182-185, 189, 193, 195, 197, 198, 199, 200, 201, 202, 204, 206, 218, 220, 221, 222, 223, 245

Louis XV, king of France, 1, 10, 13, 27, 44, 48, 60, 65, 73, 78, 80n., 81, 82, 87, 91, 100, 140, 151, 170, 182-183, 185, 189, 193, 195, 197, 198, 200, 201, 202, 204, 205, 219, 239

Louis XVI, king of France, ii, vii, ix, 1, 10, 13, 27-28, 60, 65, 73, 78, 100, 129, 146, 148, 150, 180, 182-183, 185, 187, 189, 193, 195, 197, 198, 200, 201, 202, 204, 205, 206, 219, 222, 233n.

Louis Napoleon, emperor of France, 11

Louvois, Marquis de, *see* Le Tellier-Louvois

Loyseau, Charles, 124

Luynes, Charles, Duc de, 148

Lyon, 32n., 55, 147, 227n., 244

Magistrates:

—financial, 110-113, 115, 126, 135ff., 146, 200 and n., 219, 243-244; *see also Bureau des finances; Elus; Receveurs; and Trésoriers*

—judicial, sovereign courts, 105, 110-115, 126, 198, 200, 204, 205ff., 212, 219, 243-244; intendants' families in, 117, 120, 132-134, 136ff., 143ff., 176, 184-190

—Parlementary: opposition to intendants, 7; examination and admission, 21-22, 29-33; apprenticeship, 24-29, 35-37; age of entrance, 25-31; former members in the corps of intendants, 37-49; professional ambitions, 42, 52-53; relations with and influence upon royal government, 42-51, 52, 83-86, 93-94, 125, 146; control over judicial offices, 68

—*see also* Judges *and* Parlements

Maignard (de Bernières), family, 116n., 129n., 184n.

Maintenon, Madame de, 128

Maîtres des requêtes: education in the law schools, 17-24, 91; apprenticeship in the courts, 24-29, 35-37, 49, 60-61 and n., 63, 90, 91, 92n.; prior judicial careers, 37-40, 46-50; entrance into, and process of selection, 42, 44 and n., 45-50, 53n., 60-70; pre-eminence in, and training-ground of the royal bureaucracy, 52-56, 70, 81, 86, 91-94, 93-94n.; political outlook, 53-54, 59, 68, 70, 71-72, 75, 83, 85-86, 91-94, 93-94n., 143, 209, 211, 217; prestige and privileges of, 56-58, 64n., 68, 81, 82, 117n., 120, 122; numbers, role, and functions, 57, 59, 63n., 69-70, 71-89, 93-94n., 216-217; age at appointment, 60-61 and n.; price, purchase, and inheritance of office, 61-63 and 62n., 64-69; social status and income of, 63, 67, 238, 239; origins of the office, 71-72, 93n.; length of service, 89-91, 90n.; ancestors in the corps, 112; *see also* Families of the intendants

Malesherbes, *see* Lamoignon de Malesherbes

Masonic lodges, 225

Maupeou, courts or reforms, 45, 47n., 55

Maurepas, *see* Phélypeaux de Maurepas

Mazarin, Jules, cardinal, 4-5, 6n., 7-8

Medicine, 108, 135, 136ff.

Mégret de Sérilly, Jean Nicolas, 54n.

Méliand, family, 99n.

Méliand, Charles Blaise, 64, 99n.

Merchants, 108, 112-116, 133, 135, 136ff., 204-205, 210, 245; *see also* Bourgeois and *bourgeoisie; and Roturiers*

Mercoeur, Duc de, 153

Merlin de Douai, Philippe-Auguste, 234n.

Metz, 65, 156; *see also* Parlements, provincial, Metz

Meubeuge, *see* Hainaut *and* Valenciennes

Military, 137, 222-224, 227n.; *see also* Nobles and nobility, categories of, *noblesse d'épée, and noblesse militaire*

Ministers, royal, vii, 2-3, 5, 9, 13, 41-45, 48, 51, 53, 55, 56n., 57, 58, 69, 70, 72, 79, 82, 85, 87, 91, 100, 105, 111, 112, 133, 208-209, 212, 219, 220-221, 223, 234n.; income, 239; noble origins and antiquity, 243-244; *see also* Councils, royal; Crown; *and* Intendants, careers within the royal bureaucracy

Mirabeau, Honoré Gabriel Riqueti de *(fils)*, 234n.

Monarchy, *see* Absolutism; Administration, royal; Councils, royal; Crown; *and* Sovereign and sovereignty

Montauban, 17n., 43n., 65, 88, 90

Moreau, family, 157-159

Moreau de Beaumont, Jean Louis, 6-7n., 79, 92n., 98n., 157, 162, 168 and n., 171n., 192n.

Moreau de Séchelles, Jean, 40n., 70, 79, 98n., 158, 168n., 171n., 192n.

Moulins, 40n., 41n., 65, 90n., 144; *see also* Bourbonnais

Nancy, 178n.; *see also* Lorraine

Nantes, 226-227n., 244; *see also* Brittany

Napoleon, emperor of France, 206, 214

Navarre, 82; Queen of, 151; *see also* Bayonne *and* Gascony

Necker, Jacques, 178n., 180 and n., 233n.

Noble homme, 105; *see also* Bourgeois and *bourgeoisie;* Nobles and nobility; *and Roturiers*

Nobles and nobility: opposition to intendants, 7; court nobility, 13, 108, 218-219, 223; proof of nobility, 17n., 78, 105-106, 169; ennoblement, offices and modes of, 57 and n., 58, 108-112, 117-133, 118n., 144, 161, 172n., 175-180, 178n., 195, 198-200, 205, 210-211, 226-227n., 228-230, 243-245; status and privileges of, 58, 118, 142, 197, 210, 217-224, 228-233, 233-235n.; relations with the Crown, 84, 93-94, 147, 212, 218-219,

Nobles and nobility (*cont.*)
222-224, 231-233, 234n.; noble way
of life, 105-106, 107, 108, 131, 169,
174-175, 210, 217-219, 220, 224-225;
infusion of commoners into, 105-
106, 174-175, 210-211, 221, 224-230
and nn., 232-233 and nn.; among
intendants' ancestors, 107, 115-116,
116n., 117-133, 175-176, 201ff., 210;
proportion in population, 176-180
and nn., 211, 243-245; cultural life,
213
—categories of: *noblesse de robe* (nobility of the robe), 94, 134, 137,
139-140, 143ff., 199, 201ff., 206;
noblesse de la plume (nobility of
the pen or administrative nobility),
94, 134, 137, 139-140, 143ff., 201ff.,
206, 208, 211; *noblesse d'épée* (nobility of the sword), 94, 139-140,
178, 222-223n., 223-224, 244; *anobli*,
118, 131, 245 and n.; *ancienne noblesse*, 118, 245; *noblesse inféodée,
noblesse à la tierce-foi, anoblissement par les fiefs*, 119n.; *noblesse
de cloche* (municipal nobility),
120; *agrégés*, 131; *noblesse militaire*,
178n., 245n.; *noblesse acquise et
transmissible*, 245n.; *noblesse personnelle*, 245n.; *nobles possedants-
fiefs*, 245n.
—*see also* Blois, Estates of and ordinance of; *Chevalier; Ecuyer;* Families of the intendants, noble origins
and antiquity; Fiefholder and fiefs;
Hobereaux; Noble homme; Normandy, Charter of 1470; Offices and
officeholders, ennoblement through
offices; *and Seigneurs*
Normandy, 127, 145, 147; Charter of
1470, 129, 144; *see also* Alençon;
Caen; Parlements, provincial,
Rouen; *and* Rouen

Office, ducal, 110, 243
Offices and officeholders: relationship
and attitude of the Crown to, 33,
49, 69, 101-102; appeal of, 33, 56-58,
101, 102-103, 109, 173, 225, 239;
status and privileges of, 33, 56-58,
101, 108, 109, 115, 124, 126, 173;
honorific, 56, 108, 110; prices, purchase, and inheritance of, 61-69,
103, 193-194; among intendants'
ancestors, 106, 109-115, 173, 185-
190, 204ff., 210; local, municipal,
and provincial, 108, 110-115, 126,
127, 132, 135, 136ff., 146, 178-179n.,
198, 210, 219, 227-228n., 243; categories of, 110-113; ennoblement
through offices, 119-126, 178-180,
178-179n., 210-211, 221, 227n., 229n.,
243-244, 245n.; *see also* Families of
the intendants; Household, royal;
Magistrates; Office, ducal; *and*
Venality
Orange, 22
Oratorian, 19 and n.
Order of Saint-Louis, 56; *see also* Intendants, honors, rights, and privileges
Orléans, 43n., 228n., 244; law faculty,
22; intendant of, 31n., 41n., 88 and
n., 90n., 145, 152; mayor of, 111

Pajot de Marcheval, Christophe, 41n.
Pareto, Vilfredo, 216 and n., 218
Paris, 149, 153, 154, 156, 157, 159, 161,
163, 165, 213, 225; university and
law faculty, 22; intendant of, 30,
87n., 90n., 143; native Parisians and
Parisian magistrates in the corps of
intendants, 39-45, 47-49, 97-103,
98n., 99n., 147; appeal of capital,
41-42, 97, 101-103; lieutenant-
general (of the police), 55, 56n.;
prévôt des marchands, 55, 65; ennoblement of Paris magistrates,
57n., 102; sovereign courts of, 102;
échevin of, 120; custom of, 123n.;
bureau of finance, 124n., 147; *see
also* Chambre des Comptes, Paris;
Châtelet; Cour des Aides, of Paris;
Parlements, Parlement, Paris; *and*
Sovereign courts, Paris
Parlements: judicial tasks of, 35-37;
relations with the Crown, 42-45,
50-51, 83-86, 93n., 208, 209, 213,
219, 233n.; number of offices, 178n.
—Parlement, Paris: in the Fronde, 7;
apprenticeship of lawyers in, 24-
29; age and admission of magistrates, 28n., 29-31; former magistrates in the corps of intendants,

Parlements *(cont.)*
37, 39-45, 47-49, 55, 90n., 163; influence of, 42-45, 48, 50-51; relations with the Crown, 47n., 50-51, 50n., 61, 83-84, 125, 212, 231, 232; ennoblement, 57n., 101, 125, 199 and n.; ancestors attached to, 112, 145, 147, 148, 150, 151, 152, 157-158, 163, 199; proportion of noblemen in, 221, 222n.; income, 237-238, 239
—Parlements, provincial, 40; proportion of magistrates within the administration, 44-49, 51, 199 and n.; proportion of nobility in, 221; Aix, 38, 39, 40n., 55, 64; Arras (Conseil Provincial), 38; Besançon, 38; Dijon (Burgundy), 38, 40n., 151, 161; Dombes, 38 and n.; Douai (Flanders), 38, 156; Grenoble, 38, 125; Metz, 38, 39, 40n., 63, 64n., 128, 151, 165; Pau, 82; Rennes (Brittany), 38, 55, 84, 90n., 151, 153; Rouen, 38, 69n., 145, 175n.; Toulouse, 38, 40n., 85
—*see also Avocat-général;* Chambre des Comptes; *Conseillers,* Parlementary; Cour des Aides; Cour des Monnaies; Crown, relations with sovereign courts; Grand Conseil; Magistrates, judicial, sovereign courts; *Maîtres des requêtes,* apprenticeship in the courts; Nobles and nobility, ennoblement, offices and modes of, *and* categories of, *noblesse de robe;* Offices and officeholders; *Premiers présidents; Président à mortier; Procureur-général;* Sovereign courts; *and* Venality
Partenai, 156
Patriot Party, 233n., 234n., 235n.
Pau, 14n.; *see also* Bayonne; Gascony; *and* Navarre
Paulette, 67n., 102; *see also Charge; Droit annuel;* Offices and officeholders; *and* Venality
Pays d'état, 209n.
Peasant, 12, 105, 108, 113, 115, 116, 138, 220; *see also Laboureur*
Peirenc, family, 163-166; Abraham Peirenc, 164-165
Peirenc de Moras, François Marie, 31, 163-166, 168

Pension, 237-239
Perpignan, 32n., 42n., 53n., 64
Perrin de Cypierre, Jean François Claude, 31n., 41n.
Peter the Great, 140; *see also* Russia
Phélypeaux de Maurepas, Jean Frédéric, 69n.
Phélypeaux de Pontchartrain, Louis, 63, 88
Philip the Good, Duke of Burgundy, 128
Philosophes, 214; *see also* Voltaire
Physiocracy, 225
Picardy, 145, 146, 147, 148; *see also* Amiens *and* Soissons
Pierrefonds, 162, 163
Pineau de Lucé, family, 156-157
Pineau de Lucé, Jacques III, 31, 156, 162, 168
Poitiers, 30, 42n., 127, 156, 157, 244; *see also* Poitou
Poitou, 147, 156
Poland, 176 and n.
Polysynodie, 9; *see also* Regency
Pondichéry, 160
Pontchartrain, *see* Phélypeaux de Pontchartrain
Pont de Monderoux, Jean Samuel de, 41n., 116n.
Pontoise, 84
Postal service, royal, 111, 113, 137, 149, 150; *see also* Bureaus, of the royal councils
Potier de Novion, family, 153
Premiers présidents (first presidents of the Parlements), 46, 55, 64, 238
Président à mortier (of the Parlements), 152, 237
Présidial, 39n., 156, 157; *see also* Judges
Prévôt des marchands (of Paris), 55, 65
Princes, 2, 13, 80n., 93n., 110, 128
Procureur-général (of the Parlements), 31, 38, 46-47 and 47n., 74, 84, 85, 152, 156, 238
Provence, 231n., 233n.; *see also* Aix-en-Provence

Rapporteur, see Maîtres des requêtes, numbers, role, and functions; *and* Parlements, judicial tasks of

Index

Receivers-general, *see* Receveurs

Receveurs, 4-5, 7, 110, 132, 212; *see also* Bureau des finances; Elus; Magistrates, financial; *and* Trésoriers

Regency, 9, 28; Regent, 53, 54, 93n.; Council of Regency, 147-148; *see also* Law, John

Rentes, 225

Rentier, 107, 169

Requêtes de l'Hôtel, 39n., 41n., 48, 71-72; *see also* Maîtres des requêtes, numbers, role, and functions

Resignatio in favorem, 64-67, 69; *see also* Offices and officeholders; Survivance; *and* Venality

Revenue, *see* Taxes

Revolution, French, ix, 104, 211-235

Rheims, 22; *see also* Champagne

Ribeyre, Antoine de, 153

Richelieu, Armand-Jean du Plessis de, cardinal, 3-5, 7, 151

Riom, 31, 163; *see also* Auvergne; Chazerat; *and* Cour des Aides, of Clermont-Ferrand

Rodin Museum, 165

Roland de la Platière, Jean-Marie, 228n.

Roture, *see* Roturiers

Roturiers (commoners), vii, 107, 116, 129, 223, 224; *see also* Blois, Estates of and ordinance of; Bourgeois and bourgeoisie; Estates, Third Estate; Merchants; Nobles and nobility, ennoblement, offices and modes of, *and* noble way of life; Normandy, Charter of 1470; *and* Offices and officeholders, ennoblement through offices

Rouen, 85, 88n., 153, 161; *see also* Normandy *and* Parlements, provincial, Rouen

Rouillé d'Orfeuil, family, 143; Louis Rouillé, 149-150

Rouillé d'Orfeuil, Gaspard Louis, 149-150

Rue de Varennes, 165

Rue Saint-Denis, 157-159

Russia, 176n.; *see also* Peter the Great

Saint-Germain, Claude Louis, Comte de, 54n.

Saint-Malo, 244; *see also* Brittany

Saint-Simon, Louis de Rouvroy, Duc de, vii, 9, 11, 107, 114, 206

Savonette à vilain, see Secrétaires du roi

Secrétaires du roi (notaries and secretaries of the king, royal household, and Crown), 57n., 110-114, 121 and n., 122, 126, 132, 135, 136, 149, 154, 158, 160, 170ff., 178n., 183n., 199-200 and 199n., 210, 227n., 243; *see also* Nobles and nobility, ennoblement, offices and modes of; *and* Offices and officeholders, ennoblement through offices

Secretaries of state, 2-3, 53, 55-56, 58, 79-80 and 80n., 81, 82, 83, 87, 122, 220-221; income, 239; *see also* Councils, royal; Crown; Intendants, careers within the royal bureaucracy; *and* Ministers, royal

Séguier, Pierre, chancellor, 121

Seigneurs, 11, 105, 106, 107, 113, 115, 129, 132, 135, 136ff., 220; *see also* Nobles and nobility

Sénac de Meilhan, Gabriel, 54-55n., 170, 172n., 175n., 199n.

Shopkeepers, *see* Merchants

Sieur, 105, 108; *see also* Bourgeois and bourgeoisie; *and* Nobles and nobility, noble way of life

Social mobility, 12-13, 97, 99, 100-101, 115, 116, 117ff., 131, 139-141, 155-156, 162, 166-168, 170ff., 202, 204-207, 221-222, 224-230; *see also* Families of the intendants

Soissons, 64; *see also* Picardy

Sovereign and sovereignty, 1-3, 56, 59, 85, 126, 128, 208-210; constitutional sovereignty, 214, 232-233 and nn.; *see also* Absolutism; Administration, royal; Centralization; Councils, royal; Crown; Intendants, role and functions, *and* honors, rights, and privileges; *and* King of France

Sovereign courts, 125, 243; Paris, 102, 146, 148, 150; provincial, 113, 150; presidents of, 122; *see also* Chambre des Comptes; Conseillers, Parlementary; Conseil Supérieur; Cour des Aides; Cour des Monnaies; Crown, relations with sovereign

Sovereign courts *(cont.)*
courts; Families of the intendants; Grand Conseil; Magistrates, judicial, sovereign courts; *Maîtres des requêtes,* apprenticeship in the courts, *and* prior judicial careers; Maupeou, courts or reforms; Nobles and nobility, ennoblement, offices and modes of, *and* categories of, *noblesse de robe;* Offices and officeholders; Parlements; *and* Venality

Spain and Spaniards, 4, 5, 147

Stanislas Leczinski, king of Poland and sovereign of the duchies of Bar and Lorraine, 87

Subdélégué-général, 110

Substitut, 31, 37, 158

Survivance, à titre de, 65-67; *see also* Offices and officeholders; *Resignatio in favorem; and* Venality

Sweden, 177n.

Switzerland, 98

Taboureau des Réaux, Louis Gabriel, 42n.

Taille, 5, 7n., 144; *see also* Nobles and nobility, status and privileges of; Offices and officeholders, status and privileges of; *and* Taxes

Taxes, 4-6, 6-7n., 8, 57, 74, 78, 80, 93n., 101, 102, 107-110, 112; *see also* Bureau des finances; Capitation; Dixième; *and* Taille

Tax farmers, 80, 108, 111, 113, 128, 135, 136-137, 159, 160, 161, 170ff., 204, 210

Terray, family, 105

Terray, Antoine Jean, 17n., 43n., 90

Terray, Joseph-Marie, Abbé, 90

Thiroux, family, 161-162; Jean Louis Thiroux de Lailly, 62n.; Lazare Louis Thiroux, 161

Thiroux de Crosne, Louis, 85, 88n., 161, 162, 168

Tocqueville, Alexis de, 11, 107, 212, 218

Toulouse, 120, 244; *see also* Languedoc *and* Parlements, provincial, Toulouse

Touraine, 147, 149; *see also* Tours

Tournai, 156; *see also* Hainaut

Tours, 29, 84, 149, 169

Tradesmen, *see* Merchants

Traitants, see Tax farmers

Traitement, 237-239

Treasurers-general, see *Trésoriers*

Trésoriers, 4-5, 7, 110, 115, 124, 132, 212; *see also* Bureau des finances; *Elus;* Magistrates, financial; *and* Receveurs

Trévoux, *see* Cachet de Garnerans *and* Dombes

Trudaine, family, 111

Turcaret, 159

Turenne, Henri de La Tour d'Auvergne, Maréchal and Vicomte de, 79

Turgot, family, 105, 108, 144-146; Jean Turgot, 129, 143-144; Jacques Turgot, 144

Turgot de Saint-Clair, Marc-Antoine, 98n., 143, 144-145

Turgot de Soumons, Jacques Etienne, 65, 90n., 98n., 143, 144-145

Valenciennes, 42n., 54n.; *see also* Hainaut

Valois, royal dynasty, 102, 146; Marguerite of, 147

Venality, 33, 46, 49, 54, 61-63, 68-69, 70, 161, 178, 210-211, 223, 224, 227-228n.; inheritance of venal offices, 64-67; *see also* Commissions and commissioners, royal; *and* Offices and officeholders

Venice, 148

Versailles, 1-3, 158, 165, 218

Versoriers, see *Trésoriers*

Voltaire (François Marie Arouet), 85

Wars, 102-103, 104, 112; Thirty Years' War, 4-5; War of the Spanish Succession, 55, 103, 158, 164, 205; Wars of Religion, 102

DUE